To Strike at a King

To Strike at a King

The Turning Point
in the
McCarthy Witch-Hunts

Michael Ranville

Momentum Books, Ltd.
Troy, Michigan

Printed in the United States of America

98   97   96   3   2   1

973.921   2/97
R   BᵃT
           29.95

Momentum Books, Ltd.
6964 Crooks Road
Troy, Michigan 48098

ISBN: 1-879094-53-3

Library of Congress Cataloging-in-Publication Data

Ranville, Michael, 1943–
    To strike at a king : the turning point in the McCarthy witch hunt
  / Michael Ranville.
        p.   cm.
    Includes bibliographical references and index.
    ISBN 1-879094-53-3 (alk. paper)
    1. Anti-communist movements--United States--History.
2. Radulovich, Milo, 1927–   --Trials, litigation, etc. 3. Courts
-martial and courts of inquiry--United States--History--20th
century. 4. Murrow, Edward R.   5. See it now (Television program)
6. McCarthy, Joseph, 1908-1957--Influence.   I. Title.
E743.5.R36   1996
973.921--dc20   96-9576

To Milo

Stand tall, friend. The Radulovich name is presented to the next generation, honor intact.

Foreword by Fred W. Friendly

On October 20, 1953, "See It Now" broadcast "The Case Against Lt. Milo Radulovich." That night the face of television documentaries was changed forever.

At the time of the broadcast Sen. Joseph McCarthy and his assault on individual rights had journeyed virtually unchecked into a third year. Although some had bravely stood their ground against the senator, none had slowed his pace. McCarthy was a bare-knuckled political brawler who basked in the headlines of shattered lives and destroyed careers. How ironic, then, that history would settle on a genteel physics student, a reserve Air Force weather officer, to deliver the first blow that could stagger Joe McCarthy.

Our program that Tuesday evening held up a mirror. For the first time Americans saw what McCarthyism had wrought. The Milo Radulovich program peeled back the wretched excess of Communist witch-hunts, and what we found startled us—a son who would not abandon his frightened, immigrant father; a student with a wife and two kids, working two jobs, and attending college under the GI bill; a reserve officer who had served his country with distinction for ten years and was being discharged from the military even though his loyalty was not in question. Milo Radulovich was hardly the stuff of sedition.

I can still recall Murrow's impish grin as he thrust a *Detroit News* article my way during a chance meeting at an elevator. "Fritzl," he said—he was one of a select few who could get away with calling me that—"this could be the little picture for your McCarthy story."

"My McCarthy story," as he put it, referred to a question that was being asked of us almost daily that fall of 1953: when would Ed Murrow take on Joe McCarthy? Ed and I had discussed the matter in private many times. We agreed that when we did move there could be no margin for error, our story had to be directly on point. "See It Now" was built on a foundation of the "little picture," explaining a news event by showing the impact on one person. The McCarthy story had to be the *perfect* little picture. We were looking for a Milo Radulovich long before we knew who Milo was.

As time passed, Murrow's patience proved greater than mine. In private I began to push the matter. Ed's reticence, I suspect, could be traced to the questionable circumstances surrounding the death of his close friend Laurence Duggan five years earlier. But hesitation vanished when we found Milo.

There are many reasons why the Milo Radulovich program will always hold a special place in the hearts of our "See It Now" family. Milo was such an honest man, his story so compelling, that McCarthyites couldn't just dismiss this outrageous miscarriage of justice by hiding it behind a cloak of national security. The case of Milo Radulovich underscored that the hunt for witches had gone too far.

With benefit of hindsight, our March 1954 "See It Now" broadcast on Joe McCarthy has been credited with playing a key role in the senator's demise. There is no question that without "The Case Against Lt. Milo Radulovich" five months earlier, we never could have done the McCarthy program.

The Radulovich program will also be remembered for the role it played in shaping television documentaries. We had done stories on many of the day's pressing issues. We railed against juvenile delinquency. But who didn't abhor the wasting of lives at such an early age? We went to Korea and trained our cameras, not on the war, but on those who were fighting it. But whose heart didn't ache for a lonely

GI in a combat zone away from home at Christmas? We were proud of those programs, and countless others, but to some extent when it came to conflict we were apostles of the obvious. Our program on Milo changed all that.

Despite numerous requests the Pentagon wouldn't comment on Milo's case. We were faced with what was looming to be the most controversial broadcast to date in the history of television, and telling only one side of the story. Murrow and I discussed our uneasiness and concluded that sometimes there just aren't arguments on both sides of an issue.

Our fondness for the Radulovich program also stemmed from the fact that it epitomized what we were all about at "See It Now." It was controversial, but adrenaline at "See It Now" was the daily companion that kept our wits sharp. We had less than a week to put the program together, not an easy task in the 1953 world of television. But we learned to function with one eye fixed on a clock that went twice its normal speed the closer we got to our weekly rendezvous with 10:30 p.m. Tuesday. We believed in the little picture. And Milo Radulovich was the perfect little picture to illustrate the ravages of McCarthyism.

Milo is far more than a footnote to McCarthyism. He was a major participant, and a book on his role is long overdue. Ed Murrow and I maintained that the Radulovich program was one of the finest things we'd ever done, a rare moment in history. Four decades later I cannot quarrel with that assessment.

Of all the broadcasts I have been involved in, of all the issues I have examined, I select the Milo Radulovich program to show my students each semester at the Columbia School of Graduate Journalism. I have found no better way to illustrate the role journalism plays in a free and open society than by citing "The Case Against Lt. Milo Radulovich."

The king was dead.

On December 2, 1954, by a vote of 67-22, Joseph R. McCarthy of Wisconsin became only the fourth sitting United States senator in history to be censured by his colleagues.

The resolution to censure may have said more about the Senate than it did about McCarthy. For in the end Joe McCarthy was chastised not for his desecration of civil liberties but for the abuse he visited on his fellow senators.

Some trace the senator's demise to the Army-McCarthy hearings of the previous spring. For thirty-six days the saga of doctored photos, points of order, and contentious exchanges between usually genteel senators unfolded before a television audience of twenty million Americans. Only in its infancy, television captured the haunting admonition of Boston attorney Joseph Welch after McCarthy's attack on a young associate in his firm: "Until this moment, Senator, I think I never really gauged your cruelty or your recklessness." Then, with head in hand and voice quivering with emotion, Welch asked, "Have you no sense of decency, sir, at long last?" A brief silence followed, punctuated by applause that cascaded off the committee room walls into living rooms and bars across the country.

Others point to Edward R. Murrow's "See It Now" broadcast of a month earlier. After compiling film on McCarthy for nearly a year,

Murrow and his partner, Fred W. Friendly, allowed McCarthy to fasten a political noose around his own neck. The half-hour program showed, among other things, the senator picking his nose, giggling in a high-pitched, almost demonic fashion, and mercilessly berating those brought before his Senate committee. The contrast between the articulate, sincere Murrow and the unkempt, buffoonish McCarthy was dramatic.

Those events, and others, surely played a role in McCarthy's eventual demise. Murrow and Friendly, however, cite a broadcast in October of the previous year involving a young Air Force lieutenant, Milo Radulovich, as the turning point for Joe McCarthy and the "ism" that will forever accompany his name to the history books.

McCarthy was a bully who relished the fight. Although some had challenged him, none had inflicted any real damage. Many felt only Murrow—the broadcasting legend from World War II's European theater—to be McCarthy's match. Friends and colleagues urged him to take on the senator. But Murrow waited—for the right opportunity, for the perfect weapon, for the *little picture* that would clearly show the wretched excess of McCarthyism. Like Emerson, Murrow knew "when you strike at a king, you must kill him."

The weapon Edward R. Murrow chose to raise against Joe McCarthy was the outrageous injustice of the case brought by the United States Air Force against Lt., Milo Radulovich.

As Sen. Joseph McCarthy's season of terror moved into 1953, the country was diverging into two distinct Americas.

The first was an America that had finally shrugged aside its shackles of mourning. The bitter lesson of war, that young men and women die, had escaped few families. But now the country leaned forward.

When the "shops" work, everyone works, and in 1953 the nation's factories were humming. Emerging from the constraints of rationing, the postwar economy had finally started to pace the pent-up demand for consumer goods. Veterans and their families, long denied *things*, were making and spending money.

The iceman did not come to the suburbs—refrigerators ran on electricity. "TV dinner" had joined the glossary of food preparation. Television antennas had sprouted from rooftops. Families no longer gathered 'round the radio for an evening's entertainment. Fireside chats and a "brown bomber" with lightning hands had been consigned to history.

Factory wages, aided by a labor movement flexing its political muscle, had crept upward. From Levittown to Los Angeles, blue collar-workers now had economic viability. Taken collectively, they represented a sizeable segment of society with a sizeable amount of purchasing power that could not be ignored.

Factory workers, and those who worked because of the factories, had migrated from the concrete neighborhoods of their parents to the clay and mud of the subdivisions that ringed major cities. Rows of identical living structures, all struggling to be different, lined the graveled streets. Spindly trees, one to a yard, gave promise of a shaded avenue in the decades to come. It was dirty, construction dirty, dust and filth everywhere. But it was a parade that had refused to be rained on. It was the American dream in high gear.

Americans liked their things, and the life-style that accompanied them. The depression was something their parents had feared. Americans in 1953 had something called disposable income: they had an entertainment dollar.

High Noon, a psychological western of the previous year, was treated kindly in 1953 by the Motion Picture Academy of Arts and Sciences. Star Gary Cooper rode off with the Best Actor Award, and the movie's theme song and score also won Oscars.

In one of the more thrilling races in the long and storied history of the Kentucky Derby, Dark Star sprinted by favored Native Dancer. It took "Wild Bill" Vukovich just three hours and fifty-three minutes to win the Indianapolis 500.

The Pulitzer Prize for photography was awarded to Bill Gallagher of the *Flint Journal* for his memorable shot of a hole in Adlai Stevenson's shoe during the previous year's presidential campaign. "To William Gallagher," Stevenson had autographed the picture, "from a candidate who really is not holier than thou."*

But there was a second America in 1953, a darker America hovered over by a Russian bear who loomed as a threat to the most cherished of democratic freedoms.

A country still weary from battle was at war again. Never mind that officially it was a police action, that the troops were part of a United Nations force; the war was just as real. Korea may have been the battlefield, and the uniforms on the other side may have been those of the North Koreans and Red Chinese, but the enemy was communism—that's what was killing American boys in far-off lands whose names couldn't be pronounced.

Peace talks in Panmunjom, Korea, had produced an uneasy truce. Newsreels showed the prisoner exchange at Freedom Village where gaunt, bedraggled American POWs stumbled across the 38th parallel. The insidious nature of communism had been driven home when twenty-one of those prisoners voiced a preference for socialism over democracy and elected not to return to the United States. The turncoats surely were not of sound mind, the government said, and a new weapon—brainwashing—entered the lexicon of warfare.

In 1953, the same country that liked Ike and loved Lucy was also a nation of loyalty oaths and secret FBI files. For the first time in remembered history, the snitch had become a hero. "Naming names," previously held in the greatest contempt, was being accorded the accolade of patriotism.

*Sheryl and John Leekley, *Moments: The Pulitzer Prize Photographs* (New York: Crown Publishers, 1978), 34.

Labor unions, responsible for an increased standard of living enjoyed by many Americans, had come under suspicion as Communist front organizations. Union leaders damned the Communists and accused them of polluting the workers movement.

Going to the movies was an inexpensive and entertaining way to spend a Saturday evening. With growing regularity, though, the newsreels that preceded a double feature included film clips of nuclear explosions at Nevada test sites. Close-ups that detailed the incineration of homes and automobiles were accompanied by mushroom-shaped clouds that climbed to forty thousand feet.

Schools regularly conducted air raid drills as children were instructed what to do when Russia dropped the bomb. Civil defense agencies strongly advocated the building and stocking of fallout shelters. Radios were prenotched at 640 and 1240, points on the dial where listeners could turn immediately to receive instructions during an attack.

In 1953, *The Crucible* debuted in New York. Although he insisted his play was solely the product of an interest in the Salem Witch Trials, playwright Arthur Miller's biting satire left little doubt that his sights were trained on the House Un-American Activities Committee (HUAC) hysteria in Washington, and that he had scored a direct hit.

There were those who sought to heighten the fear of communism for their own political gain. They convinced at least 50 percent of the people that the threat of communism was so real that it warranted a sacrifice of personal freedoms.

It was a war, cold perhaps, but still a war. The casualties were those abruptly dismissed from jobs on the whimsy of charges by someone they would never face and could never challenge. They were the ones who could not marshal the financial resources necessary to mount a defense within a legal system that was alien to them. They were the ones who weren't famous enough for movie actors to fly in from the coast to show support. They were the ones whose day in court did not attract an army of reporters. They were the conscripts in the war against communism—the nondescript—the true victims of McCarthyism.

⸺⇥●⇤⸺

While leafing through a *Time* magazine from 1953, I happened on a brief article dealing with a University of Michigan student, Milo Radulovich. An Air Force reservist, Radulovich was being driven from the military through no fault of his own, but because of the suspected activities of his father and sister.

Interest piqued, I turned to my ready reference on current history, William Manchester's *The Glory and the Dream*. According to Manchester, Milo's father, John Radulovich, had subscribed to a pro-Communist newspaper written in his native Serbian language. The old man could barely speak English and wanted only to keep abreast of events in his homeland, Yugoslavia. Milo's crime had been a refusal to repudiate his family.

I quickly learned that Milo Radulovich, although a footnote in history, had not been totally ignored, due largely to the CBS duo of Edward R. Murrow and Fred W. Friendly.

On March 9, 1954, in one of their most celebrated "See It Now" broadcasts, Murrow and Friendly, primarily with footage of the senator himself, had allowed Joseph R. McCarthy to paint himself as a shallow demagogue. The program would later be deemed pivotal to McCarthy's demise.

Both Murrow and Friendly felt they never could have done the McCarthy program without first broadcasting "The Case Against Lt. Milo Radulovich" five months earlier. They wanted to attack McCarthyism but needed to do so through the *little picture*, the story of a common man who through no fault of his own had become a reluctant victim.

Milo, as it turned out, became the perfect little picture.

Unlike other incidents involving intellectuals from the China desk at the State Department, the Radulovich case was easily understood. It was about immigrants, first- and second-generation Americans, a more than common occurrence in 1953 America.

The drama didn't unfold in the population centers of New York, Washington, or Los Angeles. It was in tiny Dexter, Michigan, Main Street U.S.A., population fifteen hundred.

The central character offered no long list of published works an army of congressional committee staffers could pore over and claim subliminal Communist messages. Milo Radulovich, like thousands of other Americans, had been attending college under the G.I. Bill of Rights; he was a veteran who boasted an outstanding military record.

I stumbled on a Murrow quote. Although it was familiar, I was never quite sure of the circumstances surrounding its delivery and decided to investigate further.

With only forty-eight hours to airtime before the famed McCarthy program in 1954, Murrow and Friendly had gathered their "See It Now" team in the projection room, ostensibly to review the next-to-final edit of the footage that would make up the historic broadcast. The team, however, felt anything but historic. After six exhaustive days of combing hours of film, checking and rechecking the accuracy of statements, editing the film so that it flowed with consistency, they were tired and apprehensive.

According to Friendly, "I had sensed a certain uneasiness on the part of some members of the unit. I was not sure whether this was timidity over our confrontation with the senator or whether there was something in their backgrounds which might make us vulnerable."

The people in the projection room with Murrow and Friendly that Sunday evening weren't a seditious band of revolutionaries bent on overthrowing the government. They were working men and women with grass to mow and children who rode bicycles and needed braces. But they were also a seasoned news team, loyal to Murrow. Without him there wouldn't be any broadcast. Not wanting anything in their lives targeted that would undermine Murrow, they began to recount incidents, harmless in nature, that might lead in some obscure way to a McCarthy attack. Those confessions prompted Murrow's now famous comment—"the terror is right here in this room."

Innocent people. Frightened. Volunteering the most private moments of their lives. Perhaps no statement—"the terror is right here in this room"—and the context in which it was uttered painted a more accurate picture of the chilling fear that had engulfed America during the McCarthy era.

That drew me to the little picture and Milo Radulovich.

My friend Joe Oldenburg, maestro of research at the Detroit Public Library, informed me that Milo's sister, Margaret Fishman, was living in Detroit. I called her and, though polite, she bluntly indicated that before sharing her thoughts or files, Milo would have to give his blessing to anything that involved the *case*, as I learned it had come to be known by the family.

I discovered that Ken Sanborn, one of Milo's two attorneys, was a recently retired circuit court judge. Although he had agreed to talk with me, without Milo's approval he would share only that which was already in the public domain.

Milo, I learned, was living in Sacramento, California. Margaret agreed, although with some reservation, to give me his work address. She counseled that he was a private person, that I shouldn't be discouraged if he didn't cooperate.

I wrote him. No response.

After two weeks, I called. The reception was less than enthusiastic: "Why do you want to dredge up all that crap? That was a long time ago, nobody's interested in that case anymore."

I explained that besides himself, other people were involved in the case who had personally risked much on his behalf. Their roles, as well as his, I petitioned, should not be forgotten. My interests were not in a biography or "whatever happened to…" type effort. His privacy would not be invaded. On the contrary, I intended to focus on the ninety-five days in 1953 that encompassed his dramatic stay in the nation's limelight.

"Let me think about it," he said just before hanging up. "There was a lot of pain."

Hoping to establish a bond, I foolishly volunteered that I too had been in the Air Force. "Officer?" he quickly asked.

"Uh, no."

"Oh."

A week later he agreed to talk, setting out his one condition. "No telephone," he demanded. "I want to look you in the eye."

We met. From our first unsure steps in his crowded Sacramento apartment, a friendship developed extending far beyond any book.

With Milo's blessing, doors opened. Ruth Friendly informed me that her husband, Fred, no longer sits for interviews. He would, however, discuss Milo Radulovich. Friendly proved to be larger than life. The old newsman in him, captivated by headlines of the day, pushed aside amenities before our first interview, and without even as much as a "hello," he blurted out, "Is he a Serb?"

Joe Wershba, a CBS reporter, the man dispatched to Dexter by Murrow and Friendly forty-three years earlier, had also agreed to talk. Wershba, with his delightful penchant for digression, could—and certainly should—be a book unto himself.

Self-doubts overwhelmed me. Although I had written several articles, a project of book proportions had never crossed my mind. I was mesmerized by the McCarthy era, but my vantage point was the armchair. I certainly was no historian.

Milo and I had become close. Like many friendships, ours progressed gradually. He possesses an encyclopedic knowledge of Serbian history, with fascinating insights into the Bosnian crisis. We share a love of movies, new and old. He is a voracious reader and astute observer of politics and history. And he has a charming and devilish sense of humor.

As our relationship grew so did his ease at discussing the case. We trusted each other with many personal thoughts. I was, and still am, fearful of letting him down.

Devouring books, old newspaper clippings, magazine articles, newsreel footage, anything that pertained to Murrow, McCarthy, or HUAC, I came to a definite conclusion. The world knew only the tip of Milo Radulovich's contribution to the events of that era. Although several prominent historians had written about Lt. Milo Radulovich, his role in history had been defined by how he affected the lives of Ed Murrow, Fred Friendly, and indirectly, Joseph McCarthy.

Little was known of Milo Radulovich before a Tuesday night in October 1953, when Edward R. Murrow turned in his chair and dramatically announced, "We propose to examine, insofar as we can, the case of Lieutenant Radulovich." What manner of man was it that had already made decisions critical to the broadcast long before it caromed across the airwaves of the CBS network?

I wondered what would have happened if Milo had decided not to fight and simply acceded to the tremendous pressure by the Air Force to resign. But then what would have become of this proud Montenegrin's* children and grandchildren years later?

I wondered what would have happened if Milo had not made one more phone call in what seemed like a futile quest for a civilian attorney to represent him. But then men such as Charles Lockwood and Kenneth Sanborn would never have single-handedly straightened the backbone of a community's legal profession.

I wondered what would have happened if his sister Margaret had not remained silent and announced, truthfully or not, that she was not a Communist, and had little or no contact with her brother. But then the Constitution, for at least one American, would have lost some of its vibrancy.

*An independent principality before 1918, Montenegro was a republic in Yugoslavia. Montenegrins take a fierce pride in the fact that they have never been conquered.

What if the *Detroit News* had not taken the bold step of emblazon-ing across its front page the story of a young Air Force reservist who was being cashiered out of the service through no fault of his own? What if the government had not taken intimidating steps to quiet the eloquent editorial voice of the *Detroit Free Press* when the paper came to the defense of an American citizen who wanted only to look his accuser in the eye? But then some other accomplishment, perhaps lesser in magnitude, would supplant the Milo Radulovich story as one of journalism's finest hours.

Had any or all of those questions been answered differently, histo-ry would not read as it does today.

Learned historians have written eloquent accounts of this period. I drew unashamedly and enthusiastically from their collective works, especially to convey the social and political climate surrounding the rise and fall of Joseph McCarthy, or more appropriately, the rise and fall of the witch-hunt milieu that characterized those times. "Senator McCarthy," said Murrow, "didn't create this fear, he merely exploited it, and rather successfully."

I struggled with how best to present the story of Milo Radulovich, the story of Murrow and Friendly's little picture, the story of the first telling blow visited on Joe McCarthy.

Milo Radulovich's contribution to American history unfolded over a ninety-five-day period in 1953. I decided to tell it as it happened, one day at a time. An added feature of this approach is the opportunity it afforded to underscore that Milo's plight, however important to him, didn't occur in a vacuum. It unfolded against a backdrop of other events. Some were important—the winding down of the Korean con-flict. Some were important only at the time—the Dodger's firing of Charlie Dressen. Some were probably never important, but grabbed our attention for ten minutes, and for that reason they warrant mention.

Milo was a victim, but certainly not the only victim, of McCarthyism. By looking closer at the plight of one person, by view-ing that little picture, perhaps it will influence the way we look at those who would for their own benefit seek to assign guilt on the basis of association.

And there will always be those willing to exploit fear for personal gain.

ACKNOWLEDGMENTS

*T*o *Strike at a King* was not a solitary effort.

I enjoy the support and love of two strong, independent, and caring women. No man should be so blessed. Carol and Mara—wife and daughter—are my life's foundation. This book is as much their accomplishment as mine.

And whenever the project seemed to overwhelm, my mother's perpetual novena reached out and provided sorely needed direction. Thanks, Mom. You too, Dad.

Margaret and Al Fishman opened their home, their files, and their hearts to me. They also shared their burning love of our Constitution. Years ago their daughter, Marcia Fishman-Katzman, had the foresight to catalog reams of FBI files on the off-chance they would someday be useful. They were, Marcia. Thank you.

Bob Joseph proved time and again that one can be a wealth of information, a sagacious critic, and a best friend—and excel at all three.

Although forty years had passed, Ron Rothstein acknowledged his regret over not representing Milo. Mr. Rothstein is an extraordinarily honest man. Meeting him was one of the unforgettable joys associated with writing this book.

Joe Wershba must be thanked, not only for his outstanding reporting in 1953 but also for an ability to place his accomplishments in proper historical context.

In no need of yet another accolade, Fred W. Friendly, willingly gave of his personal time and energy so that the Milo Radulovich story could be told. Hopefully, all will now know what Fred Friendly discovered in 1953—why Milo is so special.

My other family, the one at Karoub Associates, warrants special mention. You've been carrying me for years, this just made it official. Thanks one and all, from the absolute bottom of my heart.

Marianne Hartzell, Joe Oldenburg, and the Michigan Library Association reinforced what I had known for many years—you can find it at your local library.

Without Ron Monchak and Kyle Scott of Momentum Books, both Milo and I would still be wandering in a circle. Their direction of the project is respected and admired.

Finally, a note of gratitude to Moriarty's for playing host to the Wednesday night Milo seminars. And special thanks to the esteemed faculty—Mickey, Mark, David, and MAC-Farland.

To Strike at a King

FRIDAY, AUGUST 21, 1953

V era Layton didn't think much of it one way or the other. This wasn't the first time someone had come to her door with questions about Milo.

Twice before, government people had asked about her tenant, Milo Radulovich, a physics student at the University of Michigan. On those occasions, though, the men wore dark business suits. "They wanted to know if Milo had Communist leanings," she recalls; "wanted to know if he had many visitors. They asked about his sister Margaret, too, and his dad."[1]

They asked around town as well, but didn't get the answers they wanted.

This time was different, though. The men wore military uniforms, not suits, and they wanted to talk *to* Milo, not *about* him. She directed them to the little, neat, well-kept red house that sat about one hundred feet behind hers. The surrounding grounds could easily have served as the setting for a John Constable painting.

Milo Radulovich peered cautiously from the front window as two uniformed men negotiated the long driveway that led to his house, a converted barn that sat far off Ann Arbor Street in Dexter, Michigan. One of the men was a major, the other a sergeant. Military people instinctively process rank.

Apart from family, Milo and his wife, Nancy, didn't get much company. Two children, one a newborn, a full class load at the

3

University of Michigan, and three jobs between them left little time for socializing.

In the sometimes tight-knit community of career military, the globe is a neighborhood. You never know when an old friend you served with on the other side of the world might pop in for a visit. But Milo didn't recognize them; they were not old friends, and their grim looks quickly erased any suggestion that the journey to Dexter that August morning in 1953 was anything but official.

"The major spoke and he seemed nervous," Milo recalls. "Once I knew why he was there, I understood why."

The next few minutes were a blur to Milo and Nancy. Although uncomfortable, there was a crispness to the major's demeanor as he launched into a hurried explanation of his visit. They sat and listened but only fragments seeped through. Nothing made sense.

...discharge you from all commissions and appointments held in the United States Air Force...

...tender your resignation immediately or at any time prior to final action on this case...

...or you may elect to secure civilian counsel at no expense to the government...

Milo signed in receipt of a small packet and the two men left.

Stunned—only moments before, Milo was performing one of life's most basic tasks—changing a diaper; he and Nancy read the documents and then reread them, at least five times before discerning the content.

In the cold, unremitting language of military parlance, Milo and Nancy Radulovich learned that after ten years of exemplary service, the Air Force was revoking his treasured commission as a first lieutenant and discharging him from the military.

But why? *His* loyalty to the government, the documents emphasized, was not in question.

The charges, or Statement of Reasons, contained two long, awkwardly crafted paragraphs describing activities of his father and sister.

The common thread was that Milo had maintained "a close and continuing association" with both, and, according to Air Force Regulation 35-62, a copy of which was included in the packet of information left by the major, that was forbidden.

Milo's father, Jovan (John) Radulovich, was accused of subscribing and contributing to the support of *Slobodna Rec,** a publication associated with the American Slav Congress, which had been designated Communist by the attorney general. John Radulovich was also charged with "spread[ing] Russian and Communist propaganda in the factory" at his place of employment, the Hudson Motor Car Company.

This was ridiculous, Milo thought. A Communist? His father could barely speak English. The notion of his spreading Soviet propaganda in the factory was preposterous. Besides, John Radulovich loved this country, even kept a picture of Franklin D. Roosevelt over the mantel in his house.

Although he did not subscribe to *Slobodna Rec*, he read it, but he also read *Srbobran,†* its anti-Communist counterpart. Far from sinister, his purpose was simply to keep abreast of events in his native Yugoslavia, and both publications were written in the familiar and comfortable Serbian language of his homeland.

Margaret was cited in the Statement of Reasons for participating in picket lines: one protesting the Book-Cadillac Hotel's refusal to provide lodging for Paul Robeson—a singer, actor, athlete, and civil rights activist —the other opposing an indictment of twelve Communist leaders under the Smith Act. She also was charged with attending a conference opposing "deportation hysteria," and a gathering commemorating the twenty-fifth anniversary of the *Daily Worker*.

Sure, Margaret was involved in various political activities, but since Milo's enlistment in the Aviation Cadet Program in 1943, a year before his graduation from Detroit's prestigious Cass Technical High School, the only time he ever saw her was at his parents' house while

*In English, *free expression*
†In English, *defender of serbs*

home on leave. And that was just for supper, they didn't talk politics. Close and continuing association? Hardly!

The Air Force did provide options, limited as they were.

He could resign with an honorable discharge.

That wasn't as simple as it sounded. A closer examination of AFR 35-62 indicated that although the discharge would officially be honorable, his file would forever bear the stigma "resignation in lieu of elimination from the service."

He could answer the charges in writing.

This option would afford the opportunity to submit evidence that would justify his retention. "Justify your retention"—the phrase was numbing. After ten years of outstanding military service, after several commendations for excellence in the performance of duty, after just returning from a top-secret assignment in Thule, Greenland, for which he was handpicked, Lt. Milo J. Radulovich could no longer serve his country unless he *justified* it.

Or he could request a hearing and fight the charges.

Milo was the son of hardworking immigrant parents from Montenegro. Responsibility for family coupled with a strong sense of justice and patriotism coursed through the Radulovich veins.

Milo was currently on reserve status in the Air Force and studying physics at the University of Michigan; working in weather was his chosen occupation, the way he would someday provide for his family. The road to a career in meteorology was not easy. After he had completed undergraduate studies in meteorology at New York University, success now hinged on a degree in physics, a difficult course of study. But Milo was an excellent student, exhibiting an aptitude not only for the tough curriculum but also for the complexities of weather.

The study and forecasting of weather, however, was inextricably tied to government. With a personnel file indelibly stamped "resignation in lieu of elimination from the service," he would have little hope of fulfilling his career ambition. He could not let the charges go unchallenged.

Before she met Milo, Nancy Radulovich was Nancy Jane Tuttle from Lewiston, Maine. "There was never any question for me," she says. "What they were trying to do was wrong. We were going to fight, that's all there was to it."

Milo echoes her sentiments. "I wasn't going to go out without some kind of fight. This was a smear on me. I didn't want to just write a letter and forget about it, or slink off into the darkness."

Lt. Milo J. Radulovich and his wife, Nancy, decided they would fight the charges and request a hearing. First, however, Milo would have to talk to his father.

⟞⟩●⟨⟞

Milo and Nancy Radulovich and their daughter Diane had moved to Dexter a year earlier. They rented an apartment from Vera Layton and her husband, Floyd. After a ten-year stint in the United States Air Force, Milo was attending the University of Michigan under the G.I. Bill.

Although a suburb of Ann Arbor, Dexter proclaims its own identity. The tiny Michigan community of fifteen hundred was wary of strangers but quickly accepted the young serviceman and his family. "They just fell right in," says Vera Layton. "They were Dexterites."

Knowing that he had been in the Air Force tempered any concern the Laytons would have about strangers wanting to know about Milo. Those military people, it seemed, were always asking questions about one another anyway.

Besides, people liked them. Milo, in addition to his classes, worked two jobs to support his family. Nancy was a telephone operator on the night shift in Ann Arbor.

"Nancy was a fun person," says Vera. "She was home during the day and we became good friends." The Laytons also owned a small rental property behind their big house. When Kathy was born that previous May and the little house became available, they were only too happy to accommodate their young tenants' need for space and privacy.

———————⟶⦁⟵———————

The Detroit Lions, reigning NFL champions, journeyed to Syracuse, New York, on this evening for a preseason game with the Pittsburgh Steelers. Coach Buddy Parker had only five tune-up contests left to evaluate several rookies, among them center Charley Ane, All-American guard Harley Sewell, and linebacker Joe Schmidt.

The Steelers, fresh from a convincing victory over the Bears, boasted a passing attack that rode the arm of quarterback Jim Finks.

John Radulovich wouldn't show it, but Milo knew his father would be frightened.

The elder Radulovich kept an inquisitive eye on events in his native Yugoslavia. As proud as he was to be an American, he was reminded by vivid accounts from the old country that government could be oppressive as well as protective.

His family, the dignity of the Radulovich name, was everything to John Radulovich. Milo couldn't tell his father over the telephone that people sought to bring dishonor on his house. It had to be in person. Moreover, the charges made it clear that although Milo's background was not the issue, his father's certainly was.

Even though his sister, Margaret, her husband, Al, and his mother and father were coming to his house the next day for dinner, Milo drove to Detroit to tell his father of the previous day's visit from the major and the sergeant.

"It was hot," he recalls. "I remember we went down the basement where the tiles on the floor made it cooler."

Milo recounted the previous day's events to his father. He valiantly tried to interpret the contents of papers he didn't fully understand himself. Then came the difficult part. John Radulovich was part of the charges; Margaret too.

Milo told his father that his subscription to *Slobodna Rec* was specifically mentioned in the Statement of Reasons. So was the *Daily Worker*.

That wasn't all. John Radulovich was also charged with spreading Russian and Communist propaganda at the Hudson Motor Car Company, where he had been employed for more than twenty-five years. Milo's loyalty was not in question, but because he maintained a "close and continuing association" with his father and sister—whose loyalties were very much in question—he was considered a security risk.

Did they know, John Radulovich asked his son, that he read *Slobodna Rec* only because he wanted to know of events in his homeland? Did they know he also read *Srbobran*, the pro-West paper that leaned to the Monarchists?

Did they know that he was a loyal American who kept a picture of Franklin D. Roosevelt over his mantel, that he was a proud member of United Auto Workers Local 154 but was not a Communist?

Did they know that he donned an American uniform and proudly fought for his adopted country in World War I? "Even if my native Yugoslavia should attack this country today," he said emphatically, "I would fight, old as I am."

⸺⸺►◦◄⸺⸺

This was not the first time John Radulovich had encountered a hidden enemy since coming to America in 1914.

Stories circulated in Detroit's cliquish Serbian community that before 1923 when he sent for and married Ikonija Mijatovic, he had another wife and family in Montenegro. Although there was no truth to the rumors, it provided him with a lifelong alert that someone was trying to destroy his name. "I think somebody commits a sin against the eighth commandment," said the elder Radulovich, referring to those who would bear false witness against him.

In 1914, at age twenty-six, John Radulovich had emigrated from Montenegro, an independent kingdom (later part of Yugoslavia), to join a cousin, Radosav "Reddy" Radulovic, in the United States of America. A shepherd and a soldier in the old country, once in the promised land he found his way to southern Ohio and went to work in the coal mines. His nieces and nephews affectionately remember him as "the lawyer," a moniker traced to his assumed role of teacher to the young ones. At the knee of Jovan Radulovich, the Serbian children of Belmont Two mining camp not only learned the language of their beloved Montenegro but also the country's proud history and culture. Throughout his life he stressed education to his own children, vowing their lives would be more than "a strong back and a number nine shovel," a favored expression that drew on harsh memories of life in the mines.

He loved his new country and, after enlisting in the Army, served proudly when America entered World War I.

Milo's sister, Margaret, was born in 1925 at the Fairpoint Mining Camp in southeastern Ohio; Milo was born two years later in Detroit. After ten years in the mines, "Tata," as he was known by his children, moved to Michigan, convinced that the educational and career opportunities would be greater for his family.

Becoming a citizen in those days of heavy immigration was not automatic. John and Ikonija attended night school to learn about the Constitution, the three branches of government, and the history of their new country. The courses were taught in English, making the already difficult path to citizenship an even more demanding struggle. They eventually acquired their citizenship papers, but John was never comfortable enough with English to read it for pleasure. Nonetheless, a burning curiosity drove him to wrestle valiantly with the daily newspapers.

Life was not easy in Detroit for John Radulovich and his family. He went to work for the Hudson Motor Car Company in 1926, but employment was anything but steady. There was a period of four years when he did not work at all. A proud man with a growing family, being without a job took a great toll on him.

Both Milo and Margaret recall gifts from the "Goodfellows," and trips to the welfare office with a wagon or sleigh to get big bags of flour and beans. Their case worker was Miss Russell. Remembered fondly by Margaret, Miss Russell ranked third in the unofficial line of authority behind her parents and teachers. "I wanted a Shirley Temple dress," Margaret says, "but I got a welfare dress." The highly visible, volunteer-driven Goodfellow organization provided certificates that were exchanged with participating merchants. "One year I got high-top boots that had a special sheath for a penknife on the side," Milo says. "I thought those were just about the best boots a kid could ever have."

During the depression an unemployed John Radulovich would go to the Hudson Motor Car Company where Mr. Thall at the employment office would occasionally give him work. But someone, presumably someone close to the family, reported him for making money on the side and, after a visit from the welfare worker, his makeshift employment ended.

John was industrious. His hands responded to a keen mind. Shortly after moving to Detroit he made a down payment on a house. Admittedly, it wasn't much when he bought it: one floor, no central heat, no basement. But with the help of neighbors he dug a basement, laid a foundation, put in sewer pipes, and eventually built a second floor. With bare hands and innate intelligence, he transformed the shack into a home for his family.

Land contract payments were frequently late, sometimes missed altogether. Twice the landlord was about to foreclose, and twice Tata was able to borrow money at the last minute from a bachelor friend, who also hailed from Montenegro. The third time, John was saved by the Home Owners Loan Corporation, a depression-era program created to avoid foreclosures. From that day forward, a picture of Franklin D. Roosevelt was prominently featured in John Radulovich's home.

Like others during the depression, John Radulovich did what had to be done to care for his family. With an old Ford Model T truck, he sold ice from an icehouse he built on a vacant lot. Later he added candy bars and ice cream to his product line. At one point, when the lights were turned off for failure to pay the bill, the ever-resourceful Tata crudely rigged the meter, a common practice during the depression. Other times light was provided by old lamps fueled with five-cent-a-gallon kerosene Milo recalls lugging home.

Through it all he was unequivocal in his support of the union. As difficult as times were, he was consoled by the fact that it was worse in the old country. His standard of living in America was higher than he had ever known and it was because of his union.

It mattered little to John Radulovich that many of his union brethren openly professed their support of socialism. The attraction organized labor held for the followers of Marx was understandable. Communists heralded worker dignity, called for improved working conditions, demanded unemployment insurance and social security, and insisted on a distribution of part of the proceeds to the workers who generated them—the very things unions were seeking in their fight for recognition.

Charles Nusser, a party member in the thirties, points out that during the depression, communism did not carry the onerous stigma that would encase it twenty years later. He indicates the attraction of communism had nothing to do with Karl Marx or any complicated question of doctrine. "People were starving in this country. We went to bed hungry every night," he says. "The Communist party was trying to do something about it. When somebody had their furniture thrown out on the sidewalk, the Communists would organize people to pick it up and put it back in. They organized people to go down to the relief bureaus, to go down and fight for relief and unemployment insurance. That was the appeal of the Communist party."[1]

John Radulovich was never a Communist. He was, however, a union man and a ready and willing participant in the famous sit-down strike of 1937. Along with fellow workers at the Hudson plant, he "sat" for thirty days.

In late 1936, American-worker frustration was brimming. The United Auto Workers requested to meet with General Motors Executive Vice-President William S. Knudsen to discuss a general collective-bargaining agreement.

Company policy at General Motors, for both executives and workers, was tightly controlled by upper management. By indicating it would be pointless to meet because local concerns were handled by individual plant managers, Knudsen's response mocked the union request.

While labor leaders pondered their next move, the rank and file decided the time for pondering was over.

The production lines of American factories were manned by many first- and second-generation European immigrants with strong ties to relatives and friends in the old country. Sitting down on the job as a means of protest had garnered worldwide attention years earlier when Welsh and Hungarian miners refused to come to the top until their wages were increased.

On December 28, 1936, workers in Fisher Body Plant Number 1 in Cleveland sat down while automobile frames passed them by unattended. Within hours, Fisher Body Plant Number 2 in Flint followed suit. Over the next few weeks, workers in the great automobile plants of Pontiac, Oakland, Kansas City, Atlanta, and Detroit all joined their fellow workers in one of the greatest displays of solidarity in the history of the American labor movement.

Management did not anticipate a long strike. These protesters were Communists, they said, not real Americans. Public opinion would surely alight to the company. Jobs were scarce. Any number of men would be willing to trade places with the ungrateful strikers, wages and working conditions be damned. Further, these upstarts were not only challenging authority but flouting a tenet of the republic, the sanctity of private property. They were trespassers as well. Nevertheless, management did not sit by idly and wait for the tide of public opinion to eject strikers from their plants.

In Flint, National Guard machine guns were mounted as a show of force.

Harry Bennett, Henry Ford's bodyguard, hired an army of thugs for the inevitable moment when the strikers would storm the Dearborn plant.

Workers wrapped wet leather tightly around lead pipes in preparation for the confrontation. Margaret Fishman recalls her father coming home from the "thirty-day war," his union button securely fastened to the makeshift weaponry that was never called to service.

Henry Ford was outraged at worker impudence. Twenty years earlier the elder statesman of automakers had shocked the business world with his announcement of a five-dollar day for production workers. Now the ungrateful sons of those employees had seized his plant. Such effrontery could not be tolerated.

The strikers were careful not to destroy any company property. When heat was turned off in the factory, they did calisthenics and roller-skated. Family members defied police lines and with improvised pulleys hoisted food and laundry through broken windows. Margaret recalls her mother and brother, Sam, going to the Hudson Motor Car Company with food and clothing for her father.

She also recalls her agitation at the family who stayed with them during the strike. "They were from Montenegro," Margaret remembers, "mother, father, and three children. The father was a former Detroit police officer. He kept saying it was the Communists who were leading the strike, and thought the Army should be called out to end it. Here he was, living in our small house with his three kids, eating our food, and not paying a cent. And he's criticizing the actions of my father."

Anger aside, Margaret laughs when recalling one of the children. "He wasn't all that old, but must have weighed a couple of hundred pounds. They were all on their way to California where they thought this kid was going to be the next Fatty Arbuckle."

After forty-four days that included skirmishes between workers and police, a number of ignored court directives, and the refusal of Gov. Frank Murphy to order the National Guard to eject the strikers (despite heavy pressure from the companies), General Motors agreed to meet with the UAW. The strike was over: the union was recognized.

It's difficult to believe that John Radulovich's loyalty to his union was strengthened beyond what it was before the strike. In the years after, even with a halting command of English, he would speak out forcefully on behalf of his union. Many of those who shared that passion also attempted to bring his union under the banner of communism.

The well-publicized strike did have a lasting impact on his twelve-year-old daughter, Margaret. The union won. Big business, the company, had been brought to its knees despite court orders and threats to personal safety. The victory was important to her father's self-esteem. His days of begging for work were over.

<hr>

"If he had told me not to fight this, I wouldn't have," Milo says of the discharge. "I would not have put him through it."

John Radulovich was proud of his son. Milo was a man of distinction, not just any soldier but an officer. He had proudly signed the statement of permission enabling his seventeen-year-old son Milo to enlist during World War II. And although he didn't fully comprehend Air Force Regulation 35-62 and something called a Statement of Reasons, John Radulovich quickly discerned there were those who sought to bring dishonor on his family.

He gave Milo his blessing to fight.

———⇒➤●◄⫘———

In Washington, Sen. Joseph R. McCarthy had requested Postmaster General Arthur E. Summerfield to provide him with figures on how much money the government spent subsidizing distribution of the *Washington Post*, the *Wall Street Journal*, and the *New York Communist Daily Worker*.

According to McCarthy, Summerfield had earlier asked Congress for $240 million to make up the difference between handling costs and the mail rates paid by the nation's newspapers and magazines.

It was the third time in a week that McCarthy had attacked the *Washington Post*. In his letter to Summerfield, McCarthy said, "I requested the information on the Washington Post as a paper typical of those which feel that freedom of the press means freedom to deliberately lie and to twist and distort facts." He went on to say, "While some arguments can be made in favor of subsidizing a general distribution of truth, there certainly can be no legitimate argument in favor of subsidizing dissemination of deliberate falsehood."

"Certainly," McCarthy emphasized, "there can be no reason for using tax money to pay for the distribution of the *Daily Worker*."[2]

They knew each other, McCarthy and Summerfield. Three years earlier their paths had crossed on a far different issue.

Looking to tap Ed Nellor's extensive credentials as an investigator of Communists, McCarthy had been wooing the *Washington Times-Herald* reporter to join his personal staff as a speech writer. Nellor and fellow *Times-Herald* reporter George Waters had coauthored the historical Lincoln Day speech that had catapulted McCarthy to national prominence. The reporter, however, had already accepted a position with *Look* magazine and turned McCarthy down. Summerfield, a member of the Republican National Committee and a prosperous Michigan auto dealer who advertised heavily in *Look*, successfully urged the magazine to hire Nellor and then place him on permanent loan to McCarthy free of charge.[3]

———⟩⟩●⟨⟨———

President Dwight D. Eisenhower told Air Force Association convention-eers in Washington that now, more than ever, America must build the best air force in the world. The president's remarks were delivered by Air Force Secretary Harold Talbott. Talbott charged Congress with being "penny-wise and pound-foolish" by cutting servicemen's benefits so much it would cost $2.6 billion in the next year alone to replace trained men who refused to reenlist.

Valued by the Air Force for its lobbying clout on Capitol Hill, the association numbered thirty-five thousand veterans in its membership.[4]

Dinner that Sunday was at Milo and Nancy's. Ostensibly the family gathered to celebrate the recent arrival of Kathy, their new niece and granddaughter, but now there were other things to discuss as well.

"My first memory of the case," says Margaret, "was that Sunday in Dexter when Milo showed us the letter from the Air Force."

Margaret, Milo felt certain, would be angry.

Brother and sister had seen little of each other since Milo enlisted in the Army after graduating in 1944 from Cass Technical High School in Detroit.

Leaving Dexter that Sunday, a concerned and confused John Radulovich wondered how they could do this to his boy Milo.

Margaret Radulovich Fishman girded one more time to protect her constitutional right of free speech.

———————<><>———————

It had not been a good year for Al and Margaret Fishman. Julius and Ethel Rosenberg had been sentenced to death for conspiracy to commit espionage. In June, the Fishmans drove to Washington, D.C., to join others in protest of the scheduled execution. Sensing victory when U. S. Supreme Court Justice William O. Douglas granted a stay, they motored back to Michigan. On the car radio they learned that Chief Justice Fred M. Vinson had called together his colleagues on the high court and vacated the stay. The Rosenbergs were dead. "That really affected us," Al recalls. "Then two months later there was Milo's case."

Although many old-country customs did not survive the immigrants' journey to America, one did. Men ruled their families. The Radulovich home was no exception.

"We know today it wasn't right," Milo explains, "but while women did the dishes, the men went off into the other room to talk politics. That's just the way it was." The men relived ancient battles, more often than not accompanied by the mournful sound of a *gusla*, the stringed instrument played by Montenegrins for centuries.

Although respectful of her father and the customs that governed and brought order to his life, Margaret Radulovich burned with her own strong political beliefs. She would not be relegated to the kitchen.

She had joined others in protesting the Smith Act, which markedly reduced the rigid legal test for treason and enabled the well-publicized prosecution of twelve alleged Communists.

She had protested the Book-Cadillac Hotel's refusal to provide lodging for Paul Robeson, the civil rights activist and singer, and his party.

She had protested her country's treatment of the foreign born.

Now the same forces she protested had set up camp on the doorstep of her family. Margaret Fishman was indeed angry.

"I had broken no law," she says, "only exercised my constitutional right to free speech. There was no justification for the government's action against Milo. He had done nothing wrong. If I've done something wrong, then come after me, not him."

———————

While the Radulovich family groped for reasons and wrestled with a course of action this Sunday, American involvement in Korea stepped to the headlines of the nation's front pages.

Although it was officially labeled a police action, the media settled comfortably on calling it a "conflict." To those who fought in Korea it was a war. Bombs were dropped, prisoners taken, and shots fired in anger.

People died too. Since June 25, 1950, the date Communist forces in North Korea made their incursion across the 38th parallel and invaded the Republic of Korea, 25,604 Americans had been killed in action.

Now, more than three years later, many of those soldiers had begun their long journey home. The troop ship *Marine Carp* had pushed away from the dock at Inchon, Korea, on July 9. Eighteen days later a truce between North and South Korea was signed. But the signatories were wary.

Terms of the agreement stipulated that neither side was to increase its military strength during the truce. When the accord was signed on July 26, the Communists did not have bombers in North Korea. As American prisoners passed through "Freedom Gate," they brought back reports of new twin-engine, swept-wing bombers and the show they had put on over the North Korea capital of Pyongyang long after the truce had been signed.[1]

They brought back other reports as well, of those who conspired with the enemy to gain temporary comfort or food. Newspaper articles told of the hatred some prisoners harbored for fellow prisoners who "squealed" on them to the Communists.[2]

They also brought back reports of atrocities committed by their Communist captors. One American soldier was lashed to a pole and left to die in the sun because he would not confess to germ warfare. Another was chained to a wall in such a way that he could not stand or sit.[3]

Other stories told of returning GIs and emotional reunions with family and loved ones. Reporters couldn't interview all returnees; some were too sick, others bore severe emotional scars.[4]

Sidney Karbel couldn't figure out why Margaret Fishman didn't just announce to the world she wasn't a Communist. As far as he was concerned, that would have been the end of it. For Margaret, though, it went far beyond any statement involving her political philosophy. The issue for her was the Constitution itself. "If we have a Constitution," she says, "then let's use it."

Margaret Radulovich Fishman loved the Constitution—her Constitution. It was more than just an elegant charter revered by school children for the graceful manner in which it had presided over her country for nearly two hundred years. "To me," she says forcefully, "it is a document that lives and begs for use, a powerful forum that safeguards the rights of individuals to speak out and challenge their government."

As Margaret arrived for work at the law offices of Karbel and Eiges where she was a legal secretary, the Constitution was very much on her mind. Shortly after the office opened for business, a hasty meeting was called. In attendance were Margaret, her two employers, Sidney Karbel and Herbert Eiges, and another lawyer in the firm, Ron Rothstein.

The three people that sat with Margaret at the Karbel and Eiges conference table all held her in special esteem.

22

"Herbert Eiges looked upon Margaret as a daughter. He was a bachelor with no children of his own," says Rothstein. "When he was your friend, he went to bat for you."[1]

"Karbel was pretty much the same way," Rothstein continues. "He wasn't quite as close to Margaret as Eiges was; nevertheless, he was a man of great honor."

"If I needed another sister," Rothstein says, "I'd want Margaret to be my sister."

Margaret told them of the charges against her brother. She said it wasn't anything Milo had done, but because she chose to exercise her right of assembly and free speech, her brother was being cashiered out of the Air Force. Milo, she emphasized, was not a security risk. He was accused of nothing more than "a close and continuing association" with his father and sister.

"Mr. Karbel couldn't figure out why Margaret couldn't tell somebody that she wasn't a Communist," Rothstein recalls.[2] "He was puzzled by the fact that she couldn't end it all by saying 'I'm not a Communist'."

Rothstein, a Navy veteran, originally thought the charges against Milo were inflated in their importance. "They were going to kick him out of the reserves," he says, "and I thought what the hell is the big deal? Who wants to be in the reserves?"

The conference lasted well into the day. The three lawyers tried valiantly to persuade Margaret to craft a statement that would help her brother. She wouldn't budge.

"I just couldn't do it," she says of the statement. "I have a right to be a Communist if I want to be a Communist. I can be anything. If I break the law, then they have to come after me, not my brother."

"I'm a pragmatic guy," offers Rothstein. "Most Americans are pragmatic. The Raduloviches are different. Honor is everything."

Rothstein remembers when he was representing "a group of ethnics" and the judge chastised him for not understanding his clients, that money didn't mean anything to them, it was all honor.

"You can say that about the Raduloviches. Honor. It's everything," Rothstein says. "Sometimes there's a conflict between honor and your best interests. It's no contest with these folks [Radulovich family]."

Of the meeting that day, Margaret says wryly, "I held my own."

———→◦←———

Vera Layton had grown close to her troubled tenants, particularly Nancy. Working two jobs and attending school, Milo was often gone. Nancy, although she worked nights, was around during the day.

"Nancy was very upset," Mrs. Layton recalls. The Laytons, and others living in Dexter, were very supportive of the young serviceman and his family.

"We simply didn't believe it," Layton says. "We were not the least bit suspect of Milo."

———→◦←———

By all accounts, Canada's first Shakespeare Festival had been a resounding success. The farming community of Stratford, Ontario, population 19,000, had attracted more than 53,600 Canadian and American theatergoers during the six-week run.

Drama critics were effusive in their praise of the festival: "a genuine contribution to Shakespeare," wrote Brooks Atkinson of the New York Times.[3] Alec Guinness and Irene Worth, in particular, were singled out for their performances.

Up to a week before opening night, festival organizers were deep in debt and had feared a major flop. But once under way, an explosion of ticket sales prompted an extension of the festival from five weeks to six. Organizers admitted they would have rejoiced at a 60 percent capacity for the run: the performances played to 97 percent capacity. The unexpected influx of cash prompted the formation of a committee whose first task would be to determine whether the festival should be an annual affair.

TUESDAY, AUGUST 25, 1953

U nable to afford a civilian attorney, Milo sought military counsel.

As he prepared to visit the Judge Advocate General's office at Selfridge Air Force Base in nearby Mount Clemens, Milo Radulovich faced an uphill battle.

Although never reticent about defending his honor, when it came to challenging authority Milo didn't intentionally place himself in harm's way. "I was nervous and scared," he points out. "It is so difficult to explain to people today, especially young people, how fearful we were of authority."

If the situation were different, if Milo had no responsibility except to himself, the apprehension wouldn't have affected his thinking. "If I was single," he says, "it might have been different."

But he wasn't single. He was a twenty-seven-year-old husband and father of two beautiful little girls, one an infant. Nothing came before his family. "I had to take into account my ability to provide for them," he says.

From the standpoint of his family name, his career, and his conscience, Milo Radulovich really had no choice.

The trip to Selfridge had a twofold purpose. Milo was to meet with his military lawyer, but he also needed to officially acknowledge receipt of the charges.

And he was going to tell them he intended to fight those charges.

Lt. Milo J. Radulovich had determined he would not accept the tainted honorable discharge accompanied by the damning phrase, "resignation in lieu of elimination from the service."[1] Nor would he write a letter that would likely never leave his file *justifying* why he should not be discharged from the Air Force. He informed the Air Force that his decision was to accept the option to appear before a hearing board and avail himself of military counsel.

The meeting with his assigned military counsel, a second lieutenant with law school credentials from Harvard, did not go well. Milo asked how many cases like his had the young lieutenant defended. Four, came the response. How many had he won? None. "That pretty much decided it for me," he says with smile. "Those weren't the kind of odds I was looking for. He also told me 'you've had it. They got you pegged to start with, no matter what you say. All I can do is read your record.'"[2]

The military lawyer then went off the record and took Milo into his confidence. He urged him to seek civilian representation. The panel that would hear his case, advised the lawyer, would comprise three colonels. He doubted any of the defense counsels in his office would risk a burgeoning military career by challenging three full birds, one of whom, Col. William L. Doolan, Jr., was their commanding officer and would preside as president of the tribunal.

Regarding that visit Milo says, "The guy did me a favor by telling me to get a civilian lawyer. He didn't have to do that. I really appreciated his honesty. It turned out to be a great piece of advice."

———⇒➤●◄⇐———

On the day Milo Radulovich met with his military counsel, Detroiters read an emotional account of the first prisoner of war from their city to return home. Army Sgt. Edward Hewlett, in a North Korean prison camp for the past three years, had not set foot in Detroit for five years. After calling his brother, Hewlett waited more than an hour before his family finally arrived.[3]

A memo from Maj. Donald H. Smith to 1st Lt. Milo J. Radulovich, AO 589 839, AFRes, stated in part, "Officer desires to appear before a hearing board with military counsel appointed on his behalf."

It was now official. There would be no voluntary resignation and no letter of justification for the files.

According to a report by a special committee of the American Bar Association, it was the duty of lawyers to defend clients accused of subversion. That posture, editorialized the *Detroit News*, "is a reaffirmation of the basic American concept of justice for all."[1]

According to the report, "The very fact that reputable lawyers are willing to appear is added evidence of the strength and health of our system and a further good answer to the enemies of that system at home and abroad."

The editorial concluded that the American Bar Association had sent a message of comfort to the lawyers "who have been reluctant to accept cases for fear they would be suspected by the public of sharing the view held by those who seek their services."

Police in the communities making up the greater Boston area stepped up their search for Sylvia Plath, described as a "brilliant Smith College senior," who disappeared from her home. Reportedly near nervous collapse, Plath left a note saying she was going on a long hike.

THURSDAY, AUGUST 27, 1953

They would find the money somewhere. They had to. Securing a civilian attorney was no longer a luxury, it was now a necessity. But lack of money, Milo and Nancy quickly learned, was not their biggest problem.

⟹➤●◄⟸

"We were continually arguing," says Ron Rothstein of his relationship with Margaret Fishman. "Continually. I was amazed our employer put up with it."

Ron Rothstein and Margaret Fishman joined the Detroit law firm of Karbel and Eiges within a few months of each other in the spring of 1951. "She was very suspicious of me when we met," says Rothstein. "We came from different worlds. Yet I sensed her outstanding qualities as a human being. Margaret is very sensitive to, very knowledgeable about, and deeply interested and involved in politics."

Rothstein had prepped at a military academy, taken his undergraduate degree from the University of Michigan, and then graduated from Harvard Law School. "I was from a comfortable Jewish family," he says of his upbringing.

Margaret was the daughter of poor but proud immigrants. There were times when she didn't have electricity or enough to eat.

Yet their relationship grew into a friendship with a solid foundation of mutual respect. Margaret suggested to Rothstein he consider representing her brother, Milo. Ron Rothstein said no, and became the first lawyer to reject Milo Radulovich's request for legal representation.

"I [am] ashamed to say, in my heart I was a red baiter," he recalls. "I was influenced by a book, *Darkness at Noon*, by Arthur Koestler, that describes how evil the Communist system was. I couldn't take people's jobs away, but I gloated when it happened because they were my political opponents. I'm ashamed of it now, very much ashamed."

Rothstein also deeply regrets his decision not to represent Milo. "I should've done it but I just didn't feel up to it," he offers.

Personal politics aside, Rothstein is quick to point out there was still a valid reason for turning down Milo. He felt strongly his being Jewish would significantly hamper the case. "You know the anti-Semites," he explains, "are always trying to brand the Jews as either Communists or international bankers, or both."

Rothstein was more sensitive than most to the anti-Semitism of the era. Was it a residue from Father Coughlin?* "Hell yes," he responds. "But Father Coughlin was just the tip of the iceberg. I can still remember my first interview after law school when I was asked if I was a Hebrew. This was in 1951."

---

*Fr. Charles E. Coughlin entered the public limelight in 1926. After his church in Royal Oak, Michigan, burned to the ground, Detroit radio station WJR had offered him free airtime to raise money for a new church, the Shrine of the Little Flower. Four years later, his church rebuilt, Father Coughlin and his "Golden Hour of the Little Flower" had become a Sunday night mainstay on CBS radio.

While Coughlin's popularity grew, his message had become more strident and blatantly anti-Semitic. An early supporter of FDR, he broke with Roosevelt in early 1935 and called for the president's elimination by the use of bullets. He claimed at that time "the New Deal" had become "the Jew deal."

In early 1942, Coughlin's anti-Semitism reached such extremes that the National Association of Broadcasters urged stations to cancel their contracts with him. Many did. On May 1, 1942, Coughlin was silenced by the Vatican. The message to the flamboyant priest—to cease all public pronouncements under threat of defrocking—was delivered by his religious superior, Archbishop Edwin Mooney. Father Coughlin obeyed the directive.

The Red baiters," he continues, "could be pretty good anti-Semites too. There was no civil-rights movement in those days."[1]

The Detroit Tigers announced the signing of Claude Agee, an eighteen-year-old outfielder from Blythedale, Pennsylvania. Scouted by Ed Katalinas, Agee was the first Negro ball player in the Tiger organization.

Agee, formally signed by the assistant farm director, John McHale, hit .419 and five home runs in his senior year. McHale and Katalinas saw Agee play the previous June while scouting Tiger bonus baby Al Kaline.[2]

In a speech before the American Bar Association in Boston, Atty. Gen. Herbert Brownell announced his intent to place the Lawyers Guild on his official list of subversive organizations.

Brownell indicated that although the sixteen-year-old guild "originally attracted some well known and completely loyal American citizens," it is now fully committed to the Communist party line.

The guild had been notified that in accordance with new procedures, it was entitled to a hearing before being added to the list of subversives.[3]

MONDAY, AUGUST 31, 1953

Against a backdrop where 50 percent of Americans supported Joe McCarthy, and the unions of his father and neighbors were suspected of strong Communist influence, Milo Radulovich sought the services of an attorney to prove he was not a security risk to the government.

He hit the bricks. For nearly a week now, Milo had been on foot in downtown Detroit. His quest had taken him in and out of tall buildings, up rapidly moving elevators, down long corridors to law firms with many names on their doors. He asked efficient receptionists if he might see a lawyer, and waited patiently while they juggled calls.

Occasionally a lawyer would spend a few moments with him. Some promised they'd get back to him, but they never did. Detroit's legal community, and its collective feet of sand, underscored that the Red scare was real.

"Most said they didn't have time for me," Milo says with a degree of disgust. "One guy came right out and told me he wasn't about to get his career besmirched by getting involved in this Red thing. Another was a little more blunt. He just said, 'What do you think, I'm crazy?'"

His concern was mounting with each passing day. Time had grown precious to Milo. The world didn't stop just because the government was trying to throw Lt. Milo Radulovich out of the Air Force. There were still classes to attend, chapters to read, papers to write.

The bills were still there too, as well as the two jobs he was working that enabled him to pay those bills. Milo was being pulled in several directions. Kathy's cradle still needed rocking, while Diane rightfully expected her father to be a dad. There was little time for Nancy.

For Milo Radulovich, or anyone else cloaked in Communist-related charges, it was not a good time to need an attorney. The law offices he entered had already been visited by reports and resolutions from both the American and Michigan Bar associations. Those earlier visits did not bode well for him.

In 1950, the Michigan Bar Association had mirrored its national counterpart and stepped up its efforts to rid the bar of Communists. Resolution 14 had reaffirmed the State Bar of Michigan's position "as vehemently opposed to Communism and its treasonable doctrines."[1] The resolution let it be known that those who traveled the same roads would also not be welcome: "[Resolved] That Communists and those SYMPATHETIC TO OR practicing its teachings be barred from all government service; federal state and local...[Resolved] That Communists and those sympathetic to OR PRACTICING its teachings be barred from teaching in the schools, colleges, and universities of the United States."[2]

Spurred on by a resolution of the American Bar Association that called for "disbarment of all lawyers who are members of the Communist party of the United States or who advocate Marxism-Leninism,"[3] the Michigan Bar Association had formed a special panel to study disciplining "disloyal members." Not only did the final report echo the ABA recommendations but it also called for the commissioner of the Michigan State Police and the state attorney general to forward information to the Michigan Bar Association that might be helpful in preparing charges for disbarment proceedings.

In 1952, the Michigan legislature had approved the Little Smith Act, legislation that made *advocating* overthrow of the government a felony punishable by life imprisonment. Even more chilling to lawyers, the Michigan bar report had specified that in situations involving violations of the Little Smith Act, "it is not necessary that criminal conviction precede the petition for disbarment."

The report had prompted a lengthy debate, but it was eventually approved by a wide margin.

Writing on the disbarment report a few months later, E. Blythe Stason[4] asked, "Why undertake to disbar attorneys guilty of disloyal acts—acts that may not necessarily be related to the administration of justice?" Because, he points out, the antics associated with tactics in cases involving charges of disloyalty call for a housecleaning in advance instead of waiting for the shambles to take place.[5]

———◦———

The charged anti-Red atmosphere of Detroit went far beyond its legal community. In late February 1952, the House Un-American Activities Committee had visited the city and, according to one witness, played a role in accelerating passage of a state law mandating registration of all Communists.

At the crest of its power in the early fifties, HUAC had set its sights on communism in the labor unions. Michigan, with its abundance of organized autoworkers, should have provided some noteworthy conquests. But Detroit had not treated kindly those who sought headlines in their battle against the domestic Soviet. The committee was hungry for what it felt was a long overdue victory against labor in its own backyard.

The committee came to order amid rumors that because of suspected Communist infiltration, an administrator was about to be placed over Local 600, the United Auto Workers' largest unit. Union officials lamely claimed that a directive ordering the officers of Local 600 to appear before the International Executive Board had nothing to do with HUAC's probe of communism in the labor movement and its visit to Detroit.[6]

During the week-long hearing, the stage was dominated by Coleman Alexander Young, a black man, whose stature was already approaching legend in Detroit's Black Bottom district. Young stubbornly refused to accord the committee, dominated by white southerners, the deference to which it had become accustomed. A gifted and facile speaker, Young totally rejected the path of silence recommended by his attorney George Crockett. He reasoned the committee wanted to hear his views, else they would not have asked him to testify.

The first to feel the brunt of Young's acid tongue was the committee counsel, Frank Tavenner. Young directed Tavenner, a white southerner who spoke with a decided accent, on proper pronunciation of the word Negro. Bristling at the committee counsel, Young instructed "that word is 'Negro' not 'Niggra'".[7]

Tavenner responded, "I said 'Negro'. I think you are mistaken."

Young retorted, "I hope I am. Speak more clearly."

The committee Chairman, John Wood, then interjected himself. "I will appreciate it if you will not argue with counsel."

Young refused to be intimidated and responded to Wood, "It isn't my purpose to argue. As a Negro, I resent the slurring of the name of my race."

"They knew they were doing violence to the word," Young recalls. "I knew they could speak more plainly than that."[8]

"Do you consider the activities of the Communist Party un-American?" Tavenner asked a few minutes later.

"I consider the activities of this committee un-American," Young retorted.

Further into the hearing he again crossed swords with the chairman. Wood told Young, "For your information, out of the 112 Negro votes cast in the last election in the little village from which I come, I got 112 of them."

Young fired back "I happen to know, in Georgia, Negro people are prevented from voting by virtue of terror, intimidation, and lynchings.

It is my contention you would not be in Congress today if it were not for the legal restrictions on voting on the part of my people."

Later, he cut Congressman Donald Jackson off in mid sentence. "If you think," Jackson began, "the lot of the Negro, who have in 80-some odd years come forward to a much better position…"

"Mr. Jackson," Young sharply interrupted, "we are not going to wait 80 more years, I will tell you that."

Of his performance, the *Detroit News* wrote: If the Soviet Politburo ever issues an award for contempt of the U.S. Congress, Mr. Young should be one of the leading candidates."

A phonograph recording of his appearance was given broad circulation in the Black Bottom district of Detroit.

⟫●⟪

The Michigan legislature approved the Michigan Communist Control Law, or the Trucks Act as it came to be known. Sponsored by Kenneth Trucks, a Republican from the west side of the state, the bill mandated annual registration of all Communists. Such registration must include, among other things, home and business address, occupation, sources of income, and the names of others known to be Communists. Failure to register or making false statements was a felony punishable by up to ten years in prison.

Files compiled under the act could, at the discretion of the state police, be opened to the general public. Further, the attorney general was empowered to transmit a file to a person's employer.

The act also prohibited Communists from working for state or local government or from appearing on a Michigan ballot.

Should a dispute arise regarding someone's Communist affiliation, the Trucks Act specified that taking the Fifth Amendment was prima facie evidence that "such person is a communist or a knowing member of a communist front organization."[9]

Even before the bill had reached his desk, Michigan Gov. G. Mennen Williams indicated strong support for the measure. "The Communist party over the years," Williams said, "has not been a political party in the ordinary sense of the word, but a conspiracy."[10]

Saul Grossman, executive director of the Michigan Committee for the Protection of the Foreign Born, strongly protested the bill to Williams. Grossman, however, steadfastly refused to disclose the membership of his organization's board to the public for fear they would be harassed.

Lawyers, to the detriment of Milo Radulovich's search, remained in the news.

The American Bar Association's policy-making body, the House of Delegates, unanimously adopted a resolution urging the legal profession to purge itself of Communists. The report cited the incompatibility of membership in both the bar and the Communist party.

The Detroit Free Press strongly supported the House of Delegates recommendation. "Red lawyers," opined the paper, "have attempted to make a mockery of American justice by hiding themselves and their clients behind the protection of laws which they are seeking to overthrow."[11]

The Detroit News discussed the legal profession's dilemma, following Attorney General Brownell's decision to place the Lawyers Guild on the subversive list. Many eminent lawyers, including several prominent Michigan judges, were proudly affiliated with the guild.[12]

TUESDAY, SEPTEMBER 1, 1953

Congressman Kit Clardy announced a postponement of the House Un-American Activities Committee hearings scheduled for Detroit this fall. Clardy indicated he was currently conferring with two witnesses in New York, both of whom he expected to testify at the Detroit hearings.

The delay was prompted by a conflict with scheduled hearings in California and a European trip by several members of the committee to study governmental expenditures.

"Staff members will continue combing the tremendous amount of material that has come to us about Michigan," Clardy said.[1]

MONDAY, SEPTEMBER 7, 1953

*A*ppearing *on the CBS weekly show, "Man of the Week," the UAW-CIO president, Walter Reuther, admitted there are Communists in Ford Local 600 but only in secondary leadership roles.*

Reuther said unions must be vigilant against communism. He pointed out that every effort was being made to spot Reds in the unions and keep them from assuming positions of leadership.[1]

California Lt. Gov. Goodwin Knight had been assured by the Eisenhower administration that he would be governor before year's end. It had been widely rumored that a federal post, possibly a circuit judgeship, had been found for current Gov. Earl Warren while he awaited nomination to a Supreme Court vacancy.

TUESDAY, SEPTEMBER 8, 1953

Ernest Goodman was dismayed to find his old friend in such a state of despair.

Charles C. Lockwood and Ernest Goodman had been friends for almost fifteen years. "He was a liberal-minded person, and was independent," Goodman recalls, "one of the first lawyers around here who could be considered a consumer lawyer."[1]

Charlie Lockwood entered the local limelight in the early forties when he successfully represented a number of small, independent farmers locked in a price-fixing battle with the state's large milk producers. His son, Charles P. Lockwood, fondly recalls traveling around the state with his father while the no-nonsense lawyer talked to small gatherings of farmers regarding their case.

At one point in the case, Lockwood met with a young Teamster organizer who urged the lawyer to pursue his defense of the farmers in a far less aggressive fashion. "He was a fighter," the younger Lockwood says of his father. "He wasn't afraid to speak up to anybody." Lockwood was not intimidated, nor was he swayed by James R. Hoffa.[2]

As close as Goodman and Lockwood were, both personally and philosophically, their chance meeting should have been pleasant. It was not. Lockwood, in his characteristic blunt fashion, voiced a concern that the country was becoming a Fascist state. "He was so pessimistic about everything," Goodman says. "He was pessimistic about

41

life, about doing anything, and not only that, but the worth of doing anything."[3]

They talked for some time. Goodman tried to buoy Lockwood's spirits. "You're good," he told him. "People respect you."

When they parted, Goodman was concerned for his friend. "I was trying to get him back into the kind of political activity he had been involved in most of his life," he says. "But he was so bitter. He just felt there was no point in doing anything."

⸻⸻⸻⸻

Fred M. Vinson, chief justice of the United State Supreme Court, died after an early morning heart attack. Vinson, 63, had served as chief justice since 1946.

Initial speculation for Vinson's replacement centered on California's Republican governor, Earl Warren.

Although the decision on an attorney would rest with Milo, Margaret's career as a legal secretary afforded her an exceptional vantage point in the search for legal representation. After Ron Rothstein's refusal, she suggested Milo ask for an appointment with Ernest Goodman.

Margaret had worked for Goodman. Like Rothstein, she and her husband, Al, had also developed a warm friendship with him. Unlike Rothstein, however, Ernest Goodman had a long and impressive record of defending those accused of Communist-related charges.

Goodman's partner, George Crockett, an African American, had been summoned to New York in 1950 to represent four black defendants in the Smith Act trial. All were convicted. After the trial, Crockett and other attorneys in the case were cited for contempt. There was, according to Goodman, little or no due process in the contempt proceedings, and Crockett eventually spent four months in prison.

Wary of both the national and state bar associations' aggressive posture to rid their profession of Communist sympathizers, Goodman and others banded together to ward off disbarment proceedings against Crockett.

Ernest Goodman was no stranger to loyalty hearings, nor to the front pages of Detroit's newspapers. About those incidents he observes, "When the newspapers reported the case, the Communist's

43

lawyer was painted with the same brush as the client. The apostrophe made little difference."[1]

Apart from the fact that she respected his ability as an attorney, there was another, more practical reason Margaret thought Ernest Goodman a good choice to represent her brother—he had a good track record with military loyalty board hearings, especially those involving family relationships.

In 1947, the United States Army had taken action against Capt. Charles Hill, Jr., ostensibly for reading the *Daily Worker*, a charge the young soldier flatly denied. According to Coleman Young, "The fact is that Charlie Hill was a good soldier who never had a radical thought in his life, and they were fucking with him because he was assisting with his father's Common Council campaign."[2]

Long a prominent figure in civil-rights circles, the Reverend Charles Hill, Sr., had teamed with labor leader Stanley Nowak to form a broad left-wing coalition for the Common Council elections that year. "Reverend Hill was an old-fashioned Bible-thumping preacher whose only political concern was making things right in the sight of the Lord," Young says. "It was mind-boggling to me that the United States government would be so afraid of a man who was so good and decent."[3]

Hill's credentials included a stint as president of the National Negro Congress, a labor-oriented civil-rights organization. He was also among those called to testify in the HUAC hearings of 1952, where he appeared with counsel, Ernest Goodman.

Although Hill lost the Detroit Common Council election of 1947, Captain Hill was cleared with an apology. His attorney in the widely publicized case was none other than Ernest Goodman.

Goodman's frequent visits to the front page of Detroit's newspapers prompted his mother to relay a concern voiced by her card-playing friends that he was "doing something bad." Goodman laughs. "It was very simple to her," he says; "you're either good or bad. I just told her, 'Ma, look, you think I would do anything bad? Well, I am not. Don't believe them.'"

Milo and Goodman met. Together they reviewed the only background Milo had on the case, the sparse material delivered days earlier by the Air Force major. Success, Goodman discerned, hinged on their ability to try the case in the court of public opinion. The same newspapers[4] that had painted Goodman and his clients with a singular brush would have to be courted and converted.

If he sat at the helm of the defense, it would likely be reported as nothing more than Ernie Goodman representing another Communist.

"I told Milo," he says, "that the climate is pretty bad around here. This case is a good case that could be used to open up the eyes of people. But I couldn't get it the publicity it deserves." Ernest Goodman said he didn't think it would be in Milo's best interest if he represented him.

He did, however, have someone else in mind.

Goodman called Charlie Lockwood and briefly recounted his visit with Milo. Then he said to Lockwood, "This is the case you've been looking for, this is the case you're going to win."[5]

Ernie Goodman knew publicity was crucial to the case. Charles Lockwood wrote a column for the *Eastside Shopper*. He understood the power of newspapers and the important role a properly framed issue could play in tapping that power. Goodman also knew Lockwood possessed a talent not normally associated with the legal profession, a facility for a quick journey to the heart of an issue, an ability that would be welcomed by the hard-bitten corps of newspaper reporters covering the case. They would, he felt certain, like Charlie Lockwood.

Goodman's advice to Milo was uncomplicated: "Listen to Charlie Lockwood, he's got fire in the belly, and he's got nothing to lose."

Charles C. Lockwood, attorney-at-law, member in good standing of the American Civil Liberties Union, the National Lawyers Guild, and longtime combative advocate for the underdog, agreed to see Milo

Radulovich. Only after talking with him would he decide whether to take the case.

——➤●◀——

The Louisville Times *managing editor, Norman Isaacs, laid down the gauntlet of ethics for his colleagues. Isaacs levied charges on what he considered private corruption—the acceptance of gifts in return for newspaper coverage. The English-born Isaacs pointed out that staffers at his paper eschewed routine perks: sports writers had to pay their own way on baseball trips and women's-page editors were not allowed to accept expensive samples or other gifts.*

The taking of favors, Isaacs contended, was akin to saying newspaper space is for sale. "Newspapers that still accept travel and other expenses for covering any kind of event anywhere are accepting subsidies—or, to put it more bluntly, bribes, for their coverage. Let's be honest, or go out and dig ditches."[6]

FRIDAY, SEPTEMBER 11, 1953

They met in Charlie Lockwood's home on Detroit's west side. Although a proper man, the lawyer greeted his guest at the door in an open shirt and no necktie. Milo was uncomfortable to begin with; Lockwood's chosen manner of referring to him, not by name but simply "young man," added to his uneasiness.

Milo at first thought the sixty-one-year-old lawyer to be on the irascible side. "I learned in a hurry," he says, "that Charlie Lockwood never wasted a word. When he told you something you knew exactly what he meant. There were no shades of meaning."

They sat at Lockwood's dining room table. Milo vividly recalls the tension of that first meeting, the sandpaper feeling of his dry throat, the intimidation of "a table so big you couldn't lift it with five people." The lawyer listened stoically, allowing the nervous young airman to tell his story uninterrupted, making no effort to calm him. While assessing the arguments, the seasoned lawyer was also taking careful measure of the man.

Milo handed him the papers delivered by the major less than two weeks ago. Lockwood studied them for what seemed a long time. Then, he recalls, the lawyer looked up and said abruptly, "There's only one way to fight this and that's through the press. Are you willing to talk to newspapers, young man?'"

Lockwood's comment unnerved Milo. "I thought he was just going to represent me at the hearing," he says. "That's all I was there

47

for. I couldn't afford that type of sophisticated representation." Lockwood pressed the matter and said he had an editor friend at the *Detroit News*; would Milo be willing to talk with him? "Charlie said he was hoping for a few paragraphs on page fourteen," Milo says. "So I said sure, why not? I had nothing to lose at this stage."

Other lawyers had kept Milo at arm's length and tendered insincere wishes of luck before escorting him to the door, but Charlie Lockwood's keen instincts quickly ferreted out critical aspects of the case.

Like thousands of other Americans, Milo Radulovich was attending college under the G.I. Bill of Rights, a veteran who boasted an outstanding military record.

Milo offered no long list of published works an army of congressional committee staffers could pour over and claim subliminal Communist messages.

The case revolved around immigrants, first- and second-generation Americans. Part of the charges emanated from John Radulovich's simple desire for knowledge of his homeland. A father or grandfather who wondered aloud in broken English of the old country, yet still professed a fervent love for the United States, was more than a common occurrence in 1953 America.

The Radulovich drama wouldn't unfold in the population centers of New York, Washington, or Los Angeles, but in tiny Dexter, Michigan, Main Street U.S.A., population fifteen hundred.

The strength of the defense resided in the simplicity of the case. The plight of Milo Radulovich, Lockwood ascertained, was easily understood. Handled properly, that fact alone would be pivotal to fueling public interest and, hopefully, outrage.

There was one hurdle to the Lockwood strategy, though: John Radulovich. Going to the newspapers meant publicity, and Milo didn't know if his immigrant father was ready for a public confrontation with the government. "If my dad says no," he told Lockwood, "then I won't do it." In what appeared to be the first loosening of his stiff, emotional demeanor, Lockwood said he understood, but to get back with him as soon as possible.

The two rose and shook hands. No mention had yet been made of money. Towering over his shorter and stockier client, Charles Lockwood said there would be no fee for his services. "He said he'd do it for the principle," Milo recalls.

———————➤●◄———————

Charlie Lockwood remained reserved, almost distant, during the meeting with Milo. After he left, however, his son, Charles P. Lockwood, recalls the outrage of his father. "He was incensed that they could accuse a man for the actions of his father and sister," the younger Lockwood says. "He called it a star-chamber type of proceeding."[1]

———————➤●◄———————

Raised on a farm in South Lyon, Michigan, Charles C. Lockwood was not born to wealth. Nevertheless, his father was still able to give each of his six children a farm. Young Charles immediately sold his for tuition money to the University of Michigan. Later he attended the Detroit College of Law and in 1922 opened his own legal practice.

His brother pursued a successful career in medicine and also moonlighted as a prizefighter; at one time he was being groomed to fight the heavyweight champion, James Johnson.

During the twenties and thirties, Lockwood served as a professor of speech and oratory at his law school alma mater. There he acquired a widespread reputation as an accomplished public speaker. A lanky frame and a booming, stentorian voice reinforced the striking physical resemblance he bore to actor Raymond Massey.

His son recalls him as stern, but not brutal, with strong family ties. "He didn't run on too long," says the younger Lockwood. "My father was not a man of anecdotes."[2]

Despite pressure, Charlie Lockwood had turned down a prestigious appointment as assistant prosecuting attorney for Wayne County, which includes the city of Detroit. Unlike other lawyers who could offer the resources of a large law firm, the fiercely independent Lockwood preferred to practice alone.

——————⋙●⋘——————

Bandleader Ray Anthony emerged as the clear winner in the "Dragnet" theme sweepstakes.

Jack Webb, owner and star of "Dragnet," television's popular police drama, had steadfastly refused to allow the show's familiar theme to be recorded commercially. Finally, Webb relented, and the scramble was on to record Walter Schumann's original music. Within ten days, Anthony's version was in record stores and on the radio. Inside of a month sales had topped 500,000. Anthony, of "Bunny Hop" fame, auditioned a number of trombonists for the recording session before settling on Dick Reynolds.

SATURDAY, SEPTEMBER 12, 1953

Although he had previously advised the Air Force of his intent to seek nonmilitary counsel, Milo now informed them he had indeed retained a civilian attorney.

Charlie Lockwood went to work. The hearing on "Proposed Termination of Appointment" was set for September 22. More time was needed. Lockwood requested a postponement of the hearing until "on or after 18 October 1953."

———————

One of the nation's most eligible bachelors, Massachusetts Sen. John F. Kennedy pushed through a crowd of three thousand onlookers and took socialite Jacqueline Lee Bouvier as his wife. More than eight hundred guests jammed St. Mary's Catholic Church in Newport, Rhode Island, to witness the nuptials. Later, more than twelve hundred well-wishers gathered for a reception at the three hundred-acre Newport estate of the bride's parents.

The ceremony was performed by the Most Reverend Richard J. Cushing, archbishop of Boston.

Kennedy, a Harvard graduate, was the son of Joseph P. Kennedy, former ambassador to the Court of St. James. The bride, a Vassar graduate, was the daughter of Mrs. Hugh D. Auchincloss of Newport and McLean, Virginia, and John V. Bouvier of New York.

A West Coast honeymoon was planned.

———————⇒⊃●⊂⇐———————

Of the top ten television programs of 1953, only "Dragnet," Jack Webb's paean to police officers everywhere, and "Fireside Theater" offered a diversion from lighthearted fare.[1]

The comedy of former vaudevillians Jackie Gleason, Milton Berle, and "the one, the only, Grroouucho" monopolized newly purchased Philco and Dumont television sets.

Earlier in the year, Dwight David Eisenhower had been sworn in as the thirty-fourth president of the United States. Also taking the oath was the new vice president and longtime Communist fighter, Richard M. Nixon. Millions watched on their televisions as, Eisenhower, the war hero from Abilene, vowed to uphold the Constitution.

The night before Eisenhower's inauguration those same sets were tuned to CBS and "I Love Lucy" in what was to date the most watched program in television history. America's favorite redhead and her Cuban bandleader husband, Desi Arnaz, were presented with an offspring. Little Ricky now graced the household of televisions's number-one rated show.

———————⇒⊃●⊂⇐———————

In his biography of Walter Winchell, Neal Gabler describes the gossip columnist's relationship with FBI Director J. Edgar Hoover: "No two men so fully appreciated the value of secrets—of finding them, deploying them, protecting oneself from them."[2]

Their relationship was joined in August 1934, when Hoover intervened to secure a long-coveted commission for Winchell as a naval intelligence officer. Three weeks later Winchell, even though he had the scoop of the century in the crime of the century, reciprocated by demurring and allowed Hoover to announce that Bruno Hauptmann had been arrested in the Lindbergh kidnapping case.

Shortly thereafter, Gabler says that "rumors were swirling around New York, that Winchell was so tight with Hoover that the columnist was getting information from the bureau before official press briefings."[3]

"Winchell was probably the first nationally known radio commentator developed by the FBI," says former Assistant Director William Sullivan. *"We sent Winchell information regularly. He was our mouthpiece."*[4]

Although the friendship between Hoover and Winchell was genuine, it was nurtured by a mutual love of the clandestine. Winchell's column and broadcasts were dotted with endless Hoover trivia, feeding the director's insatiable ego. Hoover, in turn, supplied valued tidbits to the nation's most famous gossip; some of the items were even newsworthy. *"The source, although he always denied it, was Edgar [Hoover] himself,"* writes Anthony Summers, in his biography of Hoover. *"Hoover was almost like another press agent submitting material."*[5]

———————⟫●⟪———————

On the same show in which he revealed a Russian-based plot to assassinate him, Walter Winchell included a "blind" item that HUAC was holding secret sessions in California to investigate the entertainment industry. *"The most popular of all television stars,"* Winchell said, *"was confronted with her membership in the Communist Party."*[6]

At home that night listening to the show, Lucille Ball pondered who it might be. Desi Arnaz was playing poker when a friend called informing him of the Winchell item. To Arnaz, the item was anything but "blind."

Later in the evening, friends and supporters gathered at the home of Lucy and Desi to discuss damage control.

Preparing his upcoming case, Charles Lockwood carefully began a studied review of Air Force Regulation 35-62, which prohibited "a close and continuing association" with persons, including relatives, suspected of disloyalty to the government of the United States of America.

———◦———

The Lucille Ball story dominated America's headlines.

Television's top comedienne, as the story unfolded, had registered to vote as a Communist in the 1936 primary election, "but only because Grandpa wanted all of us to."[1] At the time, Lucy was twenty-four and a budding Hollywood star. She adamantly denied ever being a member of the Communist party.

Records show Ball signed a nominating petition for Emil Freed, Communist party candidate for the 57th California Assembly District. She indicated that her grandfather, Fred C. Hunt, now deceased, made all the political decisions in the family and the petition was signed only at his insistence.

Her husband, Desi Arnaz, told reporters that the only time Lucy had ever voted was the previous year, and that her ballot had been cast for Eisenhower. The only thing "red" about Lucy, he said, was her hair.

Congressman Donald Jackson, a vigorous participant in the Michigan HUAC hearings in 1952, was quick to exonerate Ball. "There is no evidence that Miss Ball is or ever was a party member," Jackson said to a packed press conference. "The committee is satisfied and does not intend to question Miss Ball further."[2]

When queried about the swiftness in clearing Ball of any wrongdoing, Jackson responded, "the Committee is departing from its usual procedure so that fact may be separated from rumor and no damage be done Miss Ball."[3]

TUESDAY, SEPTEMBER 15, 1953

"We Still Love Lucy,"[1] proclaimed the headline above the editorial in the *Detroit Free Press*.

Minimizing Lucille Ball's brief jaunt from the entertainment section to the front page, the *Free Press* relegated the affair to that of zany comedy. "It sounds like a family whose doings, with a little polishing by a script writer, could be made pretty entertaining,"[2] said the paper.

After dismissing the public case against Lucy, the *Free Press* went on to challenge the motives of those who would question her loyalty: "Much less funny is the irresponsibility of congressional investigators who risk compromising an individual's professional standing by giving weight and publicity to such a piece of bygone and doubtless regretted trivia."[3]

Milo Radulovich wondered aloud how his case differed from that of Lucille Ball's.

Harry Lunn knew. "She admitted she was wrong," says the editor in chief of the *Michigan Daily*, the University of Michigan's highly regarded student newspaper. "That was the difference between her and Milo."[4]

Charles Lockwood needed additional time, not only to prepare his case but also to let the wholesale injustice of the government's charges against his client percolate with the newspapers. But the government was not about to cooperate.

The request to delay the hearing until on or after October 18, 1953, was officially rejected. "You are advised," said a memo to Milo from Maj. Donald Smith, "that we are unable to postpone the hearing for such a long time."[5] The best they would do is one week. The hearing was now set for September 29, 1953.

FRIDAY, SEPTEMBER 18, 1953

Michigan Sen. Homer Ferguson resurrected campaign rhetoric from the previous year and blasted Adlai E. Stevenson for his softness on communism.

Ferguson, pinch-hitting for the ailing GOP chairman, Leonard Hall, keynoted a Republican women's regional conference in Chicago. Ironically, during the previous two days, Democrats rallied in the same locale, with both Stevenson and Michigan Gov. G. Mennen Williams featured as speakers.

Ferguson's prepared remarks noted Stevenson's speech from the day before: "To me it was an alarming document—alarming because it appears plain that the eggheads will never learn about Communism.[1] It is difficult to discover exactly what Adlai Stevenson is advocating, but anyone who has read the speech will have to admit that the old softness toward Communism which has marred his wing of the Democratic Party is still with us."[2]

Ferguson defined "egghead" for the wildly partisan crowd as "a person with both feet planted firmly in midair on any issue."[3]

The GOP senator also blasted Williams, who chaired a symposium on agriculture during the two-day Democratic gathering. Citing the Michigan governor's complaint that cuts in military spending were tightening up employment, that farm income was down and economic conditions terrible, Ferguson countered with, "These gentlemen [Stevenson and Williams] offered no alternative. But I imagine many a mother asked herself what their solution would have been—to keep the war in Korea going?"[4]

Williams was a rumored challenger to Ferguson for the 1954 Michigan Senate election.

The conference also examined some political races for the upcoming year. The congressional seat of Kit Clardy, HUAC member from Lansing, Michigan, was assigned "marginal" status, meaning his previous victory was less than 5 percent.

MONDAY, SEPTEMBER 21, 1953

Charlie Lockwood arranged a meeting for Milo with a friend on the editorial board of the *Detroit News*. Although he was not comfortable talking to reporters, Milo told his trusted counsel he would cooperate in any way that would help the case. But there was an important person he had to see before visiting the paper.

A month earlier Milo had driven into Detroit from his home in Dexter for what he knew would be a difficult conversation with his father. Now another equally difficult journey had to be undertaken.

Why John Radulovich, Milo wondered. Why were they doing this to his father? He certainly was not the propaganda machine described in the Statement of Reasons. Milo recalled the tremendous surge of pride experienced by his father during the war when the old man was tapped to become a member of skilled trades, the elite in the corps of automobile factory workers. After attending classes, he became an internal grinder. "He was so proud," Milo recalls. "He felt like he was really somebody in the plant. I think those couple of years were some of the happiest of his life."

He also remembered his father's unselfish patriotism. Shortly after the war, Michigan's automobile factories were glutted with returning servicemen. Layoffs were announced and would be implemented on the basis of seniority. John Radulovich, with service dating to 1928, was not slated to lose his job, but when he discovered a number of disabled war veterans were, he volunteered for layoff. "He just said it was the right thing to do," Milo remembers. "Some rabble-rouser."

If John Radulovich were to tell Milo he did not want to make the fight with the Air Force public, that would have been it. Milo would simply inform his attorney they could not go to the press.

Standing on the same cool basement tiles where father and son had conversed weeks before, Milo spoke of his trust in Charlie Lockwood and of the attorney's belief that the story must be told to the press. After explaining why taking the case public would benefit him, they examined the consequences. "I told him this would be in the paper, your name would be in it," Milo says of their talk. "It was a tough conversation. But if he said no, then I never would have gone to the papers."

"The old-country types of his generation," Milo explains, "were hat in hand in America to the bosses. He was a foreigner who couldn't speak English. Authority was a big thing. And now here's the United States government coming down on him."

News from the old country told of the terror, of arrests in the night, of imprisonment without trial. Government, John Radulovich knew all to well, could be a formidable enemy.

In the end, John Radulovich's apprehension over being named in an official document, of fighting his government on the pages of American newspapers, was far less important to him than the integrity of his family name. "He said yes," Milo recalls, "but he was pretty shook up about it."

"Where Are They Now," asked Newsweek. Preston Tucker, whose rear-engine dream car failed to penetrate the nation's tough automobile market, was reported to be living in Ypsilanti, Michigan, and operating a moderately successful machine and tool company with his mother. Bankruptcy debts resulting from his ill-fated "Tucker Torpedo" were slowly but consistently being repaid.[1]

TUESDAY, SEPTEMBER 22, 1953

For a paperboy in Detroit, delivering the *Detroit News* was the best job in town, especially during the depression—the customers paid. That regularity of payment instilled in Milo and Sam Radulovich, *Detroit Times* carriers both, a belief that the *News* was the paper of Detroit's upper class.

The irony was not lost on Milo. The immigrant's son, raised in a family of blue collars and callused hands, was about to become a story in the same paper that he had long aspired to deliver.

Save for a few wasted moments with feckless lawyers, talking to the *Detroit News* represented his first opportunity to sway the opinion of someone who already wasn't on his side; to defend himself with someone who mattered, someone who could help explain to the world that he wasn't a security risk.

Don't despair, Charlie Lockwood had told him. They were only looking for a paragraph or two on page fourteen. Even if just a few people took notice, that's a beginning, he said. They could build from there.

Nevertheless, Milo was anxious. The strategy of going to the press was fraught with far too many unknowns. Already weary to the point of exhaustion, his mind was swimming. This whole thing could backfire.

This was real life, not the movies. A movie buff, Milo wondered what if the reporter wasn't as conscientious as James Stewart in *Call Northside 777*.

The *News* was a conservative paper. What if the reporter was an ardent anti-Communist? Hostile? Tried to trip him up with his own words?

The family name could be muddied. Despite John Radulovich's blessing, Milo knew a negative article would break his father. The proud Montenegrin would never understand.

What if the article was favorable; would it antagonize the Air Force and hurt his case? What if it was unfavorable; would it hurt the case?

His father's admonition clear in his mind to do what must be done to protect the Radulovich name, Milo arrived at the offices of the *Detroit News*. After a brief handshake with Charlie Lockwood's friend, he was ushered to the desk of a reporter, Russell Harris.

No stranger to hand-to-hand public combat, Charlie Lockwood advised his client to be straightforward. Answer questions directly, don't try to manipulate the reporter. The facts in your case, he sagely counseled, were strong enough for the story to stand on its own two legs.

Long ago Milo learned the value of uncompromising integrity from his parents. "Sure, I was nervous," he recalls, "but I decided if I was honest, God would guide my answers. Besides that, I really didn't have anything to lose."

They talked for three hours. Milo recounted that day when the dour-looking major and sergeant appeared on his doorstep. He talked about the options and why they weren't really options. Together they dissected the Statement of Reasons, the undocumented transgressions of his father, and his sister's exercising of her constitutional right of free speech. The reporter, in turn, grilled Milo on his background as well as that of his father and sister.

"He was really thorough," Milo says of Harris. "He knew about the internal politics of the various nationalities in Detroit, and that impressed me." He was heartened by Harris's decision to send a photographer home with him for a picture of the family.

Milo had never been interviewed by a reporter. He thought it went well and said as much to Charlie Lockwood when he called to brief his attorney on the meeting with the *Detroit News*.

———⟫●⟪———

Paring their roster for the September 27 regular season opener against the Pittsburgh Steelers, the Detroit Lions released George "Pat" Summerall, former University of Arkansas end and kicker.

WEDNESDAY, SEPTEMBER 23, 1953

Milo Radulovich left for school that Wednesday morning a worried student carrying two jobs, fourteen units of physics and math, and a growing concern for his family's future. He returned home that evening a celebrity. "The phones started ringing and wouldn't stop," he recalls. "The wires had picked up the story and reporters from all over the country were calling."

As was his daily routine, Milo met a couple of buddies for coffee in the morning before class. Today, however, the friends were smiling, almost giddy, and greeted him with the news that "your kiddies are all over the paper."

It was more than his kiddies. The headline emblazoned across the *Detroit News* screamed U.M. STUDENT FIGHTS EXPULSION FROM AF.[1] A large picture of Milo, Nancy, and the children sat atop the cut line, "Suspicion Mystifies Lieutenant, Wife." Three front-page columns were devoted to Russell Harris's story.

The opening sentence set the tone for the entire article: "A young Air Force reserve lieutenant, charged with no disloyalty himself, faces trial and expulsion from the service at Selfridge Field next Tuesday because he has 'maintained a close and continuing relationship' with his father and sister."[2] From Milo's standpoint, it could not have been better.

65

Later that morning, as he walked into his Russian class, Milo's instructor, a short, stout woman with a heavy accent, shook her finger at him playfully and said, "Yoou've been a baaad boy."

John Radulovich learned of the article while walking home from work with his good friend, Walter Vosko. Milo's brother's Sam rushed to meet them on the sidewalk and breathlessly delivered the good news. Although not given to public displays of emotion, John Radulovich was pleased and thankful that Russell Harris had preserved the dignity of his family name.

Milo Radulovich was news. Placid life as a student, at least temporarily, was over. Radio stations were calling. Russell Harris was calling for a follow-up story. Gayle Greene of the *Free Press* was calling. Alice Silver of the *Michigan Daily* was calling. Tom Joyce of the *Detroit Times* was calling. Elie Abel of the *New York Times* was calling. Charlie Lockwood was right, the public was interested.

One call, though, was not from a reporter.

Among the many readers that morning was a young lawyer from nearby Mount Clemens, Michigan. Ken Sanborn remembered Milo Radulovich from their days together in the Aviation Cadet Program at Michigan State College ten years earlier.

Other lawyers couldn't put enough distance between Milo and themselves, but Sanborn offered his help. "The charges were ridiculous," he says. "So I called and offered to become cocounsel."

Milo still smiles at Sanborn's gift for understatement. "I was amazed when he called. The first thing he says is 'Milo, you didn't tell me you were a Red.' He had a great sense of humor. But I sure was grateful."

Today Sanborn eschews any hero labels. "Actually," he says, "Milo was one of those special sort of fellows everybody liked. He was no Communist."[3]

Ken Sanborn privately admitted to some misgivings. "I remember thinking before I called," he says, "that this thing was shaping up as a Communist trial."

As a staunch and proud Republican, the politically conservative Sanborn could hardly expect joining the case to benefit his fledgling law practice. "At that time," he points out, "it wasn't particularly popular to represent someone that had been accused of being a Communist. There were other attorneys doing that kind of work and I wasn't, frankly, interested. But there was no rhyme nor reason for them to be picking on Milo. After some soul searching I decided to give him a call. It just seemed like the right thing to do."

Sanborn was also a first lieutenant in the Air Force Reserve. He served in the Judge Advocate General's office at Selfridge, the same office that Milo had visited earlier. His status differed little from that of the lieutenant who had ignobly urged retention of civilian counsel. Moreover, Sanborn's commanding officer was none other than Col. William Doolan, the man tapped to preside over the tribunal empaneled to hear the case against Lieutenant Radulovich.

With both his private law practice and military career at stake, Kenneth Sanborn, attorney-at-law—Lt. Kenneth Sanborn, USAF—indicated to Milo that, like Charlie Lockwood, he would not accept a fee. "No hero indeed," Milo says. "Ken Sanborn deserved a medal."

Sanborn knew Michigan Sen. Homer Ferguson. He chaired the Macomb County Young Republicans, and as a youngster was Ferguson's paperboy. That relationship, the lawyer felt, would give him swift passage for a private audience with the senator. Once Ferguson was made aware of the facts in the case, Sanborn was convinced that he would surely come to Milo's defense. Ken Sanborn called Homer Ferguson's office and said he needed to talk to the senator as soon as possible.

Homer Ferguson enjoyed a well-cultivated reputation as a fervent anti-Communist. After the elections of 1950, Owen Brewster of Maine attributed the seven-seat GOP increase in the Senate to Joe McCarthy and his "ism."[4] Among those rushing to McCarthy's side was Homer Ferguson, who publicly exchanged subversive lists with the controversial Communist fighter on the floor of the Senate.[5] A year later, the

Senate Judiciary Committee was forming yet another subcommittee to investigate internal security matters, an effort Sen. Pat McCarran of Nevada was named to head. Membership was balanced by party, but the collective philosophy of the members was decidedly conservative and anti-Communist. One member, Senator Ferguson of Michigan, was considered one of the ultraconservatives on the committee.[6]

Among Ferguson's more difficult but prestigious duties in Washington was that of chairman of the Senate GOP Policy Committee. As such, he was the chief liaison between Republican Senate members and the White House. "Success or failure of an administration program," writes Carl Muller, "can depend considerably on how adroitly and capably the policy chairman performs."[7] Although the responsibility and pressure to perform was great, so too were the rewards. Namely, as the Eisenhower standard bearer in Congress, Ferguson was accorded quick and frequent passage to the president and top White House officials.

A month earlier President Eisenhower indicated he would visit Michigan on behalf of "my good friend Homer"[8] should Ferguson decide to seek reelection, an all but foregone conclusion. Ferguson, at the time, had been on a "progress report" tour of the state on behalf of the president. Given Ferguson's connections with the White House, Sanborn speculated, who knows what might happen?

There wasn't much time. In six days Col. William Doolan would bring to order the hearing on Lt. Milo Radulovich.

Ferguson's secretary was most helpful, quickly locating the senator in Grand Rapids, Michigan, where he was speaking to the National Association of Manufacturers at the Pantlind Hotel. Later that day he was scheduled to appear at a fishing tournament in Algonac, Michigan. Fortunately his travel route would bring him within minutes of Sanborn's house. Certainly he would make time for Ken Sanborn.

They met near the corner of Grossbeck and Hall roads on M-59, the main east-west corridor through Macomb County, which was situated northeast of Detroit. "Homer and his driver pulled in ahead of me," Sanborn remembers. "Homer got out and walked back to my car."

They talked for some time, Sanborn laying out the charges against Milo, pleading his case as to why they were preposterous. "I told him the Air Force was making a mistake," Sanborn says of their conversation. "I even pointed out that the Air Library at Maxwell Air Force Base in Alabama had a copy of the *Daily Worker*." Ferguson listened intently but wasn't about to go out on a limb for Milo. At meeting's end, the senator told Sanborn that he wanted to know immediately if there were any evidence Milo was not being treated fairly.

"He was very kind throughout the meeting," Sanborn says, "but he was just a supporter of the Air Force, of the government. Finally, he said, 'Well surely, Ken, you don't think the Air Force could be wrong.' I said, 'Homer, they certainly are.'"

Given Sanborn's knowledge of the case and relationship with Ferguson, his expectations for intervention by Ferguson had been great. "I was personally disappointed that he didn't get involved in it because I had hoped that he would take my word that Milo was an honorable individual," Sanborn said of the meeting. "I think he was just willing to be a so-called company man and take what the Air Force said. I think he was just afraid to get into it. It was just so controversial, and he didn't want to talk against the military."

⎯⎯⎯⎯⎯⎯⎯⎯

The pressure, understandably, was getting to Milo. He was fighting fatigue and depression. His daily schedule, already bursting with two jobs and a full load of classes in the demanding University of Michigan physics curriculum, now had to accommodate still more time to prepare for a hearing, a hearing that could affect the rest of his life.

He was angry, too. He had done nothing wrong. The Air Force's programmed response, that *his* loyalty was not in question, was beginning to ring hollow. Then why were they doing this to him?

When he asked for help, the doors of hypocritical law offices slammed in his face. "Defenders of the Constitution?" Milo scoffs. "Why, these people were nothing more than parasites with comfortable law practices that enabled them to remain aloof from the Constitution."

Then two people, lawyers both, bounded into his life, and his spirits soared. One was a stranger, a proper man with a commanding presence and crusty demeanor who had been practicing law since Warren Harding was president. The timbre in his voice matched the fearlessness in his heart. He was not intimidated by the government: that buoyed Milo's confidence.

The other was a friend from the past, a conservative Republican who held no quarter with Communists. His unselfish presence was the sole product of a firm belief in Milo's innocence. That comforted him, and did so at a time when he sorely needed comforting.

"Ken Sanborn and Charlie Lockwood," Milo says, "renewed my faith in the legal profession."

What a day. If he had scripted it himself, there would be little change. With the kids in bed, the phone finally quiet, just he and Nancy, Milo read the story again. Russell Harris, Milo concluded, had written one hell of an article.

As anticipated, Harris was precise, but he also looked at the world through Milo's eyes.

The article thoroughly examined the charges against his father and sister. Readers learned John Radulovich read *Slobodna Rec*, the pro-Tito publication, but also discovered that "he bought the opposing paper, the anti-Communist one. . .he wanted to know both sides of everything."[9]

Far from being a sinister Communist sympathizer, Milo was painted, as Charlie Lockwood predicted, with an all-American, patriotic brush. He was described as "a short, intense, thick-browed and sparkling-eyed young man who speaks in American slang and who has little apparent knowledge of political jargon." Moreover, much was made of Milo's student status and the concern for his immigrant father, who was most apprehensive of governmental authority.

Margaret's history of public protesting, and the charges stemming from those activities, were not glossed over. Harris quoted directly from the Statement of Reasons, which specified her "adherence to the Communist Party line," her opposition to the Smith Act, and outrage over a Detroit hotel's refusal to lodge Paul Robeson and his entourage. Unlike the Air Force, though, Harris afforded Milo the opportunity to respond: "I never see my sister except at an occasional family gathering. . .and I've never talked politics with her in my life."

Milo's official Air Force personnel file was also probed. It included commendations from his commanders, and cited his outstanding service at Crystal Two and Thule, Greenland, the secret Arctic base. His request for an active-duty assignment in Korea shortly after the conflict had broken out was also mentioned. Harris let Milo speak for himself, and the airman bolstered his patriotism stock: "If I felt I was a risk, even in the least way, I'd quit. But I'm getting axed."[10]

Comment from the Air Force was cryptic. A spokesman cited AFR 35-62 and its provision for an honorable discharge without stigma. But, as Harris pointed out, the blank discharge form sent Milo included a stipulation, "resignation in lieu of separation," hardly a ringing endorsement without stigma.

For the first time since the major and sergeant appeared on his doorstep more than a month ago, Milo felt better about his chances of winning the case. The *Detroit News* was a conservative, staunchly anti-Communist newspaper; Russell Harris was no patsy, but a tough, experienced reporter. He had taken Charlie Lockwood's advice and presented the facts of his case without embellishment, and the response was favorable. Maybe, he thought, just maybe, there was hope.

———————➤●◄———————

Former first lady Eleanor Roosevelt's speech at the University Christian Church in Des Moines, Iowa, was abruptly canceled when she was declared persona non grata by church trustees. "It would just be a lot of politics," the trustees said as they denied use of their auditorium for her address. [11]

It was the stuff of a great story: an all-American boy with an outstanding service record as the victimized underdog, vague references to informants and secret government files, a hardworking immigrant family with the hint of a checkered past, a sister with Communist leanings who refused public comment. In the vernacular of newsrooms across the country, the story was getting legs.

On the day after Russell Harris's explosive article, the *Detroit News* continued its outspoken support of Milo. "Justice Nods" read the title of its penetrating editorial.

> The Air Force alleges the lieutenant is a poor security risk because his father and sister are suspected of Communist sympathies. The Regulation says grounds for dismissal shall be "close, continuing association" with a Communist, but it also provides that guilt shall not rest on "fanciful or ingenious doubt or conjecture."
>
> The father in this case is accused of reading a Communist newspaper; the sister of supporting certain Communist causes. The lieutenant has had a long and impeccable record of service in the Air Force. The letter informing him of the proceedings to compel his resignation admitted that no question of his own loyalty is involved. Yet he is to be discharged. What could be more fanciful or more repugnant to justice and common sense?

> To prove loyalty, must a son report to the FBI that his father
> is reading Red literature and then dissociate himself from his
> family? If that is not what the Air Force is saying, what is it
> saying?[1]

Not to be outdone by the competition, the *Detroit Free Press* head-lined its second front page with "Flier to Fight AF Ouster Move." An increasingly belligerent Milo is quoted as saying, "[T]aking action against me because of my relationship with persons under suspicion seems ridiculous. A person can pick his friends and associates, but has no choice in his parents or relatives."[2] As the story unfolded in news-papers across the country, readers also learned that Milo quickly con-cluded the offer of legal assistance from the Air Force was at best a cosmetic overture. He turned to a civilian lawyer shortly after his appointed military counsel structured his defense on the premise that he must "bare your soul."[3]

The story had also become part of "all the news that's fit to print." Writing in the *New York Times*, Elie Abel focused on how the charges were holding Milo's career captive, pointing out that he had been offered a job with the Navy but couldn't accept it, "because they would wash me out as a bad security risk if I were expelled from the reserves."[4] The *Times* also noted the marked similarities between the case against Milo and that of Capt. Charles Hill, Jr., two years earlier, and that the charges against the fellow Detroiter had been dismissed.

Although his name was deleted from the original article, reporters quickly found John Radulovich. Described as "speaking in a mixture of his native Serbian and English and near tears," he told a reporter, Tom Joyce, "My wife and I have been loyal Americans ever since we came to this country. It's my country. It gave me food and clothing for my wife and children when I couldn't find work during the depres-sion. I don't care about myself, but why should my children suffer when I've done nothing wrong?"[5] He also referred to an unknown enemy who turned him in to the FBI, an enemy of years past who spread malicious rumors involving a so-called other family in the old country, an enemy who "broke the Eighth Commandment."[6]

———————⋙●⋘———————

Margaret Radulovich Fishman knew that sooner or later she would have to comment. Although she was comfortable with the reason for her silence, the motive was not being communicated. The *News*, for instance, indicated that "the lieutenant's sister refused to help."[7] "That wasn't it at all," she argued. "I wasn't refusing to help, but my views were simply irrelevant. I hadn't been accused of anything. Whatever my political thinking might be I don't see why it should reflect on my brother."[8]

"I was trying to avoid the press," Margaret says. "I hadn't worked out in my own mind what I was going to say." After pondering a statement for a few days, she finally released it to the newspapers.

True to form, she minced few words. After defending her father's patriotism and indicating there had been little contact with her brother over the past eight years, she attacked what for her were the underpinnings of the case against her brother.

> We have heard of guilt by association, this is something new and more horrible, this is GUILT BY RELATIONSHIP. My brother is guilty of being my brother.
>
> It seems that McCarthyism has set new standards in our land. In order to prove one's loyalty, one must denounce one's own father, sister or entire family if need be, and thus prove oneself a "good American."

The statement, as expected, prompted calls from the press. Reporters came to her house; one in particular angered her. "I was left wing," she points out. It was not a secret. We've always had a lot of books. There was this *Detroit Times* reporter who kept looking at my possessions for evidence that I was a Communist. He totally missed the point."

———>●<———

Although the Milo Radulovich story was traversing press wires and appearing in newspapers across the country, it still belonged to Russell Harris, the reporter who broke it. His front-page, follow-up article the next day demonstrated why.

The Ken Sanborn–Homer Ferguson meeting was prominently featured. Sanborn pointed out that Ferguson wanted to be kept informed of events in the case. If there were any evidence Milo was not getting a fair hearing, the senator indicated he would take it up with the Defense Department.

For whatever reason—his halting use of English, the charges levied against his integrity, the drawing of a political sword on his family—John Radulovich trusted few beyond his inner circle of family. But this reporter from the *Detroit News* was different. He knew Detroit's Serbian community, and unlike those in government, he had listened to Milo. Harris wrote what he saw and knew, not what the government wanted him to write. Although John Radulovich was cautious, he trusted him.

Russell Harris visited John Radulovich and coaxed an incident from him involving the expulsion of his other two sons, Walter and Sam, from a special Serbian school. Bringing the event to light inched closer to supplying critical missing pieces of what was rapidly becoming a confusing puzzle. Why Milo? Why the Radulovich family?

Just before and after World War II, two forces fought for control of Yugoslavia and the hearts of Serbian people around the world: the Monarchists, under the leadership of Draza Mihailovic, and the Communist partisans of Marshal Josip Tito. After 1943, the United States supported the Tito regime.

Margaret recalls her dad supporting the Mihailovic forces until, as she puts its, "all of the sudden my father started talking about someone named Tito." Several school officials, however, remained loyal to

Mihailovic. Within their community the Tito supporters were called Reds.

Then came the incident at school. In 1944, Walter and Sam Radulovich, like many other children in their community, attended classes at the Serbian Orthodox Church. At the beginning of one session, the teacher asked the children to stand and sing a battle song in praise of Mihailovic's Chetnik fighters. The Radulovich brothers refused. When asked why, Walter, the older brother, said he wouldn't stand for any other national anthem than the "Star-Spangled Banner." Those who wouldn't acknowledge the Mihailovic loyalists, the teacher announced, had to leave. The boys were put out of school and told not to return, that they were from a Red family.

Rumors abounded: "Don't go near John Radulovich's house, it's being watched," said Margaret. She firmly believes the shunning of her father emanated from the school incident. "My father was humiliated," she continues. "He wrote an article about the expulsion in this newspaper he was accused of reading [*Slobodna Rec*]."

John Radulovich did support the partisans of Marshal Tito. "The father," Harris writes, "said he believed that perhaps the Air Force had misunderstood a racial and nationality problem for a political one. 'I told the boys to refuse'," said Radulovich. 'They did and they were expelled. Perhaps this comes from that.'"[9]

⸺⸽⸺

While they dutifully chronicled the annual fall rush and endless get-acquainted smokers, the staff of the *Michigan Daily* also kept a watchful eye on the clacking Associated Press Teletype machine in their office. Besides the university community, the product of their daily labor also served, in effect, as the paper of record for the Ann Arbor area. This added dimension gave the student journalists entrée to the arena of national and international news, a challenge they relished and took most seriously.

Twenty-year-old Harry Lunn was especially proud of the senior editorial staff that gathered about him for the 1953–54 academic year, his tenure as managing editor of the *Daily*. "Collegial," was the way Lunn characterized his management style. "I was not a Hearst-like figure," he says. "Someone had to be in charge, but we decided things collectively."

A conservative from Detroit, Lunn's support of Eisenhower over Stevenson in the 1952 presidential campaign was not well received in the predominantly liberal and sometimes cliquish community of the *Daily*; it almost cost him the prestigious managing editorship. "In the end," he says, "there were people willing to do the right thing."

Two years earlier, as a sophomore reporter for the *Daily*, Lunn had gone to Lansing to cover Douglas MacArthur's speech to the Michigan legislature as the retired general weaved his way eastward to what eventually culminated in the famous "old soldiers never die" farewell to Congress. The previous year he covered the HUAC hearings in Detroit, carefully noting the performance of California Congressman Donald Jackson. It came as no surprise to Lunn when Jackson raced to exonerate Lucille Ball of any wrongdoing only ten days before. "She confessed," Lunn explains of Jackson's rapid forgiving. It was that simple for Harry Lunn.

Among the senior staff was a young woman from Washington, D.C., Alice Bogdanoff Silver. Her parents were close friends of Herbert Block, who cartooned with distinction as Herblock for the *Washington Post*. "Herblock knew Alice," Lunn says. "He was a big hero for her." Three years earlier Herblock had created what was to date one of history's most renowned eponyms. On a barrel of mud, supported by splattered buckets, he sketched the term "McCarthyism."

"Alice was our in-house liberal, our in-house lefty," Lunn says admiringly of Silver. "She was the great liberal, Jewish, Washington-based conscience of the staff. When the Rosenbergs were executed in June, it was like the death of her own parents."

Alice Silver brought the case of Milo Radulovich to the attention of her colleagues on the *Michigan Daily*. Her pleading on behalf of Milo was warmly received by the senior editorial staff.

Exercising his "first among equals" prerogative, Harry Lunn wrote the Radulovich story himself. Even though he was from a self-described "very uptight Republican family," there was no real decision whether the *Daily* would support Milo. "It was evident to all of us," Lunn says; "this was a complete injustice."

Although rare, a front-page editorial in the *Daily* was not unheard of, usually employed in extreme cases, but at most only two or three times a year. Because, Harry Lunn said, "the Radulovich case was easy in the sense that it was so absurd," the decision was made to do a front-page editorial.

On the morning of September 24, beside a front-page article by Lunn on governmental charges brought against physics student Milo Radulovich, *Michigan Daily* readers were bluntly informed in an editorial signed by the seven-member staff that "the Air Force charge is open to serious question." The editorial went on to challenge the fairness of the proceedings, suggesting the outcome was in all likelihood predetermined, and that the university should demand a fair review. Finally, the student editors trained their sights on the trade-off between national security and individual rights:

> Radulovich's case is a pertinent example of security considerations being carried beyond the point of safeguarding the nation to the point of discouraging vital government personnel. In terms of the country's future, this is an equally great security risk.

The announcement that day from Panmunjom, Korea, was unsettling. Twenty-three GIs, one from nearby Lincoln Park, Michigan, chanted Communist slogans and vowed they would never return to the United

States. American observers and allied soldiers were caught off guard as the prisoners rode in Russian-made trucks and sang the Communist anthem, "The Internationale," on the way to their mandatory three-months' neutral custody.

A spokesman for the turncoats said that they "loved our country and our people." But they would never return, he said, "while the voices that shouted the loudest and get the most publicity are those of Senator McCarthy, the book burners and those who demand preventive war."

"Are we going south?" one of the turncoats shouted. "Noooo!" his comrades responded in unison. "Are we going north?" the impromptu cheerleader asked. "Yeesss!" came the collective reply, as they delighted in the shocked look on the faces of American observers.[10]

———————⟶⦿⟵———————

The White House today announced the resignation of a former New Dealer turned Republican, Emmett J. Hughes, from his $15,000-a-year post as chief presidential speech writer. Hughes, 32, returns to Life magazine as a senior editor. Another New Dealer, Bryce N. Harlow, 37, has been named his replacement.

Hughes was generally credited with supplying Eisenhower with the idea during the previous year's presidential campaign of going to Korea. Friction developed after the election between Hughes and several more-conservative cabinet members.

B uoyed by his conviction that the charges against Milo lacked substance and that the Air Force had not long ago dismissed similar charges against Capt. Charles Hill, Ken Sanborn held out hope that Sen. Homer Ferguson would intervene in the case. But the wary lawmaker kept his distance. Sanborn did, however, extract a commitment from Ferguson to intercede if it appeared Milo was not being treated fairly.

True to his word, Ferguson called officials at Selfridge for details on the case. His office issued a statement indicating "if there is any evidence the boy is not receiving a fair hearing, I will take the matter up with the Defense Department immediately." An obviously pleased Ken Sanborn parroted Ferguson's pledge to reporters.

***

Charlie Lockwood was not accustomed to playing the role of media darling. His newly arrived-at fealty with the press apparently was not misplaced. In one of its strongest editorials to date, the *Detroit Free Press* said:

> It may sound callous to say so, but we almost hope that the Air Force has a great deal more information than it has made public to support its claim that Lieut. Milo J. Radulovich, Air force reservist, is a bad security risk. Otherwise, it is our fear that the Air Force and the Government of the United

81

States is going to look very, very foolish....If the measure of a man's loyalty to his Country is to be determined by the associations or political beliefs of members of his family, there will be very few of us who will be safe....

If this sort of thing is to be standard practice, we can all live in terror of the informer. A person can be convicted by whisper or by innuendo. Legal process will have no more meaning than it did under the secret police of Hitler and now of Malenkov. The protection of individual rights will become nothing more than a fiction believed in by no one....No matter what the outcome of this case, Lieut. Radulovich has been done irreparable damage....If Lieut. Radulovich has done anything which would cast doubt on either his loyalty or his security status, he should be properly dealt with, but it should be done in the open and not in a star chamber session....The responsibility for this affair should be fixed and its instigator promptly dealt with. That person, whoever he is, appears to us a far worse security risk than Lieut. Radulovich.[1]

More information emerged on John Radulovich.

"A frightened old man admitted Thursday that he belonged to an organization that was later tagged 'subversive'" began an article in the *Free Press*.[2] The story went on to point out that *Slobodna Rec*, the Serbian paper with the official subversive label that figured prominently in the charges against Milo, also sponsored an organization whose membership roster included John Radulovich.

"The Free Word had a club. I belonged to it," acknowledged the father. "The club was called subversive so I dropped it. I have not paid dues in four years, not attended meetings. I never did attend many meetings."

Although admitting to reading the controversial paper, the elder Radulovich once again stressed that he also read *Srbobran*, the pro-West publication.

John Radulovich was quick to state that he was not a Communist, had never been a Communist. "I am a Democrat," he said, "and I don't even mind Mr. Eisenhower's government." Upset that his patriotism was in question, he went on to say, "Even if my native Yugoslavia should attack this country today, I would fight them, old as I am."

They fired Al Fishman.

Husband of Margaret Radulovich Fishman, brother-in-law of Lt. Milo Radulovich, Al Fishman was fired from his job at the Hudson Motor Car Company.

According to the well-crafted union contract, any time before the ninetieth day of employment, a worker is subject to termination, no explanation required. After the ninetieth day, however, the worker is welcomed into the brotherhood of labor and dismissal is anything but easy. Al Fishman was fired upon completion of his eighty-ninth day of employment.

Fishman's eighty-nine-day tenure of employment was without incident. "I was doing everything I was supposed to do," he says. "There was no complaint about my work." At shift's end, his foreman quietly pulled him aside and said, "You're being terminated as an unsatisfactory employee."[3]

Although an admitted left-winger—he and Margaret's courtship ran concurrent with their membership in the Marxist-centered Labor Youth League—Al Fishman's nodding acquaintance with the public limelight could be traced to one thing: his wife had been referred to as "Mrs. Al Fishman" in several press accounts during the past week.

About the firing, Fishman says, "It was the publicity around the case, I am certain of it. I can't prove it."[4]

Guy Nunn called that afternoon. Nunn was the popular Sunday morning host of a Detroit television talk show, "Meet the UAW," that focused on issues of importance to the United Auto Workers. Charges levied because of purported statements by "brother" John Radulovich while working at the Hudson Motor Car Company fell neatly into Nunn's category of interest. Ken Sanborn, Charlie Lockwood, and Milo were asked to appear on the program sometime in October.

The heavy concentration of press, though welcome, also gave Ken Sanborn pause for concern. He needed to know if there were boundaries within his canon of legal ethics to guide him in the media jungle that was enveloping the case. Prompted by the Nunn invitation, he sought counsel from his legal peers in Macomb County.

Jewel E. West, president of the Macomb County Bar Association, eschewed a personal opinion and sought the refuge of Wilber Brucker, former Michigan governor, attorney general, and current chairman of the Ethics and Illegal Practice Committee of the State Bar of Michigan.

Not surprisingly, Brucker's advice fell heavy on the side of the government. West, relaying Brucker's opinion, wrote to Sanborn and indicated "that any attorney-at-law had a right to appear on television or radio and discuss general matters with regard to the law or facts but that he must not answer over radio or television specific questions as to the law or as to what one individual's rights are or what he could do, either directly or indirectly. (I think that this would include expressing an opinion.)* Mr. Brucker further stated that an attorney should not advertise in any manner over the air and that he should not make any statements over the air that might bring the courts or any departments of our government into disrepute."5

* Parenthetical comment from West.

Charles C. Lockwood, who did not hold Brucker in high esteem, sought no official beacon to guide his public deportment.

In news from Hollywood, Paramount Pictures announced that Bing Crosby and William Holden will star in a movie version of the Broadway hit The Country Girl. *Crosby will play the role of an aging, alcoholic musical-comedy star.*

SATURDAY, SEPTEMBER 26, 1953

Milo was handily winning the public fight. Charlie Lockwood maintained that when it came to matching wits in the media, the military was a clumsy opponent at best. Strikingly similar press reports from around the country, both articles and editorials, chanted their support for the victimized airman.

The previous evening, just four days before Col. William Doolan would call the proceedings to order, the Air Force declared the hearing off-limits to the public. Calculated or not, timing of the announcement raised troublesome questions of motive. Coming as it did on a Friday night, the surprise ruling ensured that news of the closed session would arrive in the homes of Americans on Saturday, that one day in the week when affairs of state traditionally give way to affairs of family and household chores.

Without legal substance in the charges against Milo, public outrage, deftly articulated to date by the press, had proved to be Lockwood's most effective weapon. "Before the bar of public opinion in this country," he had earlier declared, "it is the Air Force that is now on trial rather than Lt. Radulovich."[1] Prohibition of press coverage of the hearing, an order that came directly from Air Force headquarters in Washington, D.C., dipped deeply into Lockwood's arsenal.

Accompanying the order to close the hearing—in what rapidly had become a programmed staple in official remarks issued by the Air

Force regarding the case—was the comment that "Lieutenant Radulovich was in no way suspected of disloyalty himself."[2]

—————⇒➤●◄⇐—————

Famed pianist Artur Rubenstein's scheduled concert before a sold-out house in Mexico City was canceled. Nobody had remembered to bring a piano.

SUNDAY, SEPTEMBER 27, 1953

On Sunday, September 27, just two days before the hearing, several threatening phone calls came into the home of John Radulovich.

Fielded by Sam Radulovich, Milo's younger brother who lived with his parents, the calls were thought to be those of a crackpot. Sam immediately phoned Charles Lockwood, who in turn advised that the police be contacted at once. "There must have been a lot of reporters hanging around the station looking for a story," Sam said, "because they were at the door before the cops." A twenty-two-year-old engineering student at Lawrence Institute of Technology, Sam told police that the caller said, "We're going to get all of you. You Commies think you can come over here and take control of the country. But you'll see. We'll take care of you."[1]

Sam indicated the caller repeated the threat about seven times during a fifteen-minute period. One call, however, differed from the others. It was from a woman with a German accent who said, "Tell your lawyer not to say bad things about Hitler."

Police agreed with the brother that the calls were more than likely the work of a crank. As a precaution they ordered stepped up patrols in the area.

<hr>

In overwhelming numbers Dexter residents signed a testimonial petition supporting their neighbor, Milo Radulovich. Circulated by Madeline Lewis, manager of a local dry-cleaning shop, the petition read: "Mr. Radulovich and his family have been residents of the village of Dexter, Mich., for over a period of one year and we believe him to be an honorable, upright citizen, true to his country—the United States of America."[2] The petition was forwarded to Radulovich's attorney, Charles C. Lockwood.

That afternoon, Bert Rechichar's first ever field-goal attempt in professional football was good for a National Football League record of fifty-six yards and keyed a Baltimore Colts 13-9 win over the Chicago Bears.

Milo and his two attorneys had been meeting regularly in Ken Sanborn's law offices. Barring the ability to review the government's case against Milo, and to cross-examine the witnesses used to make that case, neither lawyer was optimistic.

Issued on May 2, 1949, Air Force Regulation 35-62 mirrored the security-conscious era in which it was created. Although amended at least six times before reaching the doorstep of Lt. Milo J. Radulovich, its central purpose never wavered: to provide an orderly, if not intimidating, process to escort from the military members of the Air Force whose loyalty or security had been called into question.

Despite a wholly defensible rationale that the military must operate under a different, more strict, judicial code than the civilians they are sworn to protect, the Air Force, to date, had commented only sparingly on the Radulovich case. When it did, statements were unusually stiff and generally cited the often invoked nebulous justification for military behavior: *for reasons of national security*. Inevitably, official comment would also contain a robotlike disclaimer that Lieutenant Radulovich's personal loyalty to his country was not at stake.

Although the fairness of the case against Milo—being held responsible for the actions of his father and sister—had fired public support on his behalf, the regulation under which he was charged was receiving scant public attention.

90

For a nation that boasted a judicial system holding sacred the rights of an accused, the case against Milo Radulovich dramatically underscored the most pronounced difference between civilian and military jurisprudence, namely, in the presumption of innocence. Being cited under AFR 35-62 meant that instead of divining flaws in the government's case against him, Milo and his attorneys were in the untenable position of justifying why he should be retained in the Air Force. In the eyes of the Air Force, because he had been charged, Lt. Milo Radulovich was already guilty; he must now prove his innocence.

AFR 35-62 could intimidate. The respondent (accused) first learns of pending Air Force action under the regulation in a document ominously titled "Notice of Proposed Termination of Appointment or Enlistment."[1] The first sentence in the notice reads in part, "Pursuant to. . .action has been initiated to discharge you from all commissions and appointments held by you in the United States Air Force." It goes on to offer options, the first of which is immediate resignation.

The specific charge against Milo involved a provision that afforded a discharge under honorable conditions.[2] However alluring the opportunity to put the case behind him and move on with his life, for Milo it was no option at all. With the offer of an honorable discharge came a stipulation that his record would forever include the proviso, "resignation in lieu of separation from the service." Agreeing to such a condition meant his chosen career in weather, a career inexorably tied to government, was over. More important, though, letting such a proviso go unchallenged meant a blemish would be visited upon the Radulovich name. More than a month earlier, when Milo delivered the painful message to his father that there were those seeking to harm the family, John Radulovich reached deep into his proud Montenegrin heritage and used the Serbian word *chast*, which means "honor," as he gave his son the blessing to fight. Milo wouldn't, he couldn't, walk away with a taint attached to his family name.

Another option open to the respondent involved answering "the charges in writing within thirty days of his receipt of the notice, and to submit in connection with his answer, such statements, affidavits, or other documentary evidence to justify his retention as he may desire."[3]

Milo Radulovich's file spoke volumes of his devotion to duty and of the trust bestowed upon him by the Air force. A review of his record showed recent classified duty in Greenland that required a top-secret clearance, laudatory performance evaluations from superior officers, and, as evidenced by repeated requests for duty in Korea, a willingness to stand in harm's way for his country. That record had been ignored and Lieutenant Radulovich was being told he must have even greater documentation to "justify his retention" in the Air Force.

Compounding his frustration and sense of justice, Milo learned the Air Force could mount a formidable case against him and then *for reasons of national security* deftly step aside when challenged to produce the evidence collected to create that case. According to AFR 35-62:

> Hearings will be conducted in such a way as to prevent unauthorized disclosure of classified information or compromise of investigative sources or methods. No disclosure will be made which may compromise the identity of confidential informants. Classified information in the file will not be disclosed to the respondent or his counsel or any other person not cleared for access to such information without express authority from the Director of Military Personnel, Headquarters USAF.[4]

The determinant of who is a "confidential informant," what is "classified information," and who is "cleared for access" was the Air Force. The government had, within the comfortable confines of AFR 35-62, charged Milo Radulovich with being a security risk, demanded his resignation, and then denied him the right to face his accuser.

The final option was "to request a hearing before a hearing board."[5] At that hearing, a respondent could choose to be represented by military or civilian counsel. Military counsel would be appointed, civilian counsel would be retained at the respondent's expense.

Although the military has a specific name for it, and it is expressly forbidden, *command influence* is not unique to the military. Affecting the actions of an underling through subtle, and sometimes not so subtle, suggestion is as old as the supervisor/subordinate relationship. Its application to the military, however, particularly within the Judge Advocate General setting, can be disastrous to the judicial process. The term *command influence* never expressly surfaced during Milo's conversation with his military appointed lawyer, but it did hover.

Defensible or not, AFR 35-62 severely strained the American sense of fair play.

Implied or not, a case could be made that the regulation under which Milo and countless others had been charged created a comfortable one-way path leading to acceptance of a judgment by convenience.

And whether it was politically popular or not, Charlie Lockwood and Ken Sanborn intended to make that case.

"I often wonder," Milo says, "how many guys before me in similar circumstances jumped at the chance to go quietly with an honorable discharge just because it was easier."

———————◄►●◄————————

Preparing a defense without knowing the charges, and whence those charges came, would be difficult under the best of circumstances, but virtually impossible under the constraints of AFR 35-62.

Charlie Lockwood and Ken Sanborn couldn't defend their client; he wasn't guilty—a point the Air Force reinforced at every opportunity. The case for the defense had to focus on proving that the allegations against John Radulovich were groundless, and that Milo's contact with his sister was anything but "close and continuing."

The charges aimed at John Radulovich, the family believed, were preposterous. From the Statement of Reasons:

> [I]t is reported that you have maintained a close continuing association with your father, John Radulovich, who is reported to have, during 1948, and for an unspecified period of time thereafter, at or near Detroit, Michigan, subscribed to and contributed to the support of the Slobodna Rech [*sic*], (pro communist newspaper published in Pittsburgh, Pennsylvania), and that he also received copies of the "Daily Worker." Since 1946, while your father was employed at the Hudson Motor Car Company, Detroit, Michigan, it is reported that he endeavored, on occasions, to spread Russian and Communist propaganda in the factory....The "Slobodna Rech" [*sic*] has been designated by the House Committee on un-American Activities as a publication designated to "work for the organization of the American Slav Congress." The American Slav Congress has been designated by the Attorney General of the United States as Communist.

"If he was spreading Communist propaganda in the plant," Milo sardonically observed, "it must have been in Serbian."

Yet there was enough political foment in Detroit's cliquish, close-knit Serbian community for someone to embellish or even fabricate charges against John Radulovich. It certainly wasn't the first time, and likely not the last, that he had endured empty claims directed at his reputation. But the defense team was confident that once the culprit was known and motive discerned under cross-examination, the Air Force would have no alternative but to realize that the charges were without foundation, that this was an affair of the Serbian community and should not reflect on Milo's military career. Besides, the defense would clearly show that John Radulovich loved his country, and even though he was a staunch Democrat and supporter of President Roosevelt, he had a deep and abiding respect for President Eisenhower.

Further, John Radulovich's reading of *Slobodna Rec* was for keeping up with events and people in his native Yugoslavia. He also read *Srborban*, the pro-West paper. Surely, at the appropriate time those factors would be taken into consideration.

Finally, there had been a mistake. Although the *Daily Worker* had been delivered to the home of John Radulovich, it was addressed to and meant for his daughter, Margaret. Attorneys Lockwood and Sanborn concluded that the Air Force would simply have to drop this charge. Be that as it may, Ken Sanborn pointed out that the *Daily Worker* was in the Air Library at Maxwell Air Force Base, Alabama.

The charges involving Margaret were not so easily dismissed. From the Statement of Reasons:

> In October 1948, your sister participated in a picket line at the Federal Building, Detroit, Michigan, protesting the Smith Act and the indictment against the twelve Communist Leaders;

> In November 1948, your sister picketed the Book Cadillac Hotel, Detroit, Michigan, protesting the refusal of the hotel to house Paul Robeson and party;

> In November 1948 and March 1949, your sister attended and participated in classes held under the auspices of the Michigan School of Social Science on the American labor movement;

> In December 1950, your sister attended a National Conference against "deportation hysteria", and acted as a registrar of this conference sponsored by the American Committee for the Protection of the Foreign Born and the Civil Rights Congress of Michigan;

> In February 1949, at or near Detroit, Michigan, your sister attended a mass meeting commemorating V. I. Lenin, and celebrating the 25th Anniversary of the "Daily Worker", and the 1st Anniversary of the "Michigan Worker".

> In July 1949, at or near Detroit, Michigan, your sister attended a social gathering of the Labor Youth League of Michigan, affiliated with the National Labor Youth League to launch a recruiting drive for new members.

In late 1948, shortly after returning home to Detroit from a three-year stint at the Yugoslavian Embassy in Washington, D.C., Margaret joined the Young Progressives of America. No role was too small for her. She would run the mimeograph machine, lick stamps, whatever needed to be done. When the Progressive party decided to sponsor a program involving Paul Robeson, Margaret dutifully helped publicize his appearance. Robeson, a close friend of Coleman Young and frequent Detroit visitor, enjoyed vaulted celebrity status as his booming voice and message of racial dignity caromed off the walls of Detroit's black churches. When the prestigious Book-Cadillac Hotel refused Robeson and his party lodging, Margaret was incensed and readily joined those who protested the hotel's action.

Although she was cited in the Statement of Reasons for picketing the Federal Building a month earlier for protesting indictments in the Smith Act trial, Margaret maintains taking up a sign and marching around the Book-Cadillac in November 1948 was her first-ever act of civil disobedience. "I hadn't been there [the Progressive party] that long, and hardly knew anyone," she says. I just did it because it was the right thing to do. I never had any black friends in my life. I never had any contact with black youth."

Robeson and party eventually found their way to the open arms of Detroit's Gotham Hotel. Margaret continued to raise her voice in public protest.

She wanted to learn more about the history of America's labor movement and took classes at the Michigan School of Social Science, where the subject matter was given a Marxist bent. The Michigan School of Social Science had been designated Communist by the attorney general of the United States.

She had a burning curiosity about Marxism and joined the Labor Youth League, where, coincidentally, she began seeing and eventually married Al Fishman. The Labor Youth League had also been designated Communist by the attorney general of the United States.

She was concerned in general about "deportation hysteria" but in particular about the rights of children whose parents had been deported. Her mother's stories of hooded horsemen riding through their mining camp home in southeast Ohio shouting, "Popavich, Radulovich, sonafabitch" remained far too vivid. She joined the American Committee for the Protection of the Foreign Born and the Civil Rights Congress of Michigan, and organized a one-time picket of the White House. Both groups had been designated Communist by the attorney general of the United States.

She believed strongly in a free and open press and attended a meeting celebrating the twenty-fifth anniversary of the *Daily Worker*. The *Daily Worker* had been designated by HUAC the "chief journalistic mouthpiece of the Communist Party of the United States."

The Statement of Reasons said Margaret's actions clearly "indicate her adherence to the Communist Party line."

There would be no quarreling over the charges against Margaret. Save for a few minor discrepancies over dates and places, they were accurate. "I didn't hide a thing," she says, "because I had nothing to hide." But, she is quick to point out, "I broke no law. If I did, then they should have come after me, not my brother."

With stern resolve, she adds, "I have never advocated arms."

Milo's attorney, Ken Sanborn—1st Lt. Ken Sanborn, United States Air Force Reserve—brought to the case an intimate working knowledge of military procedure and law. As a reserve officer he was assigned to the same Judge Advocate General's office from which the hearing board was selected, the same office that had provided Milo with "off the record" counsel to seek a civilian attorney.

It was the day before the hearing, and Milo and his attorneys still had not been allowed to examine the government's case, nor had they been provided a list of the witnesses used to make that case. Sanborn and cocounsel Charlie Lockwood felt ill-prepared. They needed more time; Sanborn was confident fairness would prevail and he could get it.

After reviewing Air Force Regulation 35-62, Sanborn concluded a recess was clearly justified. The Air Force had not adhered to key provisions in the very regulation they were using to justify discharging Milo from the military. Sanborn felt the Air Force was vulnerable primarily in areas related to the accumulation of material in preparation of the Statement of Reasons. That evidence, he believed, should have been shared. He would cite the provisions, note the Air Force's failure to comply, demand the evidence, and then request time to prepare the case. It was very clear to him.

Given Milo and his attorneys' concern over the veracity of the charges in the Statement of Reasons about his father, they should have taken consolation in one of AFR 35-62's key provisions directing the Air Force not only to make an effort at proving his innocence but also to share the origin of evidence accumulated in preparation of the case against him. The regulation specified:

> Investigations by activities of the Air Force Establishment will develop all relevant facts in favor of, as well as against, a suspected or accused person. Sufficient information will be reported about informants whose identities are not disclosed to permit adequate evaluation of the information furnished by them.[6]

No such information had been received.

Milo and his legal team should also have taken comfort from another provision specifying that the "'Statement of Reasons' will be in sufficient detail to enable the individual to prepare his defense and will be as complete as security considerations permit."[7] Even a conservative interpretation meant that those who challenged his father's patriotism would be made to justify their accusations. What possible breach of national security could occur by asking John Radulovich's accusers, presumably his fellow factory workers, to repeat their remarks on the record?

The hearing board would apply the standard of "reasonable doubt" to determine whether Milo was a security risk. By reasonable doubt, the regulation states, "is intended not fanciful or ingenious doubt or conjecture, but substantial, honest, conscientious doubt, suggested by the material evidence or lack of it in the case."[8]

Built on the tried and trusted "fellow travelers" theme, nothing was creative in the government's case against Lieutenant Radulovich. He certainly would not be the first victim of "erring on the side of national security." Without the opportunity to study and evaluate the charges, and their derivation, disproving "reasonable doubt" would be a most difficult task.

⟹⟩●⟨⟸

With events of the past five weeks criss-crossing at breakneck speed through his mind, Milo slept little the night before the hearing. Since that first day when he peered from his front window at the two uniformed strangers who walked up his driveway, he viewed the case as an assault on the family unit. "My first reaction," he recalls, "was to circle the wagons, familywise."

He was angry that his father had been dragged into the case. "My dad was scared to death," Milo says. He adds, with uncharacteristic rancor, "His deal was all bullshit."

Did Milo wonder why Margaret just didn't say she wasn't a Communist? "I never felt like 'what did she get me into?'" he says. "Even though we were raised in the same house, we didn't all think alike."

Asked again if he wondered why Margaret just didn't deny she was a Communist, Milo says, "I felt in my heart of hearts that she had done nothing illegal."

Asked a third time he finally concedes, "Yes, I thought it, but I didn't say it." How about Nancy, did she wonder too? "I think she said something along those lines as well," he responded, but only reluctantly.

"Even if I did say I wasn't a Communist," Margaret offered, "they never would have believed me. I was a fellow traveler."

———

The hearing to decide the fate of Lt. Milo Radulovich was closed to the public. Despite an eleventh-hour plea by his attorneys, the Air Force affirmed its earlier decision to conduct the hearing in private. According to the 10th Air Force commander, Maj. Gen. Richard A. Grussendorf, the action was taken with the concurrence of Air Force Headquarters in Washington and "primarily for the protection of the lieutenant and his family."[9]

Lt. Col. Irwin Kempner, president of the highly regarded Detroit-based Vandenburg chapter of the Air Force Association, speculated the government's decision to close the hearing stemmed from a desire to avoid embarrassment. The charges detailed in the Statement of Reasons about Milo's father and sister all involved incidents that occurred before his last assignment in Thule, Greenland, classified duty for which he received a top-secret clearance. "Opening the case to the public," Kempner suggests, "meant the Air Force and the FBI, the two agencies charged with background investigations, had failed."[10]

———

On the day before the hearing, Milo, Charlie Lockwood, and Ken Sanborn were guests on Bud Lanker's popular Detroit radio show.

Although the case was discussed, appearing on the program would long be remembered not for any pivotal statement or event, but because they were interviewed in the same WXYZ studio where George W. Trendle's "The Lone Ranger" originated and was beamed across the nation three nights a week.

While in town for the funeral of Chief Justice Fred Vinson, former president Harry Truman paid a surprise visit to the Washington law offices of his former secretary of state, Dean Acheson. Truman instructed Acheson's secretary to tell her boss that an old friend, now unemployed, had just stopped by to say hello. Balking at first, Acheson finally agreed to receive the visitor.

A journalism major at Northwestern University, Jean Kerr had joined the staff of Sen. Joseph R. McCarthy in 1948, where her work as a researcher quickly won her high regard. Over the next five years, her stormy relationship with the senator encompassed frequent firings, repeated resignations, and an abundance of argument. But on this warm Tuesday morning in Washington, D.C., Jean Kerr and Joseph McCarthy were married.

The two were known as a tempestuous pair; McCarthy's smiling and roving Irish eyes sparked many of their battles. A diamond engagement ring was said to have become worn over the years from being passed back and forth between them. No shrinking violet, Kerr did not suffer McCarthy's shenanigans in silence. To wit, according to Thomas Reeves's biograpy of McCarthy, she once invoked her friendship with J. Edgar Hoover to engineer an Alaskan transfer of an FBI agent whose attractive wife worked in McCarthy's office.[1]

Weeks earlier the couple had just emerged from yet another strained period in their relationship and McCarthy traveled to New York seeking a reconciliation. Unlike previous peace accords this one included an ultimatum from Kerr that would culminate at the altar. Smiling to reporters as he announced their engagement, America's most renowned bare-knuckle foe of communism admitted he had agreed to conditions set out by his bride-to-be, and was so happy that he forgot to exact any concessions of his own.[2] Neither would disclose specifics of the agreement.

Joe McCarthy, on his wedding day, was amid an almost unprecedented three-year stay in the nation's headlines. He was riding the crest of an extraordinary, though controversial, career. Images can tarnish, though, and seamy rumors were creeping into the nooks and crannies of Washington gossip.

Ever the student of a finely turned ankle, McCarthy, according to a reporter and friend, Willard Evans, "consented to marriage only to quash stories that he was homosexual."[3] While attending George Washington University in 1945, "Jeanie" Kerr had been voted "the most beautiful girl on campus." Later at Northwestern, she won another beauty prize. Marriage to a former beauty queen would put a quick end to that cocktail-hour sniggering.

Vice President Richard Nixon and his wife, Pat, were among the nine hundred guests and thirty-five hundred onlookers at Washington's stately St. Matthews Cathedral.* Other attendees included Massachusetts Sen. John Kennedy and his new wife, Jacqueline; presidential aide, Sherman Adams; former heavyweight champion, Jack Dempsey; and Washington socialite, Alice Roosevelt Longworth. Choosing not to join the celebrants in person, President and Mrs. Eisenhower sent greetings. Pope Pius XII transmitted a special apostolic blessing.

The bride, a Washington, D.C., native, was attended by her matron of honor, Mrs. Robert E. Lee, also of Washington. McCarthy's brother, William, a Chicago truck driver, was best man. A reception in honor of the newlyweds was held in the fashionable Washington Club at nearby Dupont Circle.

Just before departing for their West Indies honeymoon, well-wishers, Texas businessman Ross Biggers chief among them, presented the McCarthys with a new Cadillac.

*Raised a Presbyterian, Kerr converted to the Roman Catholic religion of her new husband.

———>●<———

Finally the hearing. Since August 21, the day Milo first encountered a document called the Statement of Reasons, he longed for an official forum to address the charges. His father wasn't a Communist. He had little or no contact with his sister, and certainly she had no influence over his political philosophy. Milo still hoped that once the case was carefully examined, the Air Force would realize a mistake had been made.

The evening sessions with his attorneys, the interviews with well-intentioned reporters who all seemed to ask the same questions, the waking up in the middle of the night, the constant worrying about his family, the clutching feeling in the pit of his stomach, the uncertainty—it was all past. The long-awaited opportunity to tell his story, to defend himself, was here.

Far from the popping flashbulbs and army of political well-wishers on the steps of St. Matthews, Lt. Milo Radulovich and his wife, Nancy, dropped five-year-old daughter Kathryn off at his parents' house and motored their way to Mount Clemens, home of Selfridge Air Force Base. Milo and Nancy drove a four-year-old Ford.

Since history's first military commander bellowed the first order to the first conscript, attempts to dupe the foot soldier have met with little success. Such was the case at Selfridge that Tuesday morning.

Dressed in civilian clothes, a nervous and apprehensive Milo Radulovich stepped from his car behind Building 303. GIs were everywhere, whistling and waving their support, some hanging out of windows, others just milling around awaiting his arrival. Milo was stunned. Even though a lack of space in front of the building forced Milo to park in back, they still found him. "What a morale lifter," he recalls.

Building 303, designated the hearing locale by the Judge Advocate General's office, was indistinguishable from countless other wooden office buildings on the base. The GI reception was warming, but the long, sterile, rectangular structure served as a sobering reminder to Milo that this was still very much the military.

Unable to join her husband in the hearing room, Nancy sat and waited in an adjacent office, knitting a purple shawl to pass the time. After seeing to her comfort, Milo and his attorneys navigated the narrow hallway to the hearing room.

Room 114 was small, with no trappings that would suggest legal proceedings. Three tables adorned the room: one for the panel of judges, one for the respondent (defendant) and his counsel, and one for the recorder (prosecution) and stenographer. A witness chair was positioned to face the judges. One of the first things Milo noticed was that the judges' table was slightly elevated.

At the appointed hour—0900, September 29, 1953—Col. William L. Doolan, Jr., flanked by Colonels Enoch O. Paulson and Earl Willoughby, called to order the security-risk hearing of Lt. Milo J. Radulovich. Besides Milo and the judges, the only other people in the room were his attorneys, a stenographer, and Maj. Donald H. Smith, officially designated the recorder.

Sanborn knew Building 303 and Colonel Doolan. Building 303 was where he reported for duty as an Air Force reserve officer. While on duty, his commanding officer was none other than Col. William Doolan. "Bill Doolan was a quiet, easygoing sort of fellow," Sanborn recalls, "not a laughing, joking type of individual. I think as a lawyer he was embarrassed at the whole proceeding."

"But I didn't know him all that well," Sanborn chuckles, "First lieutenants don't socialize much with full colonels."

Doolan spoke first, laying down the ground rules: "This Board is not a court of law, and the strict rules of evidence and court procedure are not followed." He went on to point out that this was a show-cause hearing, that the Air Force had "examined the information and evidence available to it" and determined that Milo "should be separated from the service as a security risk."[4]

Ken Sanborn knew exactly what Doolan was saying. As suspected, the burden would be on Milo to justify his retention in the Air force. There would be no presumption of innocence.

Explaining for the record that one possible outcome of the hearing would be for the panel to recommend a court-martial, Doolan went to the philosophical heart of the government's case. "That [a court-martial] would be appropriate in a case where there was some affirmative, definitely affirmative, act on the part of the individual. There is quite a distinction between a charge of disloyalty and being a security risk. You understand that due to pressure of family [you] could invoke acts on the part of an individual that he would not otherwise do."

Charles Lockwood, according to his son, cared little for military brass and took an immediate dislike to Doolan. If the colonel's comments were meant to intimidate, Lockwood's counterpunch was evidence he would not be browbeaten.

A broad smile crosses Milo's face as he recalls Lockwood's opening salvo: "They said he had fire in the belly, and boy, were they right."

In carefully measured tones, the combative consumer lawyer weighed in with an attack on the skewed nature of the proceedings, accusing the board of already having reached a verdict. "We do not feel this defendant will get the fair and impartial hearing that we have been assured," he said. "The Air Force has made its mind up as to the guilt of Lieutenant Radulovich, and he is presumed to be guilty rather than innocent, and because of that he is denied the rights he is entitled to as an American citizen, and to his day in court."

With increased intensity Lockwood then trained his sights on the panel of judges: "The Board has to examine itself, following no rules of procedure or evidence. Anything goes, any statement can be introduced and there is no way of opposing hearsay evidence." Leaving no doubt as to the depth of his contempt for the entire process, Lockwood's booming voice filled the room: "This man's fundamental rights as a citizen are involved in this proceeding, his very means of livelihood are involved....I wish to challenge the Board for cause and want to have it shown in the record that I object to the entire proceeding. The whole thing is repugnant."

Confronted with a belligerent civilian attorney who at first volley let it be known that he was impervious to military protocol and rank, Doolan was not about to turn the other cheek. He lectured Lockwood on the nature of an officer's commission: "I might say a commission in any of the services is not a vested right but is held at the pleasure of the President." Then he pointed out, "I can understand that in the strict concept of trials and so forth it presents a procedure that is not in accordance with a trial and probably is not in accordance with such procedure because it is not a trial. That is the difficulty you are having and as I had the first time I read the regulation."

"What is it, Colonel," Lockwood fired back, "if it is not a trial?"

"It is an administrative board hearing," Doolan replied.

Refusing to cede the point, Lockwood continued his harangue on military procedures, contending that Milo "is entitled to every safeguard and protection due him as an American citizen...and to say that anything goes which is practically the situation under those regulations, to me that is a shocking situation."

While Charlie Lockwood contested the board's procedures, as well as its right to even exist, Ken Sanborn maneuvered for the appeal. "I knew we would probably lose the case and the transcript would go to a higher authority," Sanborn reasoned. "So I had to put it all on the record. We were going through the hearing developing a record for the appeal."

"Here we have the situation," Sanborn pointed out to the trio of judges, "where the Department of Personnel made the findings based upon some statements from some individuals, maybe crackpots, and we have no chance to investigate into them....We understand that it is not a trial but it is certainly different from our concept of the law. Hearsay evidence is admitted and everything else to arrive at your recommendation, and now it is up to us to prove the respondent's innocence....We were furnished with a copy of the charges and that is all, and certainly to any attorney that is highly insufficient to establish a case. However, the Air Force has deemed it sufficient to set up this hearing. The purpose of the hearing is to determine whether or not the respondent is a security risk. We would like to proceed with the case on that basis."

Before Doolan could respond, Lockwood picked up the attack. "Is it true, Colonel, this Board has decided among its members that Lieutenant Radulovich is already guilty of these charges and it is now up to him to exonerate himself?"

"No sir," Doolan countered, "it is not true that the Board has come to any conclusion. The Board is presented with what you would have in civil practice as a ruling to show cause."

"Without examination, Colonel, there is no way I know of that a judge and jury can hold a man for trial for cause," Lockwood responded. "You don't make him come in and free himself. You go through rules and procedure....We are dealing with an American citizen here and he is presumed to be innocent. We are not behind the Iron Curtain, we are in America and he is entitled to that presumption and the Air Force Regulations do not provide that."

Cognizant of both the appeal and the need to examine the government's case, Sanborn pointed out to Doolan that "before you can get an order to show cause, you have to petition the court and inform the court that a certain situation exists, and it has to be true and not merely alleged....We want the whole case the government has and the right to go into it to set up our defense. That's what we are here for today otherwise we are not interested in starting."

Sidestepping Sanborn's request, Doolan offered, "The statement of reasons is a synopsis of the confidential investigative file."

Lockwood then queried, "And there is nothing new or different other than what we have been apprised of?"

"That is true," Doolan responded.

Pointing out that not only were the charges unsupported but also did not even constitute a crime, Lockwood moved for a dismissal. Doolan promptly overruled the motion, stating, "He [Milo] has not been charged with anything. It is a question of whether or not in view of these facts…"

"Don't call them facts, Colonel," Lockwood interrupted. "I object to the reference to subversive statements, made by someone, as facts.…They are simply allegations, unsupported charges. We don't know who made them. We don't get the chance to see these people in person and cross-examine them. These crackpots or enemies, whoever made them and transmitted them to the Air Force, we don't have them to consider. To take them as facts is unwarranted and I want to object to that."

Lockwood would not let loose of Doolan's references to facts, to which the colonel responded, "Perhaps I have referred to them as facts when more appropriately I should have said reports or allegations."

Sanborn, mindful of the appeal, inserted for the record: "The regulation states that the defendant has the opportunity to cross-examine any witnesses. The Board has to place that amount of value on the reports and as a practicing attorney, they are merely reports, because we don't know what they are. We are in the dark as to them.…Now as it stands there are certain things said regarding members of his family, but in themselves I am surprised if they set up any presumption he should be considered as a security risk."

Sanborn then deftly introduced Milo's top-secret clearance into the record, awarded after his father and sister were purported to have committed the indiscretions delineated in the Statement of Reasons: "He [Milo] has eight years of service and participated in various classified matters while he was in the service until June 1, 1952. The Air Force didn't seem to think anything was wrong at that time and these allegations were at a time prior to that."

Lockwood then resumed his offensive: "If we proceed it will be over objection of counsel and Lieutenant Radulovich. Any proceedings taken from this time will be over objection."

Doolan perfunctorily indicated that "any objection would be necessarily overruled."[5]

Apart from Ken Sanborn's gentle steering of the discussion toward placing critical appeal items on the record, the hearing, to this point, had little structure. It consisted primarily of thrust and parry between Lockwood and Doolan—Lockwood expressing outrage over the lack of judicial safeguards for his client, Doolan patiently instructing counsel that the hearing is administrative and not governed by the rubric of civilian courtroom procedure. Typical of the bantering was an exchange where Doolan revisited the nature of a military commission: "We have to recognize that the holding of a commission is a privilege rather than a right." Lockwood promptly responded, "Driving a motor vehicle is a privilege, but before they can take away a driver's license they must put in their case."

The rudderless hearing next drifted into a discussion of the *Daily Worker*. The Communist-oriented publication figured prominently in the Statement of Reasons. John Radulovich was cited for having it delivered to his house, while Margaret had been accused of celebrating its anniversary.

Ken Sanborn directed attention to the *Daily Worker* when he stated, "I hope I am not being premature by looking at some of these things [the charges], such as a person subscribing to a paper. We don't even know whether or not he [John] even reads it. It is ridiculous. You can find a copy of *The Daily Worker* in any library." From the transcript:

> Lockwood: You will find it in the library at the University of Michigan. Maybe that is a subversive institution too, I don't know.
>
> Sanborn: I have often thought I would like to read The Daily Worker.
>
> Lockwood: The editor of The Free Press reads it every morning and also The Wall Street Journal.
>
> Sanborn: I think of the thousands and thousands of loyal Americans who read The Daily Worker and won't know if

their loyalty is questioned. A situation like this means that if a person subscribes to The Daily Worker he will be labeled a communist, subversive and all sorts of names. I am afraid of this fear of what to read, fear of what to think. . .and this Board sits and determines a person is a reasonable security risk because a relative read The Daily Worker on the allegations of some person who we can't cross-examine.

Only forty-five minutes into the hearing, the prosecutor requested a recess. In the corridor, Ken Sanborn, showing uncharacteristic agitation, remarked to a reporter, "This is repugnant to any justice we know." That same reporter also observed, "Radulovich smoked furiously during the lull."[6]

When Colonel Doolan brought the hearing back to order, it was with an obvious resolve to provide some structure. He immediately called for a formal introduction of the charges. This brought a boisterous but unsuccessful objection from both Lockwood and Sanborn.

Lockwood then renewed his motion to open the hearing to the public, which Doolan quickly denied, indicating, "The General* has ruled the hearing should be closed due to procedures and to avoid public reflections concerning the respondent and his family."

"The General doesn't need to worry about the respondent and his family. They would welcome an open hearing," Lockwood pointed out.

Objections notwithstanding, Colonel Doolan instructed Major Smith to introduce the government's case. From the transcript:

> Prosecutor: I would like to introduce into evidence as Exhibit F, the classified, investigative file.

> Doolan: It will be received and will be considered by the Board.

> Sanborn: It is being received as a closed envelope?

> Doolan: It is a confidential investigative file.

* Tenth Air Force commander, Maj. Gen. Richard A. Grusendorf.

> Lockwood: It is a report to the Air Force by someone or some agency, is that right?

> Doolan: It is a consolidation of reports by various investigative agencies of the Government.

> Lockwood: Of which the respondent [Milo] is not informed, does not see, and has no way of knowing what it is except as found in the statement of reasons?

> Doolan: That is correct.

A few moments later:

> Sanborn: I am having trouble getting away from the concept that this is not a trial. It is like the case where you lay a file before the judge and saying this is a classified file. We have no right to cross-examine, no right to look at the things in the file, no right to any of the evidence. I do want to make that objection.

> Lockwood: There's the government's case in a sealed envelope. Take it or leave it.

Ken Sanborn, the more sanguine member of the defense team, showed an atypical bit of unraveling as Doolan pointed out that, technically, the envelope was not sealed. Piqued, Sanborn proceeded to describe in detail the envelope as being wrapped in a rubber band with Scotch tape around the edges. He then said directly to Doolan, "I would think this very repugnant to the concept of practice of law, you having been a practicing attorney for 32 years."

Classified or not, sealed or Scotch-taped envelope, it mattered little. The case against Lt. Milo J. Radulovich was now on record. Milo and his attorneys were officially in the position of having to refute charges they couldn't see, much less evaluate or challenge. "This infuriated me as a lawyer," Sanborn recalls.[7] "We felt we had a loser when we went into the hearing. When they placed the sealed envelope on the table, which was their entire case, I knew we had a loser. All we could do was make a lot of noise inside the hearing and state how unfair this was."[8]

Charles Lockwood pulled the hearing from its focus on security risks and jurisprudence and introduced the underlying political variable of communism. "This is in line with the Congressional Inquiry investigation," he said. "Unsupported charges are made against him and then McCarthy says, 'here it is, free yourself of guilt.' How anyone is to free himself of guilt under those circumstances I don't know."

Doolan responded, "As you understand, Mr. Lockwood, this* has not been disseminated to the public in any sense of the word at any time by the Air Force. Even with all the publicity given the matter, the Air Force has remained silent."

Both attorneys leaped on Doolan's comment. Lockwood responded, "I understand that, Colonel, all too well." Sanborn quickly followed with, "The Air Force has remained very silent."

Finally, with what appeared to be some degree of exasperation, Doolan announced, "The file will be received and will be considered over the objection of counsel."

The hearing continued to wander in and out of discussions involving the government's unwillingness to share the underpinnings of their case. Again, Sanborn nudged the proceedings toward an examination of the charges, more specifically John Radulovich's subscription to *Slobdna Rec*. Critical to Sanborn's questioning is that he laid the groundwork for maneuvering Doolan into disclosing selected portions of the government's classified case. From the transcript:

> Sanborn: The first time I ever heard the name of the publication was in regard to this hearing. It is considered a pro-Communist newspaper. How do we know? Has it been listed by the Attorney General?
>
> Doolan: The government has an FBI file containing evidence in support of the allegation.

*The reference here is to the case itself.

Sanborn: We deny he subscribed to this particular paper. We would like to know the exact evidence to show he did subscribe to it.

Doolan: There is a statement of an FBI informant to that effect.

Lockwood: What is the basis for labeling it a Communist publication?

Doolan: As to that I cannot say how the determination is made.

Sanborn: The report was made to you and the report has been accepted as true with no examination on the part of the Board to determine whether or not the report is true....We can't accept that because it is merely a statement by an FBI informant that it is a Communist paper.

Sanborn continued his probing and elicited an admission that, besides an informant, others were also involved in preparing the case against John Radulovich. He went on to point out that *Slobodna Rec* stopped publishing in 1948 and Milo was in the Air Force until 1952.

"It is not an allegation against Lieutenant Radulovich," Doolan observed.

"All we can do is deny that he [John Radulovich] ever subscribed to the paper," Sanborn said.

"Do you deny his father was a regular reader of the paper, whether he subscribed to it or not?" Doolan asked.

John Radulovich had not been charged with reading the paper, Sanborn quickly pointed out, only with subscribing to and contributing to its support.

Lockwood: What possible difference could it make to the Air force if a person reads the paper? Is there any element at all that amounts to anything if a person reads The Daily Worker?

Doolan: One element taken with another element—

Sanborn: Taking the element if a person reads The Daily Worker?

Doolan: It is an element for some consideration.

Lockwood: Do you think we all have the right to transmit our views and publish them?

Doolan: I might decline to answer that question in that I am not on trial for my views and my personal views might not be the views of the Air Force.

Lockwood: What is the Board's idea as to the views of communism and persons who read of those views. Is it or is not a crime?

Doolan: Taken alone we would attach very little importance to it.

Lockwood: When could you give some importance to it?

Doolan: Standing alone it would receive a negligible consideration, but coupled with a number of others—

Lockwood: Is there anything on his father outside of that?

Sanborn: Also that he received copies of The Daily Worker. What do you have regarding that? Is it contained in the same report or a different document?

The prosecutor again stepped in and asked for a recess, which Doolan promptly granted. The hearing had come to order at nine o'clock that morning. Still not two hours old, and already a second recess had been ordered.

An earlier pause had been requested when the hearing appeared to be floundering. Once resumed, sorely needed structure was inserted into the proceedings. Now it appeared that Sanborn and Lockwood's skillful inquiry into the government's classified case had provoked a need for the board to discuss in private how they should respond. Moreover, Doolan had assured counsel several times, on record, that all the charges were listed in the Statement of Reasons. As Sanborn and Lockwood began rummaging through the charges with Doolan, it was clear there was much more to the case than what was in the Statement of Reasons.

Back in session, a relentless Sanborn resumed his questioning, asking Doolan if there was evidence that John Radulovich had subscribed to *Slobodna Rec*. Was the Air Force relying solely on an informant's statement?

"There is some [information] concerning other allegations," Doolan said, as still more of the classified file trickled into the record.

Satisfied that the origin of material in the file regarding John Radulovich's subscription to *Slobodna Rec* was an FBI informant, Sanborn moved on to the *Daily Worker*. "Is the evidence you have also a report by the FBI from an informant that he received copies of *The Daily Worker*?" he asked.

"That is essentially it, yes," Doolan responded.

Sanborn and Lockwood then teamed to train their questions on the specific dates the *Daily Worker* was delivered to John Radulovich's house. Their machine-gun questioning forced Doolan to pause once again and examine the classified file.

Reading from the file, Doolan said the publication was delivered on "September 29, 1949, October 1, 1949—3 copies. On the 29th, 2 copies... they were being received through the mails consecutively. I am referring to *The Daily Worker*. October 5, one copy. October 1, one copy."

Someone had been closely monitoring John Radulovich's mail, that much was certain.

After careful questioning, Doolan then admitted that the *Daily Worker* had been delivered only to Margaret, not to her father. The defense team had never denied that Margaret had received copies. The Statement of Reasons, however, had accused John Radulovich of receiving the publication.

"It would appear," Sanborn quickly contended, "the first statement [in the Statement of Reasons] that he received copies of *The Daily Worker* is incorrect. He did not actually receive them....The Statement of Reasons has to be modified." It was the first solid chink in the government's case.

Doolan, though, was intractable. Despite contradictory information supplied by himself, he refused to alter the Statement of Reasons, which strongly suggested he was not even authorized to do so. "It doesn't need to be modified," he bluntly stated.

While Sanborn continued to perform legal surgery on the government's case, Lockwood resumed his effort to draw philosophical blood.

Concerning delivery of the *Daily Worker* to Margaret at her father's house, Lockwood asked, "Suppose he [John Radulovich] had gotten copies, what's the difference? No difference if he got one, a dozen or a hundred copies....I challenge the Board to say if getting *The Daily Worker* is important. I challenge the Board to say that taking *The Daily Worker* is a misdoing or mis-anything....Because, if you take that position it is contradictory to the President of the United States. He stated definitely that we all have the right to publicize our views and pass them through the mail and for people to read it. The President of the United States himself said that in his Dartmouth speech in May."

"We are not taking any position," Doolan responded.

"You are taking the position contradictory to the President's statement," Lockwood rejoindered.

John Radulovich had been accused of spreading Russian and Communist propaganda at his place of employ, the Hudson Motor Car Company. Sanborn asked Doolan to "explain the source of that information."

Doolan responded, "We have an allegation that upon information received, in 1947, John Radulovich...was actively engaged in pro-Communist activities regarding the present Yugoslavia government,

Tito and Russia." He goes on to inform Lockwood that "this statement was received in 1949."

"But it concerned 1947. That was the year after the war," Lockwood pointed out. "Is it a crime being interested in his former country?"

"Aren't we loaning Tito and Yugoslavia a lot of money even though they are communist?" Sanborn asked.

Sanborn continued to bore in on the classified file. "As to the statement of reasons. . .if there is other information or evidence introduced, we would like an opportunity to rebut that."

Doolan again supplied information from the file: "There is evidence in the investigative file substantiating contributions to the support of *Slobodna Rec* by the father."

Lockwood asked about specific amounts of those contributions, an exchange that produced a rare lighthearted moment.

"Give us the items as to contributions," Lockwood directed. "A dollar, five dollars, or what?"

Doolan said that in the February 4, 1948, issue of *Slobodna Rec*, John Radulovich is listed as a five-dollar contributor.

"He was a piker," Lockwood declared. "The government gives billions and he gave $5.00."

Just before the lunch recess, Milo took the stand. Lockwood's initial questioning was mostly geared toward putting biographic information in the record. But he brought out that Milo's chosen field, meteorology, required contact with governmental agencies in general and the military in particular. Being tabbed a security risk, Milo testified, would pose a serious threat to that career.

Lockwood went on to ask Milo about his relationship with Margaret. Milo pointed out that the only time he saw her was occasionally at Sunday dinner at his parents' home, and that communism had never been discussed or even mentioned at those gatherings. In fact, Milo said, he had never even been alone with Margaret since he and Nancy got married in September 1947.

Meticulously placing his case on record, Lockwood turned next to John Radulovich. Milo testified that his father was an immigrant who had been in this country for thirty-nine years, had never been comfortable with the English language, and subscribed to *Slobodna Rec* because it provided him with news of his homeland and was written in the comfortable Serbian language of his childhood. He said his father was a great admirer of Franklin D. Roosevelt and that a picture of the thirty-second president adorned John Radulovich's mantel.

Besides stating that he had never seen his father read the *Daily Worker*, Milo testified that he had never heard him utter a disloyal statement against the government of the United States. His father, he said, would fight for America even if attacked by his native country.

Milo's case was simple and straightforward. His father was not the rabble-rousing Communist portrayed in the Statement of Reasons. And although she was his sister, he had little contact with Margaret; there was no close and continuing association.

Although closed to the public, the hearing spilled into the outside hallway, taking the tension with it.

Twenty-five minutes into the afternoon session, another recess was ordered. Doolan approached Milo in the cramped corridor and admonished him for taking his case to the media. "Listen, you made a mistake going to the newspapers with this story," Doolan scolded. "You're only hurting your own family. You had no right to seek to embarrass the Air Force."[9]

Although disappointed in the proceedings, Milo still held out hope that the hearing could exonerate him. His case would not be helped, he concluded, if Doolan were unnecessarily antagonized. "But, Colonel, my whole livelihood depends on this," he replied. "If I'm tagged as a security risk, I'll never be able to get a job with the government as a meteorologist. I had to turn somewhere."

An incensed Charlie Lockwood quickly stepped between Doolan and Milo. "Without this publicity this boy would have had two strikes on him before he even went into the courtroom," Lockwood shouted at Doolan. "He'd have just been cashiered out of the service and nobody would have known. Now the whole nation is interested in what happens to him."

Ignoring Lockwood, the normally placid Doolan came unnerved and continued his assault on Milo: "You would have gotten the same break if you hadn't gone to the papers. You should have quietly asked for a hearing. After it had been held you would have been sent a sealed envelope with the results and nobody would have heard about it."

The recess lasted only five minutes. Doolan's invective stemmed from an obvious distaste for the publicity generated by the case, and yet, incredulously, he fired the first verbal shell and did so in full view of the press. After the confrontation, he scurried back to the hearing room, refusing to answer reporters' questions.

The Achilles' heel of the government's case, as Lockwood had always believed, was the publicity that surrounded it. Just before the recess, a board member, Col. Enoch Paulson, had been interrogating Milo regarding his sister. Back in session, a still-agitated Doolan seized control of the questioning.

> Doolan: Lieutenant, as you know there has been quite a bit of publicity about this hearing. At the time you received the original notice, you received a copy of the regulation under which the Board was convened, did you not?
>
> Milo: Yes, sir.
>
> Doolan: I assumed you carefully studied that regulation.
>
> Milo: Yes.
>
> Doolan: To determine the procedures that were followed both in detail as to originating the allegations on the notice and the procedure of the Board hearing and so forth?
>
> Milo: Yes.
>
> Doolan: Nevertheless, prior to the hearing you have participated in rather extensive publicity consisting of trying the

issue in the press rather than doing as the Air Force attempts to do for the individual by keeping that strictly between them and giving no publicity to the allegations at any time for that matter but certainly not prior to a fair, full and complete hearing.

Milo: Yes. The newspapers contacted me originally, the Detroit News.

Doolan: Where did they get it from?

Lockwood: From the attorneys. If there is any blame to attach it is to the attorneys. The attorneys are responsible for the publicity. I felt that if a case should be brought to the public's attention, this was it and Milo had no part in that whatsoever. He hasn't wanted any part of the publicity and is in no way responsible in regards to that. I can see nothing in the regulation which prevents publicity.

Sanborn claimed the final comment in the skirmish over publicity: "The fact that the newspaper and radio men have seen proper to take the Air Force to task in the situation is absolutely no fault of his [Milo's]. I find nothing in the publicity not substantially correct."

Charlie Lockwood and Ken Sanborn had long suspected the government yearned to gracefully rid itself of the Radulovich case. But with the lieutenant's story firmly imbedded in America's newspapers, and the military featured prominently as the villain in that drama, they knew the Air Force could not just sound retreat and execute an about-face; there was dignity to consider. The Air Force needed a sign of remorse. They needed Milo to renounce his father and sister. They needed him to become a public penitent, much as Lucille Ball had.

As Doolan bored in on Lieutenant Radulovich's relationship with his sister, the tenor of his questioning solidified the lawyers' belief that leniency was in the offing if only Milo would agree to distance himself from his family.

Doolan: Have you ever in any way renounced your sister's views or indicated prior to your hearing that you were not closely associated with her as alleged in the statement of reasons?

Milo: You mean publicly?

Doolan: Yes.

Milo: I never admitted that.

Doolan: Everything else has been aired publicly.

Milo: What do you mean?

Doolan: The Statement of Reasons was aired publicly and the fact you were a good upright officer has been aired publicly and you were called upon to present your side of the case. Have you ever presented the side of the case that shows you renounced your sister's views?

Milo: Up until this time I did not know definitely what her views were, except as outlined in the Statement of Reasons.

Doolan: Couldn't you have said I don't agree with them and have not been closely associated with her?

Milo: I did state she has a right to her own opinion and still say that. She is mature, married, and has her own life. My life is my own and is on another path.

Lockwood: Do you think that renouncing her views would help?

Doolan: Not entirely.

The door was open. Milo only needed to walk through it.

"If he was willing to get up and disassociate himself from his family then they might have been able to say the situation had been corrected," Sanborn said. "It would have been a PR victory for the Air Force."

Sanborn speculated on the direction that spurning his family might take. "I presume he could have signed some sort of renunciation. All those records were secret, but perhaps he could have renounced them in some sort of letter."

But repudiating his father and sister, Sanborn hastened to point out, was never realistically considered. "It may have been an option for them," he said, "but not for Milo. Milo simply could not do that. Liberal as his sister may have been, she was still his sister. And there's no way he would have renounced his father."

Nancy Radulovich was called to the stand. Conducted by Ken Sanborn, her ten-minute testimony supported Milo's contention that since they were married in 1947, until the case began, he had never been alone with his sister or father. She had been present every time her husband visited his family and during those visits they didn't discuss politics. "They talk about school," she said. "One boy [Sam] is in Lawrence Tech and they get together on math problems and such."

Doolan tried to puncture her testimony with questions on detail. "Couldn't his father have discussed matters with him when you were doing housework or something else?" he asked.

"No," she responded firmly.

Sanborn asked Nancy if she had any political leanings. She hailed from a city and family that strongly admired the nation's only woman senator, Margaret Chase Smith. "I voted Republican," she said proudly.

"And Milo voted what?" Sanborn asked.

"I don't know," she said.

"She was a very good witness," Sanborn said of Nancy. "Easy going. Intelligent. She was not about to be intimidated."

The hearing was adjourned until 0900, October 2, 1953, the following Friday.

Several points had been made during the five-hour hearing and should have been the basis of a banner day for the defense. As it turned out, those same points were the source of frustration for Milo and his attorneys.

The defense articulated time and again their outrage over the proceedings. Milo's livelihood, the ability to provide for his family, they argued, was at stake. And he had committed no crime. Yet the government refused to allow into the hearing the most basic element of American jurisprudence, a presumption of innocence.

The defense disproved a key point in the government's case involving John Radulovich, namely that the *Daily Worker* had never been mailed to him. Yet the motion to amend the Statement of Reasons was summarily rejected.

The defense portrayed John Radulovich as a loyal American with herolike attachment to former President Franklin D. Roosevelt. His reading of the forbidden *Slobodna Rec*, they demonstrated, was because of a yearning for news of his homeland. Hardly the goading provocateur depicted in the Statement of Reasons, John Radulovich could barely speak English, a point that was not challenged. Yet, when Lockwood and Sanborn demanded the names of those who accused the immigrant patriot of disloyalty, when they railed at being denied the opportunity to cross-examine those who had assaulted his patriotism, the government refused, saying only that their case involved the use of informants. A sealed, Scotch-taped envelope emerged as the focal point of their attack.

The defense showed Milo had little or no contact with his sister over the years. The government's contention of their "close, continuing association," a key element of the charges brought under AFR 35-62, was totally without merit. Yet the government chose to ignore his testimony, and that of his wife. They sought instead a renunciation from Milo and his family.

Unfortunately morale had crested with the rebellious GI reception that morning. The tribunal seemed unwilling, unable, to acknowledge any of the concerns registered by the defense.

At day's end Lockwood summed up the proceedings for the eagerly awaiting press: "In effect," he said, "we have been presented with a batch of hearsay evidence and are asked to show that it is not true.

We're under the worst type of handicap, since we're not even permitted to know who the accusers are. The statements might be from some crackpots for all we know."[10]

The hearing not yet complete, Milo cautiously refused to confront the Air Force and focused his comments on why he was fighting the decision to release: "If I am discharged as a security risk, nine years of training in meteorology will be wasted....Practically all of this time has been devoted to direct or indirect preparation in my field. If I am discharged under a stigma, this field will be closed to me."

———————⟫●⟪———————

That evening, although exhausted, Milo took a call from Mark Reader of the *Michigan Daily*. Reader was interested in more than just the day's events. After securing obligatory quotes regarding the hearing— "there is no case and I have nothing to hide"—he asked his fellow student about attendance at class. "I'm so doggone upset," Milo said, "that I can't sit down to study. I told some of my instructors that I won't be around for a few weeks. My wife and I are getting more nervous every day."[13]

Milo's comments to Reader were grossly understated. In fact, the demands on his time had been horrendous and his studies had suffered irreparable damage. Shortly after the Harris article appeared and Milo's already frenetic schedule had been stretched even further, he went to his professors, hoping for some compassion, some patience, but found none. One asked callously, "Why don't you find a new major?"

———————⟫●⟪———————

Speculation continued whether President Eisenhower would appoint California Gov. Earl Warren to the United States Supreme Court as an associate justice or call upon him to head the nation's top judicial

*panel as chief justice. Either way, details were feverishly being
worked out in the hope that Warren could join the high court before the
fall term convened the following Monday.*

*On September 3, Warren had announced he would not be a candi-
date for another term as governor of California. It was widely rumored
then that he sat at the top of Eisenhower's list to fill the next court
vacancy. Five days later the untimely death of Chief Justice Fred
Vinson unexpectedly created that vacancy.[11]*

*Warren, running mate of the 1948 Republican presidential candi-
date, Thomas Dewey, and considered a strong opponent of racial segregation, indicated his acceptance of the offer to join the high court
after a three-hour meeting in Sacramento with Atty. Gen. Herbert
Brownell, Jr.*

—————>●<—————

As Col. William L. Doolan called to order the hearing of Lt. Milo J.
Radulovich in Mount Clemens, in Detroit federal court the trial of six
Communist leaders began.

The trial of the six leaders cited under the Smith Act with conspiring to teach, advocate, and organize an overthrow of the government
slowed over procedural motions as defense attorneys sought a bill of
particulars elaborating charges against the defendants. The
Department of Justice attorney, William Hundley, argued that the
defense was asking the government "to lay open its whole case before
the trial."[12]

Of the twenty-eight items cocounsels Ernest Goodman and Chester
Smith requested be included in the bill of particulars, federal Judge
Frank A. Picard denied all but eight. Picard urged both sides to meet
independent of the court in an attempt to arrive at an agreement
regarding the remaining points.

Referring to the previous year's ten-month Communist conspiracy
trial in New York, prosecutors voiced concern that the defense request
for a bill of particulars was only a delaying tactic.

Sen. Joseph McCarthy, presiding over New York hearings of his Senate Investigation Committee, directed two uniformed guards to remove attorney Abraham Unger from the hearing room. "Remove that man," McCarthy had shouted as Unger launched into a lengthy answer to the senator's question. Spectators in the audience hissed at Unger while he struggled with the guards. "Throw him out," one shouted.

This was not the first encounter between McCarthy and Unger. In a previous executive session of the committee, the attorney had spoken for seventy minutes without answering either of two direction questions posed by McCarthy. Once Unger was removed, McCarthy announced he would be taking action to narrow use of the Fifth Amendment.[14]

WEDNESDAY, SEPTEMBER 30, 1953

Although Charlie Lockwood vigorously defended the right of the press to speak with an unfettered voice, he was never reticent with a suggestion as to how they should exercise that right. His stormy career in the contentious arena of consumer law, coupled with a truculent style, had joined him in frequent battle with the press.

Now, however, the press had come to fight by his side. He was delighted and willing to say so. The hearing in recess until Friday, Lockwood wrote of the Radulovich case in his *Eastside Shopper* column: "I was not certain as to how much cooperation we could get from the press, but I arranged an interview. . .and hoped for the best. Within 48 hours the story of Milo J. Radulovich was being carried in every city in America...the case aroused more interest in New York City than even in Detroit."[1]

He went on to say: "I have often been critical of the press of this country, but I want to say here and now that the daily newspapers of Detroit and elsewhere recognized immediately the peril and threat presented to basic freedoms and rights and the outrageous injustice of the Air Force's position. If our press, radio and television stations will fight as militantly to protect others as they have fought to protect humble Milo J. Radulovich, then a lot of us are going to feel a great deal more confident and encouraged as to the future."

128

However real the tension—and according to Ken Sanborn, "it was tense"—when day was done the hearing's chief participants gathered in an inexplicable show of collegiality to pose for a picture. In it, Sanborn, Milo Radulovich, Charles Lockwood, and Col. William Doolan all studied with feigned interest a piece of paper held by Sanborn. Shrugging off the incongruity, Sanborn matter-of-factly pointed out, "It really wasn't Doolan's fault. He was just the closest one for us to attack. But they wanted a picture, so we accommodated them."[2]

To the right of the group shot was a photograph of a smiling Nancy Radulovich knitting a purple shawl as she waited to testify.

Milo's twenty-four-year-old brother, Walter, did as many other twenty-four-year-olds did on Wednesday nights in Detroit: he went out for a few drinks with some friends. By no means intoxicated, he did enjoy himself, not an entirely novel recreation for a young bachelor who also sported a well-deserved reputation for his ability on the dance floor.

Not long after midnight, Walter, who lived with his parents, pulled into the driveway of the family home only to be quickly intercepted and detained by two of Detroit's finest, their squad car lights strobing the street. He was asked to produce identification and thoroughly questioned. Once the officers were satisfied their detainee was in fact Walter Radulovich, he was allowed to enter his house.

Although regretting any inconvenience to Walter, given the threatening phone calls of a few days earlier, the family was grateful for the swift action of the officers.

―――――⟫●⟪―――――

President Eisenhower told reporters that if members of his administra-
tion "leaked" news to the press for what they thought were proper rea-
sons, he would not interfere with them. The president's comments
came as he was asked about news leaks involving California Gov.
Earl Warren's appointment as chief justice of the Supreme Court.

Reporters for morning newspapers also complained that the presi-
dent's practice of holding his news conferences in the morning provid-
ed an advantage to the afternoon papers. Eisenhower said he would
consider alternating between morning and afternoon, but that he
understood presidential news conferences were generally held at the
convenience of the president.

―――――⟫●⟪―――――

The official news arm of the Vatican, L'Osservatore, announced that
government officials in Poland had relieved Stefan Cardinal Wysznski
of all church duties and placed him under arrest. The fifty-two-year-
old Roman Catholic primate was taken from his Warsaw residence by
secret police and spirited to an unknown monastery where he would
not be allowed to communicate with the outside world.

According to Warsaw radio, Cardinal Wysznski, the last free prince
of the church behind the iron curtain, had been arrested for violating
provisions of the 190 church-state agreement when he protested sen-
tences received by the Most Reverend Czeslow Kaczmarek, bishop of
Kiece, and three other priests. All were recently convicted on charges
of spying for the Vatican and the United States.[3]

August Zaleski, president of the Polish government in exile, urged
the Polish people, virtually all of whom were Catholic, to remain calm.
Any action, he warned, would be viewed by the government as a
provocation and culminate in a bloodbath.

THURSDAY, OCTOBER 1, 1953

The letters started to come in.

Still a reluctant celebrity, Milo was not prepared for the public outpouring. But the mail was overwhelmingly supportive, and that braced his sagging morale.

From just across the border in Windsor, Ontario, a former United States citizen who lost a teaching job wrote that "the school trustees decided my views on race relations and civil rights were Communistic, leftist and un-un-American." He also indicated there was more freedom and tolerance in Canada and urged Milo to move there, pointing out that most Canadian universities would begin their academic year the following Monday.

Another urged Milo to resign: "Any organization which would ask you to renounce your family because of politics, doesn't deserve your loyalty and support."

Still another, a Methodist minister in Indiana, addressed the implications of Milo's case: "If an American can be so treated because his sister engages in peaceful and lawful picketing and his father chooses to read a magazine somebody calls 'radical', our fundamental liberties in this country are indeed in peril."

All the mail didn't go to Milo. From Brooklyn, New York, a telegram addressed simply "Trial Board, Selfridge Air Force Base" stated, "Let us remember we are still 'the land of the free' and not punish anyone for what his family *might* be guilty of. Even then, under our constitution, we are innocent until proven guilty."

In the "Public Letter Box" the *Detroit News* printed a missive signed simply "Mother of Serviceman," who pointed out, "I thought this country believed in the rights of the individual, but it doesn't look that way in this case. Should he be made to suffer for his family's faults?"[1]

————◆————

The hearing temporarily in recess, a bizarre twist attached itself to the Radulovich story when a recently discharged Air Force officer not only blasted government action against Milo but also charged lax security at Selfridge Air Force Base.

Former Air Force Maj. Stephen Jurkovic, who claimed he was "railroaded" into accepting an honorable discharge from the military weeks earlier, labeled the charges against Lieutenant Radulovich "ridiculous."[2]

As evidence of lax security, Jurkovic cited the results of a surprise inspection by agents of the Office of Special Investigation. He indicated that during the mock espionage maneuver, every plane and vital installation on the base had been successfully sabotaged.

When pressed for a response to Jurkovic's allegations, the Air Force did not disagree. According to the Selfridge commander, Col. James E. Johnson, "We found that as a result of this test that our security was not up to the standard that we desired."[3]

Jurkovic's public criticism of the Air Force was prompted by his anger over Col. William Doolan's personal attack on Milo for talking to the press. Concerning the Radulovich case, Jurkovic observed, "I can't see why that hearing should be kept secret as it is. If the Air Force has nothing to hide, the press should be permitted to be present."[4]

This was not the first time Jurkovic had crossed swords with his superiors. "I went through the same thing myself," he said. "Only I didn't ask for newspaper help and now after 11 years service I have to look for a civilian job."

Jurkovic recounted an incident that occurred a year earlier while he was a security officer at Wurtsmith Air Force Base in Oscoda, Michigan. One night two air policemen in his command stopped the base commander for traveling eighty miles per hour in a thirty-mile-per-hour zone. The commander claimed he had been chasing a corporal. Both air policeman, however, reported that the corporal in question had not been speeding. No charges were ever filed by Jurkovic against the commander but the corporal's car was ordered off base.

In another incident during that same period, Jurkovic intervened on behalf of a sergeant in his command who had been labeled a bad security risk because his stepmother allegedly had Communist leanings thirty years earlier. Through Jurkovic's direct efforts, which included a personal letter drafted on the sergeant's behalf, the charges were dropped.

After the speeding incident, Jurkovic's relationship with the commander deteriorated until finally he received a "poor" on his semiannual efficiency report, a death-knell rating for an officer's career. A "poor" grade is an almost certain end to promotions and usually the precursor of a request to accept a discharge.

While the Wurtsmith commander was relieved of his command and reassigned, Jurkovic was transferred to Selfridge, where he spent the last fifty-nine days of his military career.

"In the Air Force you are assumed to be guilty until you are proven to be innocent," Jurkovic charged. "That is the opposite of what this country stands for and you cannot believe it is true until it happens to you."

Maj. Stephen Jurkovic's eleven-year military career included combat duty over France in 1943 and twenty-six months of occupation in

Korea before hostilities broke out. Because of injuries from being shot down over the North Sea, he had an artificial jaw.

An Air Force spokesman in Washington stated, "The Radulovich case is strictly an administrative function and the lieutenant is getting an impartial hearing. All he has to do is prove he is not associating with the persons named and he will be cleared."[5] Assuming the statement was as carefully crafted as others throughout the Radulovich case, it represented a veiled but intriguing reference to the prospect of Milo's exoneration hinging on a willingness to distance himself from his family.

With tongue set firmly in cheek, the Detroit News proffered advice to Sen. Joe McCarthy's new bride, Jean: "Those who have hidden behind the Fifth Amendment in McCarthy's Red-hunting committee probably are predicting that the wedding of a flannel-mouthed Irishman and a converted Scottish Presbyterian can come only to a deserved end. Not us. We are in Mrs. McCarthy's corner passing out ring advice in this match. The new bride immediately should install McCarthy committee rules in her household. Those keep the witness from making long-winded explanations of his conduct and confine him to the truth—and all of it."

John Radulovich kept pretty much to himself at the Hudson Motor Company. While a strong union man he was also grateful for his job. It enabled him to provide for his family without depending on handouts from the government. He had seen too many layoffs since joining Hudson in 1926. With vivid memories of working in the mines of Ohio, he didn't complain.

The elder Radulovich stood accused of "spreading Russian and Communist propaganda" at Hudson since 1946. Despite vigorous on- and off-the-record protests, Charlie Lockwood and Ken Sanborn had been refused the opportunity to confront and, more important, challenge and dissect the motives of his accusers. They could register more objections, but to what end? Even after uncovering blatant errors in the Statement of Reasons, the hearing board had steadfastly refused to alter the charges.

Lockwood and Sanborn decided instead to call upon those who knew John Radulovich, those who had their fingers on the pulse of the Hudson community of employees, those who regarded him as a loyal union man and patriotic American who minded his own business, those who had worked with him on the line.

Save for size and structure, the Hudson Motor Car Company was indistinguishable from other automobile factories—sprawling complexes, communities unto themselves.

135

Despite great strides by the union after the sit-down strikes of the late thirties, work in the shop, especially on the line, was hard—long hours of strenuous physical labor accompanied by unyielding monotony. Heralded for the comfort it brought to the profit and loss statements of America's automobile manufacturers, for many factory workers the production line was the bane of their existence.

Life as a production worker was divided into six-minute chunks, a ten-part hour, conveniently segmented for the timekeeper to tabulate an hour's pay, a day's wage. Punching in one minute late for work translated into being docked six minutes. Twice during a shift two of those chunks were gratefully relinquished to the relief man who provided twelve precious minutes off the line—twelve minutes to use the toilet, twelve minutes to sit down for a smoke, twelve minutes to relax aching muscles.

However taxing the work, boredom was the worst part, broken only by snatches of conversation sandwiched between carefully crafted tasks performed by thousands of workers on thousands of automobile frames that slowly wound their way through noisy, poorly ventilated factories. Intimate details of family life were shared at the slightest provocation. Management was endlessly derided and cursed for their stupidity; the higher the level of management, the greater the abuse. Faded pictures of couples, and more, engaged in wildly contorted sexual acts were exchanged. Anything to spirit the mind away from the line. Anything to kill time.

Once every shift, the line groaned to a halt for thirty minutes. Relationships, forged while conversing as the unfinished cars relentlessly trudged their way to completion, were cemented during lunch break. Now conversation flowed unimpeded. Lunch was eaten with those you liked; time away from the line was too precious to be with those who annoyed.

Common to all auto plants was the oldest form of communication, rumors—rumors that raced up and down the line, rumors that bounded in and out of tool cribs, rumors that caromed off the walls of paint shops and cafeterias, rumors that traveled the plant with the speed of sunlight sprinting across a wheat field.

There were few secrets in the shop. Everybody knew the "numbers man." He plied his trade quietly, so it was no big deal. A few of the guys would run out to the parking lot during lunch and come back chewing Juicy Fruit. As long as they did their job, nobody said anything. It was all a part of life in the shop. And if someone was spreading "commie bullshit," everybody would have known that too. That would have been special grist for the rumor mill.

A unique bond evolved among those who worked together in the plant. Management, the line, too many hours, not enough hours—the common enemies were too pervasive not to feel the kinship. You knew the people you worked with, who you could trust, who you couldn't. Some still carried the scars of battling company goons at overpasses. Their bond was stronger than most.

When the hearing was called to order at 0910, October 2, 1953, Claude Edward Bland, former president and now recording secretary for Hudson's United Auto Workers Local 154, was called to the stand.

Claude Bland and John Radulovich had known each other since 1937. Their relationship had been established while working in the same department, while eating lunch together. Of his coworker, Bland said, "I never heard him dissent on the operations of this nation, its slant on democracy and never on any instance heard him agitate or instigate anything to the contrary."[1]

Bland pointed out that since Local 154 was formed in 1936 it had militantly fought the spread of Red propaganda in the plant. He also assured the hearing board that as president he would have known if anyone had engaged in such activities.

While prefacing a question to Bland, Lockwood tested once again the patience of the board president, Col. William Doolan.

> Lockwood: Under this procedure we are faced with a lot of
> blanket accusations and we have got to exonerate ourselves
> and prove ourselves. We don't know who said all these

things, they just threw the envelope down and said, "Free yourself from the blame."

Doolan: Mr. Lockwood, please—

Lockwood: I feel so strongly about this I can't restrain myself...

Doolan: Mr. Lockwood, please let's not fill the record up with more objections. You have clearly stated them earlier in the hearing.

Lockwood went on to ask Bland that if he had any inkling that John Radulovich was a spreader of communism, would he be here testifying on his behalf?

"No," Bland said emphatically. "I hate the smell of them. . . Commies and the whole philosophy. It is absolutely unthinkable that people believe in such a philosophy."

In response to a question from Doolan, Bland described John Radulovich: "I thought of him as a man who is trying to go through life minding his own business, conforming to all rules of the local union and as far as I have experienced, conforming to all the rules of the country. I have never known otherwise."

A board member, Col. Earl Willoughby, finally broke his silence and asked Bland what methods were employed to weed Communists out. The answer offered some insight into the paternal role of the union in a large automobile plant.

"There is no set method," he replied, "but I can give you an example of one case where the boys were ready to throw one man out of the plant who was spreading propaganda. . .where it had to be stopped so we definitely told him it had to stop."

"Who do you mean by 'we'?" Willoughby asked.

"The stewards in the district involved and the officers," Bland said.

"All in a party?" Willoughby continued.

"No," Bland said. "He was just told that it had to stop. He was informed that if he desired to work at the Hudson Motor Car Company he must discontinue it and he did."

Seeing an opportunity to reinforce the point, Lockwood asked, "[D]o you think it would be possible for John Radulovich to engage as has been charged on occasions in the Hudson Motor Car Company to spread Russian and communist propaganda and you not know of it?"

"I am pretty sure that I would hear about it," Bland responded.

Bland went on to say how the Hudson workers would respond to someone spreading propaganda in the plant: "[H]e would be as welcome as a skunk at a picnic."

Claude Bland stepped down.

Arwin Wheaton took the stand. As chief steward in the district where John Radulovich worked, Wheaton was expected to have intimate knowledge of activities in his area, and he testified to that effect.

Besides describing John Radulovich's quiet ways, Wheaton also gave a stirring example of the old immigrant's patriotism: "He is always a gentleman. He never says a word, never troubles us. Not only that but there are three blind veterans from World War II, one has a leg off and one with a hand off and he even agreed to give up his seniority and he was laid off and they were kept on. He always agreed they should get everything they were entitled to."

When asked what he would do upon encountering Communists in the plant, Wheaton, like Bland before him, left little doubt as to where he stood. "Throw them to hell out," he responded.

Asked about the charges against John Radulovich of spreading Russian and Communist propaganda in the plant, Wheaton responded, "I say it is a lie as far as I am concerned."

Through questioning, Lockwood also brought out that John Radulovich was told by the Personnel Department at Hudson that he enjoyed the full support of the company.

Lockwood also revisited John Radulovich's willingness to take a layoff so that his disabled veteran colleagues could continue working.

Wheaton pointed out how John wanted to avoid any fanfare, and just directed that the veterans be given what they're entitled to. "So, does that sound like the words of a subversive?" Lockwood asked.

"Hell no," Wheaton responded, "the word of a gentleman."

Arwin Wheaton stepped down.

Doolan announced that the board would meet in closed session to determine its verdict, a process anticipated to take between ten days and two weeks. Once a decision had been reached, it would be communicated only to Milo. Whether the decision would be shared with the public would be up to him.

At 1000, October 2, 1953, the hearing of Lt. Milo J. Radulovich was officially concluded.

———————

"I didn't hesitate a moment when I was asked to be a character witness for John," Bland told reporters outside the hearing room. "I've known him for a long time and I can tell you he's as good an American as I've ever seen."[2]

Asked about the UAW's position on Communists, Bland said, "Our local is always on the alert for Commies. Why, you can smell one a mile away. Mr. Radulovich is not one of them."[3]

"Any statement by the Air force or anybody else that the father is a Communist is an outright lie," Wheaton said.[4]

———————

Charlie Lockwood and Col. William Doolan tangled again.

As the colonel was coming out of the hearing room, Lockwood turned to Doolan and shouted, "This whole hearing was outrageous. I am going to recommend changes in this regulation."

Clearly agitated, Doolan shot back, "I'm sure the Air Force will be very glad to hear any recommendations you have. Personally I think the regulation is all right. If it were for me to say, I wouldn't change a word."[5]

———————>

Ever conscious of an appeal, Ken Sanborn drafted a precise, four-page brief that, with one notable exception, was a recitation of their case.

"The defense has taken the position that the allegations against the sister are wholly immaterial for the reason that no close continuing association existed between her and the respondent," Sanborn wrote. "The evidence presented was overwhelming that there is now and has been for many years past not only no close relationship or association but, on the contrary, almost no association at all between brother and sister."[6]

Sanborn pointed out that the close, continuing association between John and Milo Radulovich was unimportant, "due to the fact that all the evidence indicates that the father was and is a loyal and patriotic American who during his entire 39 years in this country has never been guilty of disloyal or subversive activities or conduct of any nature whatsoever."

Although not considered during the hearing, the brief injected into the record for the first time the case of Capt. Charles Hill. "That case," Sanborn wrote, "was almost all fours with this case. If anything, the Air Force had a stronger case against Hill." Pointing out that the charges against Hill were dropped and a formal apology made to the captain, Sanborn wrote, "The precedent established by the Hill case cannot be disregarded by this Board."

If Ken Sanborn was concerned about *command influence* or the impact that representing Milo held for his own military career, it was well concealed. His biting prose equaled the verbal venom hurled by the cocounsel, Charlie Lockwood, during the hearing.

Sanborn sent a well-aimed shot across the tribunal's bow: "The defense again points out that even if the father included among his reading a questionable Serbian newspaper, that is his absolute right and privilege and no inference of guilt or wrongdoing can be assumed because of that by this Board. This is extremely important to keep in mind because some members of the Board have indicated they believe otherwise."

Sanborn moved to stand between Milo and any punitive action stemming from Doolan's anger over press accounts of the case: "The open and all too apparant [sic] resentment and hostility shown by this Board to the publicity generated by the shocking and repugnant nature of this case must not be held against the respondent."

He bluntly labeled the government's case "whimsical, fanciful and with little or no basis in fact. It is a case that would be thrown out in any regular court without a moment's hesitation."

Sanborn concluded by showing his contempt for the proceedings: "In spite of the bias and shocking departure from all democratic and constitutional procedure, the respondent has proven himself innocent. If the testimony presented is considered at all, this Board cannot possibly hold otherwise."

Billed as the greatest technological advance in the movies since the "talkies," CinemaScope was introduced to moviegoers. The first picture filmed in CinemaScope, The Robe, *played to a first-day attendance record at Loew's Capitol theater in Washington, D.C.*

CinemaScope projected an image much larger than usual upon a curved, concave screen, producing an effect of being surrounded. The lens was originally developed by Henri Chrétien of France, who had designed it during World War I to improve the marksmanship of anti-aircraft gunners. Chrétien was in the audience for the premiere.[7]

SATURDAY, OCTOBER 3, 1953

A Tenth Air Force spokesman at Selfridge Air Force Base disclosed that, besides Lt. Milo Radulovich, two other officers were facing discharge action as poor security risks. Both were awaiting word from Air Force Headquarters in Washington on appeals prompted by adverse hearing-board decisions. Earlier, a third officer elected to accept a board of inquiry's findings and was discharged.

The spokesman said he had no information on how many officers had elected to resign their commissions and accept discharges rather than face a board of inquiry.[1]

"I wasn't overly optimistic," Milo said of the hearing, "but I felt pretty good about the case we had put on. I thought we had a real good chance of winning. I don't know what else we could have done."

The hearing concluded, Milo desperately turned to the studies that had been neglected since the Russell Harris article invaded his already hectic daily regimen two weeks earlier. Once again he contemplated dropping out for a semester, and once again he stubbornly told himself that with a little extra effort he could get caught up. But that wasn't as easy as it sounded. However noble his intent, the rest of Milo's life wasn't about to just get up and go away so he could study. There were

143

still diapers to change. The bills were there too, as well as the jobs that brought home the money to pay those bills.

The tension of the hearing had also exacted a toll. Milo was exhausted, physically and mentally. Despite the merits of his case, the Air Force had shown no inclination to drop the charges. His life might never return to the way it used to be. All this could have been for nothing.

⟹>●<⟸

It was announced that overcrowded Negro schools in the District of Columbia would be assigned twenty-two new teachers. According to school superintendent, Hobart M. Corning, the money to hire the new teachers would be transferred from accounts in the white division of the school system.

Within the system's Negro division, it was reported that class sizes were running at an average of 50–58 students per teacher. When school opened in the fall of 1952, Spingarn, the Negro high school, did not have textbooks for many classes, and there were no teachers for some classes in biology, social science, business, physical education, and foreign languages.[2]

For seven years, at least according to the charges brought against his son, "brother" John Radulovich had escaped the union's self-proclaimed airtight Communist-detection system.

Long a strident opponent of communism, the United Auto Workers were not about to suffer in silence as the Bolshevik label fell on one of its members and, by implication, on the union itself. John Radulovich, member in good standing of UAW Local 154, stood accused of spreading Communist propaganda in one of their shops. The stigma had to be excised. Lest the entire leadership of the union be branded, it had to be excised quickly.

No less a luminary than UAW International Secretary-Treasurer Emil Mazey took pen in hand to plead the case of Lt. Milo Radulovich. In a letter to Air Force Secretary Harold E. Talbott, Mazey labeled the closed hearing a "star chamber" proceeding and urged all action against Milo be withdrawn.[1]

With uncommon eloquence Mazey's pen quickly journeyed to the heart of the government's case, pointing out that action was taken against Milo because "he is the son of a man who rightfully thought that under the Constitution of the United States, a citizen has the right to read papers and books with which he disagreed, as well as those with which he agreed, and that his sister had expressed her 'right of assembly.'" He went on to say that "the disgrace and stigma which will attach to the wife and two children of Lieutenant Radulovich as a

result of these unfounded proceedings goes beyond human understanding....You do not charge the Lieutenant with attempting to influence the thinking of his father. You simply charge him with being his
father's son."

Continuing, Mazey asked, "Would you have this citizen disown
his own father because the father might not pass a loyalty test set up
by Air Force standards?...In fact, a son who does not have basic family loyalties could not be expected to be either a good citizen or a good
officer of the Air Force."

After citing similarities in the dismissed case against Capt. Charles
Hill, Jr., Mazey recalled the not too distant past: "I would remind you
that during World War II millions of servicemen were shown a series
of films by the Armed Services, praising Russia and informing servicemen of the great role Russia was playing in preserving democracy,
and of its fight against dictatorship. If the Air Force feels that a person
is guilty of a serious crime because he presumably read a pro-
Communist newspaper, then I feel that the Armed Forces is guilty of a
similar crime."

———————⏗———————

*The popular "Grin and Bear It" cartoon strip in the Sunday funnies
depicted a college football coach talking to his assistant as the team
passed before them. The caption read, "An occasional professor is
expendable. . .but I hope them Senate Committees don't come snoop-
ing around our football squad."2*

The case against Lieutenant Radulovich found its way to the pages of *Time* magazine. Nestled amid other stories in the "National Affairs" section, the article was accompanied by a photograph of Milo, Nancy, and the children. No new information was included, but the story was now officially national.[1]

Ironically, *Time*'s cover story that week featured the longtime Communist foe, Richard Nixon. In an article titled "Nixon: A Political Sinecure Becomes a Success Story," the vice president is heralded as acquiring "more real influence in Washington than any of his predecessors ever achieved, however long their tenure."

Mark Beltaire's popular column, "The Town Crier," long a mainstay on the back page of the *Detroit Free Press*, took up the cause of Milo Radulovich.

While Charlie Lockwood's public statements were replete with many references to the Nazi roots of establishing guilt by relationship, Beltaire made the same point by calling upon Rudolph Willie, former member of the German underground. Willie said government action against Milo "is a case of *Sippenhaftung*. I don't even like to translate it because the term has no place in the American language," Willie

147

said. "Actually, it means guilt by association with relatives. . . and I've seen thousands sent to the gas chambers in Germany as a result."[2]

Beltaire went on to quote an old-time airman who thought Milo should have quietly accepted the Air Force's decision to discharge him. The columnist opined, "If that's true the United States has gone to hell in a hand basket...and I for one second don't believe it. Some bungling Air Force character has got his neck in a noose and he's counting on three colonels at Selfridge Air Base to get it out...through channels of course."[3]

⸺⸙⸺

Life went on during that week of Milo's hearing.

Nothing could stop the World Series. Not peace talks in Korea. Not curtains of iron in Europe. Not the Las Vegas wedding of singer Dick Haymes to actress Rita Hayworth, the fourth such time both had vowed "till death us do part." Not security-risk hearings of Air Force reserve officers. Nothing.

Employers smiled and looked the other way as the jaunty voice of Mel Allen drifted from hidden radios and kept America abreast of its annual fall classic. Even the good and holy sisters of St. Joseph that staffed Flint's St. Agnes junior high school, relaxed their stern demeanor. Scheduled classes gave way to "special afternoon study hours" while series games were piped to classrooms over a scratchy public-address system.

Despite Carl Erskine's record fourteen strikeouts in game three a few days earlier, the New York Yankees, behind the outstanding play of their brash second baseman, Billy Martin, beat the Brooklyn Dodgers four games to two for their fifth straight World Series win. The winners' share in the subway series was $8,281 per person. Losers took home $6,178.

Jackie Robinson had hit a more than respectable .320 for the series. But his heroics, and those of other Negro Americans, could not quiet the ugly voice of prejudice. Claiming they had no open dates on their crowded winter schedule, Baltimore's Lyric Theater denied a booking to contralto Marian Anderson. Although Lyric audiences were nonsegregated, the theater had followed a traditional policy of segregation regarding performers.

That same week, Paul Robeson was feted at a ceremony in Harlem as one of seven recipients of the International Stalin Peace Prize for 1952. Refused a passport by the State Department, Robeson, the only American honored, said he hoped to collect the $25,000 prize at a later date. The award was presented by novelist Howard Fast.

In Washington, a special commission formed to study congressional salaries recommended an increase in lawmakers' pay from $15,000 to $25,000.

Rumors of President Eisenhower's failing health were quickly discounted by the White House. After his checkup in Denver, doctors pronounced the president in perfect health with one minor exception, a sore elbow, which could curtail time on the golf course.

In March 1952, the United States Supreme Court upheld a New York law making membership in a subversive organization grounds for dismissal from employment in the public school system. The previous week the New York State Board of Regents named the first two groups to come under that classification: the state and national Communist parties. Both were cited as groups that advocate overthrow of the government by force. After a ten-day grace period, any public school employee who remained a Communist party member would be subject to immediate discharge.

—————>❀<—————

In a speech to the Orange County, Virginia, Junior Chamber of Commerce, columnist Drew Pearson said the Eisenhower administration had bowed to pressure from Sen. Joseph McCarthy. Pearson's claim involved President Eisenhower's anti-book-burning speech given at Dartmouth the previous June 14.

"The Voice of America," Pearson said to an audience of more than seven hundred, "was all set to broadcast that speech. . .suddenly a

certain Senator heard about it, rushed to the White House, and the broadcast was stopped. . .because someone in the White House was afraid." Pearson went on to say, "And again it was fear which caused the President himself to reverse the importance of his book-burning speech with a public announcement. . .clearly stating that his speech at Dartmouth meant no reflection on the Senator from Wisconsin. Chancellor von Hindenberg shrank from opposing Hitler in his book-burning."[4]

The Milo Radulovich case, according to James M. Haswell of the *Detroit Free Press's* Washington bureau, was being viewed as an early test case in a new government security-check system. "The outcome, and especially public opinion on the outcome," wrote Haswell, "will show how far Air Force officials can go toward purging its Reserve Corps of persons it might hesitate to use in 'sensitive' positions if they were called to active duty."[1]

———— ⟶⊕⟵ ————

On February 22, 1949, in a speech at the Army and Navy Country Club in Virginia, President Harry Truman went to the defense of an aide, Maj. Gen. Harry H. Vaughn, who had been the target of criticism by columnist Drew Pearson. In his unbridled style, Truman startled his audience when he said, "If any S.O.B. thinks he can get me to discharge any of my staff or Cabinet by some smart-aleck statement over the air, he has got another think coming."

Former Truman aide William D. Hassett had recently written an account of his days in the White House. According to Hassett, when Truman got home that evening, Mrs. Truman had waited up for him and severely dressed him down for the inappropriate language. In fact, she was so angry with the president that she didn't speak to him for days.

The president then heard that the rector of an exclusive Washington church had indicated that under similar circumstances he might have responded in a similar fashion. "I just wish," Truman said, "that the rector would go talk to my wife."[2]

WEDNESDAY, OCTOBER 7, 1953

*F*ive men, all of whom had access to closely guarded electronic defense secrets at Fort Monmouth, New Jersey, were suspended by Army Secretary Robert T. Stevens. Thirty more employees at the Army post were under investigation for alleged security violations.

The suspensions came in the wake of an ongoing inquiry by Sen. Joseph McCarthy and his Senate Permanent Investigations Subcommittee. Several figures associated with the Rosenberg spy case were said to be involved.

WEDNESDAY, OCTOBER 8, 1953

Michigan Congressman Thaddeus M. Machrowicz announced that he had intervened in the security-risk proceedings against Air Force M. Sgt. Victor Havris, currently stationed in Bellerive, France.

On July 25, 1953, Havris was informed by the Air Force that he had been designated a security risk and would be discharged on October 20. Four days later he contacted his congressman. Machrowicz was successful in delaying the discharge date to provide Havris the opportunity to mount a defense.

Havris, who had shortened his name for convenience fourteen years earlier when he entered the Air Force, was accused of maintaining a close, continuing association with his mother, Maria Havrishko, and a brother, John. They were reported to be members of the Communist party or closely affiliated therewith. The loyalty of Sergeant Havris was not challenged.

Mrs. Havrishko, a lunchroom waitress at a Highland Park, Michigan, hospital, tearfully protested the Air Force action. "Neither I nor any member of my family ever has been a member of the Communist Party," she said. "I don't know the meaning of Communism. I know that I am an American citizen and want to be a good one. It is unfortunate, however, that children should be held responsible for any mistakes that parents might make."[1]

During the 1920s Havris's father had joined clubs where he could sing and act in plays. Those clubs, according to the Air Force, were

Communist fronts. On one occasion, when Victor was twelve years old, the father insisted both sons accompany him to an event. The Air Force contends that Victor joined the Young Communist League at that time.

The father died in 1932 and, despite Air Force reports claiming he was buried by the Communist party, Mrs. Havrishko showed receipts to reporters indicating she had paid for the funeral.

Mrs. Havrishko, a Polish immigrant who spoke with a pronounced accent, acknowledged she had bought some cheap insurance made available by the International Workers Order. "You had to pay for it in person at the IWO hall because they didn't have any collectors," she said. "When I couldn't go down myself, I sent Vic or John. They wouldn't stay around the hall but would come right home."[2] She dropped the insurance in 1944.

"I joined the party in the early thirties under a false name," admits John Havrishko. We went there when we had nothing else to do. All the kids that hung around the pool hall joined."

"My brother was never a member," he continued. "He went to dances there but he never went to the meetings. As far as most of us were concerned it was just a social club—we went because everyone else went."

Machrowicz said he had reviewed Havris's record and found nothing to contradict statements made by the sergeant and his family.

"How could he be a Communist and serve his country as long and as well as he has?" asked John Havrishko. "It'll break his heart if he has to leave the Air Force."[3]

———————

An aide to Sen. Joseph R. McCarthy snapped at reporters when questioned about his $74-a-day expenses on a recent seventeen-day European trip.

Reached in New York, Roy Cohn, legal counsel to McCarthy's Senate Permanent Investigations Subcommittee, indicated he had been too busy investigating alleged security risks at Fort Monmouth, New Jersey, to even worry about expense records. When reporters recited the exact figures he had submitted, Cohn bristled and responded, "Well, so what?"[4]

The expenses were reported by the Foreign Operations administrator, Harold E. Stassen. Stassen, a frequent McCarthy opponent, also pointed out that the FOA limits its own traveling officials to reimbursement ranging from six dollars a day in rural Germany to sixteen dollars a day in Paris.

Turmoil followed Cohn and his traveling companion, G. David Schine, throughout their trip. Although their stated mission was to investigate waste, mismanagement, and security violations at American installations in Europe, the two attracted worldwide attention by commenting on international affairs and hinting at upcoming McCarthy revelations.

One official, Theodore Kaghan, a deputy public-affairs officer under the U.S. high commissioner in Germany, was forced to resign after publicly blasting Cohn and Schine as "junketeering gumshoes."[5] *Shortly thereafter, Kaghan was labeled a security risk by McCarthy.*

FRIDAY, OCTOBER 9, 1953

Kenneth Sanborn officially informed Col. William Doolan that after careful examination he and cocounsel Charles Lockwood found the hearing transcript to be substantially correct and urged the board to make its decision.

In a related matter the *Detroit Free Press* cited similarities between the Radulovich and Havris cases, labeling both nothing more than guilt by association, pointing out that the real security risks in both instances were those who prepared the charges.[1]

Columnist Drew Pearson speculated that Michigan Sen. Homer Ferguson's maneuvering to be named vice-chairman of the newly created Hoover Commission on government reorganization was an attempt to grab political prestige. Ferguson's angling for the post, claimed Pearson, was in anticipation of a challenge for his senate seat from popular Michigan Gov. G. Mennen Williams.

According to Pearson, commission chairman and former president Herbert Hoover felt the number two position should go to a Democrat. He wanted it filled by Joseph P. Kennedy, former ambassador to England. Hoover viewed Kennedy as a safe, anti-Stevenson Democrat. However, if the post went to a Republican most commission members felt it should be awarded to Rep. Clarence Brown of Ohio, the man who wrote the reorganization legislation.

At the swearing-in ceremony Pearson quotes Brown as saying of Ferguson, "Look at him bootlicking those fellows as if he knew all about reorganization. He wants that photo to help him in his campaign....[He] didn't even read the reorganization bill before he tossed it into the hopper."[2]

According to a special seven-member committee of the Detroit Bar Association, the civil rights of Lt. Milo J. Radulovich had been violated.

Probate Judge Patrick H. O'Brien, chairman of a bar association panel formed to investigate the Radulovich hearing, said the lieutenant had been wronged on two counts: first, the basis of the Air Force case was guilt by association; and second, the hearing procedures violated his civil rights.

According to O'Brien, "We felt that the proceedings represented not only an invasion of Lt. Radulovich's constitutional rights but also the tradition of the American people as a free people."[1]

O'Brien said two members of the special panel, Ernest Goodman and Thomas Roumell, were directed to draft a resolution reflecting the committee's feelings.

⸻⊷●⊷⸻

As new developments emerged in the probe of security leaks in the Army Signal Corps at Fort Monmouth, New Jersey, Sen. Joseph McCarthy announced he would cut short his honeymoon and return immediately from the British West Indies to take control of the investigation. Only ten days of the planned three- to four-week honeymoon had elapsed.

McCarthy indicated he would preside at an executive session of the subcommittee in New York the following Monday. He would be joined in the closed-door meeting by a colleague, Sen. Everett Dirksen. According to a Dirksen aide and witness interrogator, Harold Raineville, the presence of McCarthy and other subcommittee members was prompted by the uncovering of critical information during recent questioning of Army personnel.

A number of former employees, several of them involved in a previous investigation of the atomic spy ring that resulted in the execution of Julius and Ethel Rosenberg, were called to testify.

Courtesy CBS

MILO THEN AND NOW.
Above After seeing the film on Milo, Murrow said, "This guy's got fire in the belly."
Below Milo is especially close to his grandson, Scotty. Family has always been important to him.

Courtesy Milo Radulovich

While many old-country customs did not survive the immigrants' journey to America, one did. Men still ruled their families. The Radulovich home was no exception. While respectful of her father and the customs that governed and brought order to his life, Margaret Radulovich burned with strong political beliefs of her own. She refused to be relegated to the kitchen.

Courtesy Margaret Radulovich

Above In the days of heavy immigration following World War I, becoming a citizen was not automatic. John and Ikonija Radulovich attended night school to learn about their new country. The courses were taught in English, rendering the already difficult path to citizenship an even more demanding struggle.

Opposite Page For nearly a month newspaper references to Nancy Radulovich inevitably made mention that she was strikingly attractive. In response to Joe Wershba's questions, she also proved to be a convincing force in her own right. "No, I wouldn't want him to take it laying down," she responded at one point, her eyes boring into the camera. "I don't regret anything at all—him coming forward and fighting it."

Courtesy CBS

The all-clear sign was given and the tremendous tension and pressure of the previous week broke. Friendly vividly recalls the moment: "If twenty men in a control room can figuratively lift a man on their shoulders, it happened in studio 41 that night. Technicians and stagehands came over to Murrow who was bathed in sweat and smoke, and shook his hand. Some had tears in their eyes."

They worked well together; Friendly dramatizing his reserved partner's complicated thoughts, Murrow harnessing and directing the Friendly volcano and its ongoing explosions of ideas.

Reporter Joe Wershba was dispatched to Dexter, Michigan, with the task of determining whether Milo Radulovich was the little picture Murrow and Friendly sought for their long-awaited McCarthy story. Wershba called Friendly that night: "We got our man, Fred."

Courtesy Ken Sanborn

Above With both his private law practice and military career at stake, Kenneth Sanborn told Milo that like Charlie Lockwood, he would represent him without accepting a fee.

Opposite Page Joe McCarthy and his assault on individual rights dominated American political thought in the early fifties. Many felt only Edward R. Murrow could stop him. But Murrow inexplicably waited—for the right moment, for the perfect weapon. That moment came on October 20, 1953. The weapon—the government's case against Lt. Milo Radulovich.

Charlie Lockwood never wasted a word. It was said of him that when he told you something you knew exactly what he meant. There were no shades of meaning.

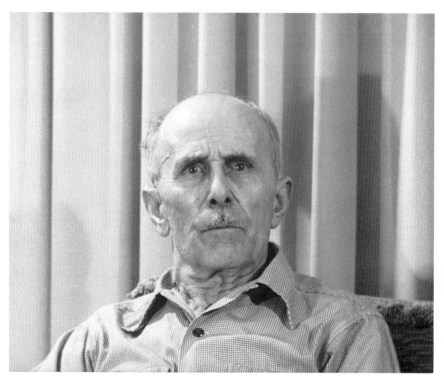

News people are noted for looking at life through suspicious and acerbic eyes. John Radulovich's brief moment on film, however, reached out and grabbed the "See It Now" team. This picture hung on the cutting-room wall of CBS for a number of years following the Milo Radulovich program.

MONDAY, OCTOBER 12, 1953

The day before the program was always hectic. There were scripts to be honed, facts to be checked and rechecked for accuracy, film to be edited. That week's program would deal with the drought in Amarillo, Texas, and would feature the secretary of agriculture, Ezra Taft Benson. Everything had to be just right, the commitment to perfection was at stake; it was every week. But even as "See It Now" prepared for the program at hand, a shroud of sorts hung over the highly touted news team. The growing shadow of Joe McCarthy loomed in the background.

In the late forties, CBS had enjoyed the prestige of housing the most undaunted of all the network news organizations. Its reputation was derived in no small part from stellar reporting on World War II's European theater by Edward R. Murrow and the team he assembled— *Murrow's boys*, as they came to be known.

With the postwar period came growing political pressure on networks and their sponsors to refrain from using the talents of those with Communist-sullied credentials, or blacklisting as the practice came to be known. CBS, writes Halberstam, seemed a willing squire to that pressure.[1]

Unlike others at CBS, Murrow and his partner, Fred W. Friendly, could claim unfettered status when it came to the content of their stories. But that independence forced the question of when they would train their vast resources on Sen. Joseph McCarthy and the wide swath

161

he had cut through individual rights on his well-publicized mission to rid the country of communism.

Their courses long since charted, only the question of when their forces would join remained: when would Murrow do battle with McCarthy?

———⟫⟪———

More than anything, Joe McCarthy feared anonymity. Until the Lincoln Day speeches of 1950, that fear was perilously close to reality.

Once every year, in February, with a sense of ritual bordering on holy, Republicans step to podiums around the country and venerate the memory of Abraham Lincoln. Their speeches are an annual reaffirmation of the Grand Old Party's close and continuing association with the president best remembered for his integrity. They also raise a lot of money.

Joe McCarthy, unlike many of his congressional colleagues whose stature enabled them to select from a number of preferred speaking assignments, had to volunteer his services, and then wait until the choice meat of the political carcass had been picked clean. Despite a reputation for ineffectiveness, the Republican Central Committee reasoned that he was still a United States senator. That would carry weight somewhere.

Five Lincoln Day speeches were booked for McCarthy in that February of 1950. Plans called for him to work his way across the country, beginning in West Virginia and concluding in Huron, South Dakota. They knew he was a poker player of some renown, and scheduled layovers in Las Vegas and Reno to temper the rigors of the trip.

Hardly a party headliner, McCarthy made his first stop on Thursday evening, February 9, at the Ohio County Republican Women's Club in Wheeling, West Virginia. During the drive from the airport, he mused with a local attorney and former congressman, Francis Love, that he had prepared two speeches, one on housing, the other on Communists in government. Which one should he deliver? History would turn on the response. The one on communism, Love advised.

Unfortunately no recordings survive and accounts differ, some markedly, as to what McCarthy said that night. His prepared remarks were released and formed the basis of a wire story that, after a stuttered start, attracted much interest as the senator completed his cross-country journey.

The speech had been a cut-and-paste effort pulled together by George Waters and Ed Nellor, two reporters from the conservative *Washington Times-Herald*.* Some of the punchier lines bore a marked resemblance to remarks given two weeks earlier on the floor of the House by California Congressman Richard Nixon. Other portions borrowed heavily from recent articles by Willard Edwards in the *Chicago Tribune*.[2]

"I have here in my hand," said McCarthy according to his released speech, "a list of 205—a list of names that were made known to the Secretary of State as being members of the Communist Party and who nevertheless are still working and shaping policy in the State Department."[3] In effect, Joe McCarthy had accused Secretary of State Dean Acheson of treason. State Department denial was predictably swift.

When McCarthy stepped off the plane in Denver, reporters descended on him for a response to the State Department denial. As he would do countless times in the years to come, Joe McCarthy bluffed. During the flight to Denver, the "205 Communists" had become "207 bad risks." He said he was misquoted. If Dean Acheson would call him in Salt Lake City, McCarthy would be glad to share the information with him. Certainly he would provide the list but unfortunately it was in his other suit on the plane. The *Denver Post* ran a picture of McCarthy intently searching his briefcase over a caption that read, "Left Commie list in other bag."[4]

*Both later joined McCarthy's staff.

That Saturday in Reno, McCarthy received a telegram from the State Department asking for the 205 names. Sensing the swelling media interest, he responded by sending a letter to President Harry Truman, released to the press, urging that Secretary Acheson be contacted directly for the list.

A good portion of the media attention stemmed from McCarthy's cavalier deployment of figures. What began in Wheeling as 205 Communists became at various intervals during the trip 57, and later 207. His explanations only added to the confusion. The 57, he pointed out, were not necessarily part of the 205. At times the 205 (or 57) were not proven Communists, only bad risks. Frequently the two terms, *Communists* and *bad risks*, were used interchangeably.

Lincoln Day speeches completed, McCarthy returned home to Wisconsin. As he stepped from the plane, well-wishers greeted their native son with applause. Joseph McCarthy basked in what was to date the greatest publicity binge of his life.

Spurred on by the warm Wisconsin welcome, McCarthy responded to probing questions during a makeshift press conference. He said that upon his return to Washington he would detail the charges levied during the previous week. The tickler sustained his stay in the spotlight.

On Monday, February 20, shortly before 7:00 p.m., Mr. McCarthy of Wisconsin took the floor of the United States Senate and held it for nearly five hours. He had brought with him, and read portions of, eighty-one separate personnel files. These persons, he maintained, held questionable credentials but were currently on the State Department payroll. The files, he claimed, had been made available by loyal Americans whose identities he would never divulge.[5]

He rambled. As he read from the files, it was readily apparent that he was seeing much of the material for the first time. Moreover, little if any evidence emerged regarding Communist infiltration in the State Department.

He obfuscated. Confronted on the authenticity of his figures, he once again darted around the numbers: 200, 205, 207, 57, 206, 81.

He attacked. When challenged by an angry Scott Lucas of Illinois, McCarthy lashed back at the Senate majority leader, ridiculing his probing questions. He said that "nothing the senator from Illinois has done here tonight indicates that he even remotely realizes the seriousness of the problem."[6] Lucas, in turn, promised a thorough investigation of every charge brought by McCarthy.

McCarthy severely strained the bounds of integrity. While reading from the files, he routinely disregarded such critical phrases as "alleged" and "reportedly." According to Reeves, "Joe altered, twisted, and improvised upon the cases he used to make them appear sinister and sensational. He recklessly omitted lines, eliminated modifiers, added phrases and exaggerated freely."

At 11:42 p.m. on February 20 the Senate adjourned.

Two days later, true to his word, Lucas introduced Senate Resolution 231, calling for a complete investigation into the charges. Wary Republicans distanced themselves from McCarthy and voted for the resolution, which passed unanimously.

After a brief scrimmage about who would chair the investigating committee, it was placed in the respected hands of Maryland's Millard Tydings. Tydings and McCarthy had previously crossed swords. On March 8, amid media fanfare rare even for the Senate, Tydings convened the special committee, and, in the process, extended Joe McCarthy's stay on the nation's front pages.

Apart from keeping the national spotlight on McCarthy, the Tydings committee would be remembered for political cartoonist Herblock's "McCarthyism" eponym. On a pile of teetering buckets dripping with tar, an unsteady barrel sat under a platform. The word "McCarthyism" was splashed across the barrel. To the right of the buckets Republican Senators Wherry, Taft, and Bridges pushed a reluctant and frightened Republican elephant. The caption, intended as a statement from the elephant, read, "You Mean I'm Supposed to Stand on That?"[7]

"McCarthyism" quickly became a colorful turn of phrase that added to the senator's growing fame. Soon "McCarthyism" was even included in dictionaries, defined by one, Merriam-Webster, as "opposition to elements held to be subversive and by the use of tactics involving personal attacks on individuals by means of widely publicized indiscriminate allegations esp. on the basis of unsubstantiated charges."[8]

Over the next three years, while the *Washington Post* and the *New York Times* assailed McCarthy for his careless allegations and lack of documentation, many Americans warmed to him. Joe McCarthy and his "go for the jugular" style had unearthed something visceral. Gallup polls indicated more than 50 percent of Americans believed he was helping the country, and only 29 percent disapproved (21 percent had no opinion).[9] His mail was voluminous. Reporters crowded his office with opened notepads and pencils at the ready. Where once he had to cajole for speaking engagements, requests for appearances now inundated his office. Handsome honoraria awaited, his fifteen hundred-dollar fee rivaled that of Eleanor Roosevelt's, one of the country's top-paid speakers.[10]

Sensitive to the political winds, McCarthy's GOP Senate colleagues, who were earlier unwilling to acknowledge him, now leaped to his side. Homer Ferguson of Michigan publicly exchanged subversive lists with him. Owen Brewster and Karl Mundt offered the resources of their staffs. Bourke Hickenlooper, from his perch as a member of the Tydings committee, became a strident McCarthy defender.

Political winds blew on both sides of the aisle, though, and the loyal opposition was not about to jump on their collective sword. At one point during the Tydings hearings, Senate Majority Leader Lucas calculated that despite the outlandishness of McCarthy's charges, only twelve Democratic senators had registered any public opposition to him.[11]

Openly skeptical at first, Robert Taft of Ohio finally provided McCarthy with the imprimatur of respectability. The highly respected Republican leader in the Senate stated, "The pro-Communist policies of the State Department fully justify Joe McCarthy in his demand for an investigation."[12]

In the fall of 1950, McCarthy and members of his staff took an active role in John Butler's successful campaign to unseat Millard Tydings. McCarthy at first snatched credit for engineering the stunning upset, then shied away from admitting any involvement in the campaign when smear tactics were alleged and later investigated by a special Senate committee.

Sen. Owen Brewster termed the congressional elections that year a triumph for "McCarthy and his ism." Across the country, victories of a number of Republicans who embraced McCarthyism, and defeats of Democrats who attacked it, were placed at the doorstep of Joe McCarthy. Newly elected Herman Welker of Idaho stated that at least seven senators owed their seats to McCarthy.

McCarthy was especially pleased over the defeat in Illinois of Senate Majority Leader Scott Lucas by Congressman Everett Dirksen. Although Lucas was more than likely done in by scandals in the Cook County Democratic machine, McCarthy still included his defeat on the roster of victories for his "ism" that year.

Amid waving signs adorned by the names of his targets—Hiss, Lattimore, Acheson—McCarthy received a tumultuous welcome as he addressed the 1952 Republican National Convention. In his nasal, high-pitched, sing-song delivery, he recited the gospel according to McCarthy: "One Communist on the faculty of one University is one Communist too many. One Communist among the American advisors at Yalta was one Communist too many. And even if there were only one Communist in the State Department, that would still be one Communist too many."[13]

Also in 1952, the Democratic presidential candidate, Adlai Stevenson, had labeled McCarthy "the most formidable presence in American life. In all countries they know of him and in all tongues they speak of him."[14]

And the country listened. William Manchester observed: "Against all logic, Americans by the tens of millions had come to regard Wisconsin's junior Senator as the symbol of anti-Communism, and as long as Communism remained an issue, he would be a hero to them. His arrogance continued to grow. Reminded that he had not replied to the committee's [Tydings] indictment, he said, 'I don't answer charges, I make them.' A reporter asked, 'Wasn't that a classified document you were reading?' The Senator snapped, 'It *was*. I declassified it.'"

McCarthy was hot and he knew it. The publicity was an opiate, driving him to make even more incredible charges. He nurtured press relationships, becoming an adept practitioner of media management. He reveled in being on a first-name basis with reporters. Many supportive but poorly documented stories were a result of his knowing certain reporters' deadlines. He would feed them information knowing there wouldn't be time to check for fear of losing a scoop to the competition. He learned who was friend and who was foe. If a friend needed an outrageous comment, he willingly obliged. In return, McCarthy invoked his senatorial privilege and inserted articles in the *Congressional Record*, in essence providing helpful reporters immunity from lawsuits.

On whether the press had covered Joe McCarthy with a reticent pen, David Halberstam caustically points out, "What McCarthy said word by word was meaningless; it was the invisible part, the inflection, the distortions of scene, the lack of follow-through, the lack of seriousness, the cumulative record or lack of record which was missing in all accounts. He made his charges and went on to his next charges, and objective journalists were considerate enough not to bother him with his record, with what he had said the week, or month, or year before."[15]

Willard Edwards of the *Chicago Tribune* candidly described the unique vantage point of a reporter with a treasured byline who had covered Sen. Joseph McCarthy in the early fifties: "I wasn't off the front page for four years."[16]

Joe McCarthy couldn't, and didn't, do it alone.

Files, in many cases purloined personnel records, didn't just appear. Love of country notwithstanding, civil servants weren't about to risk their careers by passing personal documents to Senator McCarthy.

A figure, be it 205, 57, 81, or whatever, still had to come from somewhere.

Charges against individuals, however reckless or inaccurate, still had to possess a nodding acquaintance with fact.

After the Wheeling speech, it was apparent to those more experienced at fighting the domestic version of communism that Joe McCarthy had little or no idea what he was doing. His terminology was wrong, frequently bordering on humorous; his use of figures, bumbling at best; his targets, a result of nothing more than a shotgun approach.

FBI Director J. Edgar Hoover, like many other experienced anti-Communist hands, was more than annoyed at McCarthy's sophomoric approach. Communism, to the nation's top law-enforcement officer, was a serious matter. A threat to the nation, sure, but it also afforded the director a ready tool for prying more money from Congress. According to a top Hoover aide, Louis B. Nichols, the director gave McCarthy "unshirted hell" after the Wheeling speech.[17]

McCarthy needed help. At Hoover's urging he hired a former FBI agent, Don Surine. Although involved in a prostitution scandal in New York, Surine remained a favorite of the director. McCarthy also brought Charles Kerston on board. A former congressman from Wisconsin and a strong supporter of the FBI and McCarthy, Kerston had a retinue of contacts in the federal bureaucracy that was invaluable. McCarthy turned as well to a Senate colleague, Richard Nixon, who with his voluminous HUAC files in tow, sat with McCarthy and gave sage counsel on the politics of anti-communism. Be slow and deliberate, Nixon advised, to no avail as it turned out.

With his unauthorized copy of "Appendix Nine," Hearst newspaper columnist J. B. Matthews proved indispensable to McCarthy. Developed by HUAC in 1944, Appendix Nine was a list of more than twenty thousand names haphazardly culled from letterheads, membership lists, and pamphlets of organizations deemed less than patriotic. Secretary of State Dean Acheson's wife was included as a member of the "League of Women Shoppers." Acheson admitted his wife had sent in the requisite two dollars for information on some stores in New York City. Even the committee thought Appendix Nine to be so riddled with inaccuracy that a recall order was issued and all existing copies suppressed. Matthews, however, kept his. As long as Joe McCarthy could refer to it, he would always be able to drop the name of a suspected Communist, accurate or not.[18]

The resources of the Hearst, Scripps-Howard, and McCormick newspaper chains were virtually at McCarthy's beck and call. Several of their reporters coached McCarthy and helped prepare friendly witnesses for appearances in front of the Tydings committee. They also wrote some of the senator's speeches and eventually even appeared with him at gatherings judged too difficult for McCarthy to handle alone. George Sokolsky of the Hearst newspapers, for instance, appeared with McCarthy at a B'nai B'rith meeting to answer charges of anti-Semitism.

Despite all the resources at his disposal, Joe McCarthy still carried considerable baggage.

Although the founder and publisher of the *Madison-Capital Times,* William T. Evjue, may have challenged him first and most often, Joe McCarthy had consistently displayed a reckless disregard for the straight answer. UPI's George Reedy spoke of the frustration associated with covering McCarthy: "Talking to Joe was like putting your hands in a bowl of mush."[19]

In Washington, McCarthy's drinking was legend. He carried a bottle in his briefcase and boasted of knocking down a fifth a day. Water tumblers of Scotch were chased with bicarbonate of soda. Eating a quarter-pound stick of butter, he contended, enabled him to drink more and still maintain sobriety.

Besides communism, the only real issue Joe McCarthy ever attached himself to was housing for veterans. As noble as his intentions were, a lack of moral fiber contaminated that effort. Despite conducting committee hearings around the country to receive testimony in support of the obvious—that the nation needed housing for its returning veterans—McCarthy had no compunction about accepting a gratuity of ten thousand dollars from a manufacturer of prefabricated housing. Other rumors placed him on the receiving end of a twenty thousand-dollar unsecured loan from a Pepsi-Cola lobbyist.

Above and beyond what Hoover could muster, a group of powerful people had a stake in ensuring Joe McCarthy's success. They were not drawn to him out of respect or admiration. On the contrary, of all their potential champions, they surely would not have picked the junior senator from Wisconsin.

History knows them as the China Lobby. The force that brought them together was the fall of China and their collective support for the government of Generalissimo Chiang Kai-shek. The force that kept them together, however, was their ardent, obsessive, relentless, indefatigable opposition to communism.

At first, the China Lobby eschewed McCarthy, thinking him a buffoon, a hapless, chronic gambler, a boorish drunk. As time passed, the group could not ignore his staying power in the media. They recognized in McCarthy a facility bordering on genius for drawing attention to himself. Moreover, the vehicle for his self-promotion was their issue: that got their attention. And, difficult as it may have been to accept, he was a United States senator.

The China Lobby was funded in part by right-wing newspaper publishers. Col. Robert McCormick and William Randolph Hearst weighed in as two of the more renowned check writers. The tip of the iceberg, the visible portion of the effort, consisted of prominent media personalities, such as George Sokolsky and news broadcaster Fulton Lewis, Jr. Henry Luce supported it with his publishing empire, featuring Chiang on countless covers of *Time* magazine.

The lobby's chief benefactor, however, was Alfred Kohlberg, founder of the China Policy Association, which was headed at different times by Clare Booth Luce and William Loeb. A textile manufacturer and importer, Kohlberg was a frequent and welcome visitor to McCarthy's office. He embraced the anti-Communist sentiment, but his involvement wasn't wholly ideological.

With the downfall of Chiang's government, Kohlberg's financial interests in China also collapsed. He had made millions over the years and was now able, and willing, to direct substantial contributions toward any effort that would restore the Chiang government to power. In the United States, that translated into the anti-Communist movement.

The China Lobby and the resources of its patrons, with only minor exceptions, leaned heavily to the Republican party. They felt Chiang's government would fare much better in a Dewey administration than it had under Roosevelt or Truman. GOP congressional luminaries, such as Vandenberg of Michigan, Taft of Ohio, and Styles Bridges of New Hampshire, were all outspoken supporters of Chiang.

Donations and other campaign assistance from China Lobby sources were made available to supporters. In 1950, for example, a public-relations executive on the payroll of the Bank of China took up temporary residence in California and formed an independent citizens committee for senatorial candidate Richard Nixon. *Soft on communism* charges figured prominently in Nixon's mudslinging, landslide victory over Helen Gahagan Douglas.

The China Lobby had money, media access, and a roster of prestigious supporters. They lacked only a leader, a galvanizing force the American people could identify with, rally around, and follow into battle against the Red menace. They lacked a Joe McCarthy.

Elected from Wisconsin to the United States Senate in the Republican landslide of 1946, Joseph Raymond McCarthy had attracted national attention by upsetting the incumbent, Robert LaFollette, one of the most respected political names in that state's history.

McCarthy's political baggage for the trip to Washington had included scandals involving his finances and serious questions regarding his claims of combat heroics. He had even awarded himself a nickname, "Tail-Gunner Joe." It was the type of cavalier moniker normally coveted by postwar politicians. In McCarthy's case it came to be employed with heavy sarcasm and dogged him throughout his career.

However inadvertently, Joe McCarthy—the feral, unkempt junior senator from Wisconsin—had stumbled onto the China Lobby's issue. He became their standard bearer. An adroit demagogue obsessed with his press clippings, he was on intimate terms with America's common people, the working class. He knew what frightened them; the same things terrified him. He knew what angered them; the same things outraged him. And he knew how to move them.

After the Lincoln Day speech of 1950, Joe McCarthy was news. Reporters followed him, waiting for the inevitable comment that would be the day's story. In Washington at least, there was a *McCarthy beat.*

McCarthy was great copy. He regularly complained that his enemies intentionally misquoted him. The criticisms—and there were many—evidenced his effectiveness. He would not give up his fight until the last Communist was routed from this country. And, according to a poll by George Gallup, at least 50 percent of the country believed in and supported him.

Was the Communist threat real? Were the Russians furtive back stabbers who couldn't be trusted? Was there an insidious threat based in Moscow bent on domination of the West?

Congressional witch-hunts weren't all that new. In 1938, by a vote of 191–41 the House created the original standing committee devoted to un-American activities. Conservative Texas Democrat Martin Dies chaired the panel. Over time, the Dies committee regularly stooped to bullying and demagoguery. "With strong public support and the backing of the ultraconservative Hearst and McCormick newspapers, as well as the American Legion," writes Reeves, "the committee recklessly denigrated the loyalty of New Dealers, liberals, socialists, fellow travelers, and Communists, viewing them all as essentially the same."[20] During the war, the beefy, cigar-smoking Dies became embroiled in a well-publicized fight with columnist Walter Winchell. A close ally of FDR's, Winchell claimed Dies was soft on Nazis. Dies, an avowed enemy of Roosevelt, countered with charges that Winchell coddled Communists.

Perception, so goes one of politics' oldest axioms, is reality. Real or not, keeping the Communist threat alive wasn't without political benefit for a select few.

It certainly legitimized J. Edgar Hoover's annual trek to Capitol Hill in search of money to pay for his well-publicized war against the hidden enemies of the state. If Hoover's empire expanded in the process, so be it. Within the bureau the Communist issue was known simply as the *cause*. Only two things were more important: the image of the director and the reputation of the bureau, in that order.

Opposing communism also provided a powerful reelection tool to bludgeon opponents with during congressional campaigns. The "Red Menace" had to be stopped somewhere. Why not vote for someone with a proven record of fighting the Kremlin's attempt to secure a beachhead on the Potomac? Political campaigns became litmus tests for patriotism. Patriotism was defined by the intensity of one's opposition to communism.

Communism was news. People wanted to know about Joe McCarthy, what he was doing, whom he was attacking. That need for information was created, and satisfied, by the media. Stories about McCarthy's latest roust sold newspapers, especially those in the Hearst, Scripps-Howard, and McCormick chains.

The world of entertainment and the well-publicized life-styles of its glamorous participants figured prominently in the public's ongoing fascination with communism. When well-known entertainers were called to Washington, the committee hearings served as a stage for publicity-hungry politicians seeking notoriety in the battle against communism. If a movie star testified in front of a congressional committee, surely the interrogator should accompany the actor into the headlines.

Some willingly stepped up to HUAC's microphones. Actor Robert Taylor dutifully acclaimed that he would never work on a picture with known Communists. Adolphe Menjou's testimony left no doubt to his loyalty: "I would move to the State of Texas if it [communism] ever came here. Because I think the Texans would kill them on sight."[21] Others tried valiantly to avoid testifying after receiving the dreaded HUAC subpoena. Lee J. Cobb and Sterling Hayden, resisters both, eventually joined the chorus of those who "named names."

The power of select members of the media bordered on incredible. Victor S. Navasky points out that the "political Pundits . . . used their newspaper columns as vehicles for tainting, painting and turpentining alleged reds."[22] Among those columnists was George Sokolsky, who preached the gospel of anti-communism and was rewarded with "quickly returned phone calls" from J. Edgar Hoover and the bureau's top propagandist, Lou Nichols.

The stature of Walter Winchell, a radio personality and columnist, soared with his unrestricted access to Hoover, McCarthy, and other purveyors of patriotism. When it came to identifying who would wear the label of communism in Hollywood, columnists such as Winchell and Hedda Hopper willingly served as judge and jury. How

Hollywood personalities were treated in their columns would frequently be the deciding factor for inclusion on or removal from the so-called blacklist. Along with Sokolsky, they determined not only who was a Communist but also who was a true convert and what penance should be performed by the prodigals.

Sokolsky, in particular, basked in his dual role of father-confessor and pulse-taker of patriotism. He wrote in 1947 of an exchange with actor Humphrey Bogart that publicly brought the movie tough guy to his knees. Bogart, his wife, Lauren Bacall, Groucho Marx, Frank Sinatra, and others had gone to Washington to support the "Hollywood Ten," a group of talented movie-industry people with purported Communist pasts who had been hailed before HUAC. In his column, Sokolsky criticized Bogart for his support of the ten, which prompted the actor to pen a contrite letter to the columnist.[23]

"That trip," Bogart wrote, "was ill-advised, even foolish, I am very ready to admit." After including major portions of the letter in his column, Sokolsky responded: "Confession is good for any man's soul. And you display great courage and manhood to confess error. Yes, that trip was foolish." Absolution granted, Sokolsky proffered a penance: "If you are contrite for a very foolish bit of exhibitionism, you ought to go further. You might tell us who suggested that trip to Washington. Whose brainchild was it? Who projected you and your wife to take the lead?. . . Now do something for your country that is really constructive. Tell us who suggested and organized that trip. If you have no better way, use this column for that purpose. It gets around."

Although some in the entertainment industry chose prison over naming names, the glamour they brought to congressional hearings served as fodder for the nation's headlines. With a cast of celebrities, communism as an issue enjoyed an incredible run.

Edward R. Murrow and Fred W. Friendly, made up the most formidable news duo of the early fifties. In October 1953, their fame was at its crest.

Murrow was the voice, made famous during dramatic wartime radio broadcasts ten years earlier. "This is London," he had intoned time and again as German bombers rained their devastation on the city of cities in the British Empire. "There are no words to describe the thing that is happening. The stench of the air raid shelters...This is London, being bombed again. The sound of gunfire has been rolling down these crooked streets like thunder. Half an hour ago I could read street signs in the flash of anti-aircraft batteries."[24]

Trained in speech and drama, Murrow respected the beauty and power of the written word. While others reported on the bombing of Berlin, Murrow went on a nighttime mission, describing it in vivid fashion: "The small incendiaries were going down like a fistful of white rice thrown on a piece of black velvet."[25]

So strong was his belief in the written word that over the objection of network superiors, Murrow employed print journalists, not broadcasters, to cover the war in Europe for CBS. He thought what was said more important than how it was said, and his hiring reflected that philosophy: Eric Sevareid, Richard C. Hottelet, Charles Collingwood, Howard K. Smith, and William Shirer, to name a few, all strong print journalists in their own right. "I'm not looking for announcers," he said. "I'm looking for people who know what they are talking about."[26]

The war also developed Murrow's belief in the *little picture* approach to reporting the news. Major news events, he believed, were best understood by showing their impact on one person, a philosophy sharpened to perfection years later with Friendly.

But always there were the words—the intense, compelling images created by his words. In April 1945, Murrow and CBS colleague Bill Shadel were the first reporters to enter the concentration camp at Buchenwald. "Permit me to tell you what you would have seen and heard if you had been with me last Thursday," he said in his April 15 broadcast. "It will not be pleasant listening. If you're at lunch or if you have no appetite to hear what Germans have done, now is a good time to switch off the radio, for I propose to tell you of Buchenwald." Murrow spoke of the horrible stench and of a stable built to house sixty horses that now served as a barracks for twelve hundred men. He told of encountering the lord mayor of Prague, a man he had met a few years earlier, a man he remembered well but did not recognize. He told of the children, some only six years old. "One rolled up his sleeve," Murrow said, "showed me his number. It was tattooed on his arm, D600030, it was. The others showed me their numbers. They will carry them till they die."[27]

An appearance in an occasional photograph or newsreel only added to the Murrow legend. He stood, with smoldering buildings as a backdrop, trench-coated, bareheaded, microphone in hand, without seeming regard for personal safety. He was thought to be so trustworthy, his voice so familiar, that civil-defense authorities chose him, along with Arthur Godfrey, to do official broadcasts in the event of an enemy attack on the United States.

After the war, CBS sought to reward Murrow by assigning him administrative duties and awarding him a title, vice president of news. But his heart and the "fire in his belly"—a term of admiration he used sparingly to describe someone of rare conviction—was in the *story*. His network vice presidency lasted two years, and then "Edward R. Murrow and the News" returned to radio. Murrow reported the day's events and offered commentary. He quickly regained his status as the network's premier newsman.

<hr>

In 1937, a young man of twenty-two proudly hoisted the name Ferdinand Friendly Wachenheimer onto his back and walked into radio station WEAN in Providence, Rhode Island, in search of a broadcasting job. He didn't get it. The station manager, James Jennison, claimed he was not yet ready for Providence. But the creative Wachenheimer lugged more than his name and an interest in radio to the interview. He teemed with ideas, one in particular that Jennison liked. Young Fred proposed a series of five-minute radio biographies in which listeners would be teased with facts involving a famous person and then challenged to guess that person's identity. Wachenheimer left that day with a new program, "Footprints on the Sands of Time," and a new name, Fred Friendly.

After the war Friendly made his way to New York. The city was not kind to him. He sold a few scripts, but two years passed without any real work. His most notable achievement during that period was a quiz program he sold to NBC where popular personalities of the day were challenged regarding their knowledge of current events. Critics thought the notion refreshing, but no sponsor picked it up and NBC was forced to cancel it.

Undeterred, Friendly hit on another idea. This one would come to involve the great Edward R. Murrow. And it worked.

Unlike many, Fred Friendly was not intimidated by technology; on the contrary, it fascinated him. One day, while visiting CBS, he observed technicians splicing and rearranging audio tape. He quickly determined this same process could be used to assemble the voices of history and press them into a record. With the magic of tape splicing, Roosevelt, Churchill, Huey Long, Neville Chamberlain, even Hitler, could all be brought to one room, on one phonograph.

He mentioned the idea to his friend and agent, Jap Gude, who shared his enthusiasm for the project. Friendly knew he could supply all the ingredients, save for one; he needed a great, recognizable voice, such as Ed Murrow's, to narrate it. Unbeknown to Friendly, but much to his delight, Murrow was also Gude's client, and the agent arranged for the two to meet at a dinner.

They dined at Louis and Armand's, a CBS hangout. Gude made the introduction and then receded while Friendly explained the project to Murrow. Murrow remained quiet, allowing Friendly to present and sell his idea. Few questions were asked; Murrow simply said, "Let's do it." Friendly later confessed his almost disbelief in Murrow's response. "This urbane sophisticated man saw in *me* a colleague! Me, rough on the edges, effusive, exuberant."[28]

Friendly did the lion's share of the work on the record and "I Can Hear It Now: 1933–1945" was released on Thanksgiving Day, 1948. By Christmas the somewhat less-than-affluent Friendly had received a $24,000 royalty check. Within a year the record had become the first nonmusical album in history to turn a major profit.[29] Two other similar efforts followed. Apart from their commercial success, Murrow and Friendly developed a real comfort working with each other.

Friendly went to work for NBC, where he toiled for the greater part of another year until Sigfried "Sig" Mickelson brought him and his enormous talent to CBS.

Murrow was delighted to learn that Friendly had joined the CBS team. Their successful recording venture had led to a warm friendship. Almost immediately they became coproducers of a weekly documentary radio series called "Hear It Now," a magazine of sorts for radio. Friendly wanted to do a *Life* magazine of the air, but for television, not radio. Murrow, however, was distrustful of television, a medium that featured pictures over words. If anything he would have preferred to do a *Harper's* or an *Atlantic Monthly*, but not *Life*.[30] Network chief William Paley endorsed "Hear It Now" and suggested a full hour instead of the half hour Murrow and Friendly proposed.

Although it lasted less than a year, "Hear It Now" was successful, earning Murrow a prestigious Peabody Award. But Friendly grew restless and persisted in his desire to begin charting the unmapped terrain of television. His prodding paid off. In June 1951, Murrow and Friendly agreed to coproduce "See It Now," a weekly half hour television documentary. There was only one problem: neither Friendly nor Murrow knew anything about television.

If Friendly had been a driven man before, he now was obsessed. Film became his passion. He went to the Museum of Modern Art to study film. He went to Pathé News to study film. He was an incessant interrogator. What worked? Why did it work? What didn't? Why not? Who was good? Who was the best?

They began assembling the "See It Now" team, a postwar version of *Murrow's Boys*. Friendly wanted absolutely the best, and he discovered that using Murrow's name quickly opened doors. "Ed wants…Ed feels…" became integral phrases in Friendly's eighteen-hour days. Invoking Murrow's name not only proved to be a powerful lever with which to move mountains of red tape but also enabled him to attract and hire the best television people of the day. Two stood out—not for their ability, although both were among the very best at their respective crafts—but for their initial dislike of Murrow.

In his late forties and considered one of the best cameramen around, Charlie Mack was not impressed by Edward R. Murrow. After their first meeting, he thought Murrow "uppity," better suited as a British MP than a newsman. Mack could boast of a relationship with FDR, having been the cameraman for several "Fireside Chats." The big, burly Irishman held fond memories of warm conversations with Roosevelt during shooting breaks while cameras were reloaded.[31] Charlie Mack, though, would become a strong Murrow admirer, and later earn the distinction of being known as "Murrow's favorite cameraman."[32]

Murrow and Friendly also wanted Joe Wershba on their team. Described as a bear of a man, Wershba was an excellent reporter, a student of history, and well-schooled in events of the day. And, to Murrow's delight, he was a talented writer. But of their first encounter, near the end of the war, Wershba says, "I resented him bitterly." His animosity stemmed from Murrow's war-hero status even though Murrow had never donned a uniform.[33] Like Charlie Mack, however, Wershba came to respect and admire Ed Murrow.

On November 18, 1951, "See It Now" debuted on CBS. A somewhat nervous Ed Murrow confessed, "This is an old team, trying to learn a new trade." That first program is remembered for Murrow turning to Don Hewitt and instructing him to put up a live picture of the New York harbor while another monitor focused on the Golden Gate Bridge. Two live pictures of both coasts on one screen—the technology was mind-boggling.

The Aluminum Company of America, ALCOA as it was known commercially, came to Murrow proposing to sponsor the program. Having just lost an antitrust suit, the company was eager for an image booster. It reasoned that an association with a man who was becoming a national legend would provide needed polish to that image. At the meeting, Friendly recalls, one of the ALCOA executives asked, "Mr. Murrow, just what are your politics?" Murrow replied, "Gentlemen, that is none of your business." The agreement was reached; Murrow and Friendly would do the program, ALCOA would make the aluminum.

During the next two years, the program hit its stride, as did the Murrow-Friendly partnership. They worked well together, Friendly dramatizing his reserved partner's complicated thoughts, Murrow harnessing and directing the Friendly volcano and its ongoing explosion of ideas.

Early in their relationship Friendly had used Murrow's name as a convenience: it got things done. Later he developed it into an art form. "I probably put words in Ed's mouth," Friendly freely admits, "but Murrow was more powerful than I."[34]

About their relationship, Friendly offers, "Murrow said I was his partner. I think a better term was that I was his First Sergeant."[35] There was strong speculation that Friendly was the model for Horace W. Hateful, a spiteful character on the Bob and Ray Show. Hateful was supposedly created in response to complaints from "CBS wives who resented being left alone for months on end, or seeing their husbands publicly castigated and humiliated by the never-satisfied Friendly."[36]

Given Friendly's driving personality and penchant for perfection—no fewer than six coronaries were counted among the "See It Now" staff—not many would disagree with the first-sergeant characterization.

There was, however, another Fred Friendly, a constant flow of adrenaline with a contagious enthusiasm that drove people to achieve beyond what they ever thought possible. According to Stephen Fleischman, "Friendly had the ability to make you feel as though you were the most talented guy in the world."[37] He was loyal too, willing to place himself in harm's way with network brass to protect a member of the team. According to Howard K. Smith, "Fred Friendly...did something terribly important for reporters, who, because they are looked on with distrust by executives, must have a producer who will fight for them. Fred Friendly would fight for you—and when you spend your life at a task that often seems from day to day like writing the Lord's Prayer on the head of a coffee bean, that means something."[38]

"See It Now" grew in scope and stature over the next two years. Friendly described the hectic atmosphere as "inventing the wheel on the way to the guillotine."[39] Despite early misgivings, the old hands surprised each other and did learn the new trade. At day's end they would repair to Colby's, a favored watering hole, and the moving classroom on television would continue. Of those "seminars," CBS newsman Charles Kuralt says, "he [Murrow] didn't mind a bawdy story, and could relax over a drink as happily as any man I've ever met."[40]

They tried new things; some worked, some didn't. In 1952, for example, a debate was proposed between presidential candidates Dwight D. Eisenhower and Adlai Stevenson. Both declined. "See It Now" decided instead to show each candidate delivering what was designed to be his position on key issues. In one segment, however, Stevenson's voice came from Eisenhower's mouth.

The *little picture* worked. It remained an ingrained constant of the program. "Ed believed in the little picture," says Friendly. "He believed this was a nation of little people and he befriended them in real life and on television. He loved little people who stood up against the crowd."[41]

As successful as Murrow and Friendly were, one unfought battle lurked. Joe McCarthy was never far away.

"People would come in from the Civil Liberties Union," Friendly recalls, "saying why don't you do something about Sen. McCarthy? And I could hear Murrow say, 'We will, but I'm not a minister. I'm not a preacher. When the right story comes along about McCarthyism we'll do it.'"[42] Some wanted Murrow to simply go on television and make a speech, to use the weight of his CBS pulpit to attack Joe McCarthy. "Murrow's own failure to act," says David Halberstam, "had become an issue among journalistic colleagues."[43]

Like others, Friendly thought the battle long overdue. But Friendly also knew an incident that occurred in 1948 had prompted Murrow's carefully measured steps. The image of lifelong friend Laurence Duggan's body strewn on a rainy New York sidewalk was seared in his partner's memory.

The police report of December 20, 1948, had offered no explanation, noting only that the victim was a fully dressed white male, in his early forties, with an overshoe on one foot. The other overshoe was sixteen floors up, just inside the window where Laurence Duggan stood moments before his death.

Whether Duggan had jumped, fell, or was pushed mattered little to Karl Mundt, acting chairman of HUAC. Only hours after Duggan's death, with the concurrence of his congressional colleague, Richard Nixon, Mundt had convened a special midnight session of his committee. Mundt and Nixon were the only members present.

At the late-hour meeting, reporters learned that nine years before, famed Communist snitch Whittaker Chambers had named Laurence Duggan as one of six state employees who had passed information to him. What of the other five? Mundt said he would name them "as they jump out of windows."[44]

The next day, disturbing facts surrounding Laurence Duggan's death had begun to surface. Whittaker Chambers denied not only that Duggan had provided him with secret information but also that he had even known him.

Duggan was a husband and father of four. His family had been quick to point out there was no note, he had no motive for taking his life, and emphatically had not committed suicide. Further, the police report concluded there was no evidence to suggest that Duggan had jumped, fell, or was pushed.

Ed Murrow had been close to the Duggan family. Two decades earlier, he had served Laurence Duggan's father, Stephen Sr., for three years as his assistant at the Institute of International Education. In his early twenties, shy by nature, and not yet comfortable with New York City, Murrow had been a frequent and welcome visitor to the Duggan apartment on East Sixty-fifth Street. Stephen Sr., his wife Sarah, and their three children had become a second family to Murrow.

On the morning after Duggan's death, CBS reporter Joe Wershba had received an early call at his Falls Church, Virginia, home from Murrow directing him to get a comment from Sumner Welles. Former under secretary of State Sumner Welles had worked with Duggan at the State Department and knew him well. No stranger to smear tactics, Welles, a close friend of President Franklin D. Roosevelt, was forced to resign his State Department post in 1943 because of sordid rumors involving homosexuality. FBI chief J. Edgar Hoover played a prominent role in the whisper campaign, which eventually led to a permanent severing of the director's relationship with Roosevelt.[45]

Informed that Welles was having his bath, Wershba made arrangements for a return call. In the interim Murrow had phoned again, agitated at the lack of progress. "Call and get the statement," came the icy directive. The intensity had surprised Wershba.[46]

Later in the day Murrow phoned Stephen Duggan, Jr., to tell him that evening's broadcast would be devoted to his brother, Larry. The younger Duggan, home in bed with bleeding ulcers, said of Murrow, "He sounded totally distraught."[47]

During the broadcast Murrow pointed out that "some of the head-lines that I have seen might as well read 'Spy Takes Life'—and the police have no evidence to show that he jumped rather than fell." He went on to the statement eventually secured by Wershba: "Sumner Welles, who was Duggan's chief during most of his time in the [State] Department, said 'Laurence Duggan was one of the most brilliant, most devoted and most patriotic public servants I have ever known'." Then he added, "And when he dictated that sentence over the phone, he put the emphasis on 'patriotic'."

Murrow also took the opportunity to set the record straight regarding the Duggan-Chambers relationship: "Today Whittaker Chambers says, to his knowledge, he never met Mr. Duggan. Asked if he ever named Mr. Duggan as having passed papers over to him, Chambers replied: 'I did not name Duggan as having passed papers over to me. To my knowledge, he was not a Communist."

Murrow had reserved his final volley for Mundt and Nixon and concluded the broadcast by employing his classic talent for under-statement: "The members of the committee who have done this thing...upon such slight and wholly discredited testimony may now consult their actions and their consciences."[48]

The Campbell Soup Company was enraged that the program they sponsored had been used to defend Laurence Duggan. They were not paying for "editorializing" or Ed Murrow "carrying a torch." Murrow was informed that he would have to attend a meeting to discuss the incident.

Murrow's response to the "you will have to attend a meeting" dictum took the form of a memorandum to the files: "I did not propose to discuss with...the client my news judgement...that if the client was sufficiently dissatisfied, he could, I assume, fail to pick up the option."[49]

According to Friendly, Murrow seethed over the Mundt-Nixon midnight HUAC meeting, the two congressmen gloating and notching their belts with another political victory. But this time they were gloating over the death of the son of his mentor and friend, Stephen Duggan. "Mundt," says Wershba, "was one of the more heinous people in Washington at the time. He was a real Dickensian character of smarm and slime."[50] Five years had not tempered Murrow's contempt for Mundt's claim that he would name more Communists as they "jump from windows."

Murrow didn't deny the need to engage McCarthy and that a confrontation was probably inevitable. But he was painfully aware that there was no room for error. It all had to be perfect. The perfect moment. The perfect vehicle. The perfect *little picture*. Murrow biographer Joseph Persico best captured the agony and weight of the decision when he wrote: "He [Murrow] was mindful of Emerson's dictum: 'When you strike at a king, you must kill him.'" [51]

TUESDAY, OCTOBER 13, 1953

The official announcement was predictably brief.

> After considering the complete file and transcript at the hearing, the Board found that, on all evidence, there is a reasonable doubt that the respondent is a good security risk in the position held by him as an Air Force reservist. The Board recommends that he be discharged from the Air Force reserve and that all commissions held by him be terminated.[*]

There was no additional comment from the Air Force.

While a detailed version of the verdict and a copy of the transcript were dispatched by staff car to Milo at his home in Dexter, the board president, Col. William Doolan, phoned Charles Lockwood to inform him of the panel's ruling. The two argued, Lockwood's ire again rising over the unfairness of a decision based on secret reports from protected sources quoting unnamed persons. Never wavering from the Air Force script, Doolan told Lockwood the documents remained undisclosed to protect Milo.

Officially labeled "Copy of Findings and Recommendations," the verdict was little more than a recitation of the Statement of Reasons. According to attorney Ken Sanborn, "The findings were the same as the charges. It was almost like a 'we find' situation. They just typed the same thing."[1]

[*]Air Force statement issued October 13, 1953.

"The trial board," Lockwood pointed out, "very manifestly disregarded positive and undisputed testimony in favor of vague rumor, unsupported allegations and personal hostility to the respondent."[2]

During the hearing Lockwood and Sanborn had skillfully distanced Milo from Margaret, yet the findings specifically cited a close, continuing relationship with her. "This can't be right," a frustrated Milo said of the verdict. "I proved beyond all doubt that I was not closely associated with my sister."[3]

No evidence was presented to substantiate charges against John Radulovich, yet the accusation that he had spread "Russian and Communist propaganda in the factory" was specifically cited.

Beyond the fact that it was mailed to his house and addressed to his daughter, the *Daily Worker* had never been linked to John Radulovich. Yet one of the charges in the verdict noted that John Radulovich had received copies of the *Daily Worker*—not that he had read it, not that he had subscribed to it, but that he had received it.

Although Milo was held responsible for the actions of his sister and father, the charges against them never emerged from the envelope. Yet those charges, vague as they may have been, were the foundation of findings that concluded there was doubt Milo Radulovich was a good security risk. Because of that doubt, he would forever bear the stigma of disloyalty to his government.

"I think," an angry Lockwood said, "this decision is even more shocking and revolting than what preceded it [the hearing]."[4]

"We think the transcript speaks for itself," Sanborn said.[5]

Although he was slow to anger and ever the gentleman, the verdict had severely tested Milo's sense of propriety. With uncharacteristic invective he blasted the findings. "This is the kind of decision you would have expected from the Nazi Army," he told reporters.[6] Recalling the hallway confrontation with Doolan, Milo carved out the board president for special mention: "I believe there was personal hostility on the part of one colonel hearing the case because of the publicity given to it."[7]

Milo also mentioned a chronology of events that made the verdict all the more puzzling; specifically, what took the Air Force so long to act? All the charges listed in the Statement of Reasons occurred before December 1950. Yet in March 1951, Milo had been given a top-secret clearance for a sensitive assignment at the weather station in Thule, Greenland. If he were a security risk in December 1950, Milo reasoned, surely he was still one three months later. "I still know a lot of secret information about what is going on there," he pointed out with sarcasm, "but no one seems to be worried about that."[8]

The hearing and subsequent findings, however, all seemed to hover over Milo's relationship with his father and sister. "I think that if I had denounced them," he said bluntly, "I would have gotten a different decision."[9]

The verdict took the form of twelve numbered statements. Set off in parentheses under finding number one was the comment, "(Attention is specifically invited to testimony of the respondent in response to question posed by his counsel, at the top of Page 41 of the record, 'I feel the close and continuing association is there regardless. I was born into it, he is my father and she is my sister. I can't cut the blood tie.')"[10] Finding number nine read, "No evidence or statement was introduced by the respondent refuting any of the derogatory allegations concerning his sister's associations, political idealogies or acts."[11]

Significantly, in his telephone conversation with Charlie Lockwood, Doolan volunteered that the board felt Milo had not demonstrated any willingness to temper the relationship with his father and sister.

For Milo, if exoneration was tied to denouncing his family, there was no decision. "In America," he said, "you are supposed to be able to believe what you want to. I don't believe in Communism, but I don't think I should sever all ties with my family because they don't think the same as I."[12]

There would be an appeal. Automatically the decision would be reviewed by Continental Air Command, the Air Force director of military personnel, and the secretary of the Air Force. Judge Advocate General officer Ken Sanborn was well aware that the defense had twenty days to submit further information to the director of military personnel, who, in turn, would forward it to the Air Force Personnel Board for a final review. The final decision rested with Air Force Secretary Harold Talbott.

The hearing was over. For all the hope Milo had held that it would vindicate him, the verdict made the hearing nothing more than a disappointing charade. The Air Force had taken a few public-relations hits, but from its standpoint the furor would likely die down soon and go away. In a few months, maybe not even that long, no one would remember the stubborn lieutenant with the long last name who refused to clean out his footlocker and become another quiet statistic. Ken Sanborn was hard-pressed to disagree. "I thought we had fought the good fight," he said, "but after they had ignored our evidence I didn't think we could win."[13]

⸺⸻⸻⸺

Congressman Kit Clardy's promised exposé of Detroit Communists, originally scheduled for October 26, was put on hold until at least November 30. As a rule the House Un-American Activities Committee had not been conducting hearings in cities where Smith Act trials were in process. Five men and one woman stood accused of holding membership in the Communist party, a violation of the Smith Act, and were on trial in federal Judge Frank Picard's Detroit court.

Earlier in the year Clardy was named chairman of a special HUAC subcommittee set up to conduct hearings in Detroit, Flint, and Lansing. The Michigan Republican indicated he expected to name at least two hundred persons never before publicly identified with the Communist party.

In Washington, HUAC committee members were discussing whether or not their panel would pursue claims that Communists had infiltrated the Protestant clergy. The charges were authored by the committee's former chief investigator, J. B. Matthews. Matthews, with a purloined copy of Appendix Nine under his arm, had joined the staff of Sen. Joseph McCarthy's Investigating Committee.

The Brooklyn Dodgers fired their manager, Charlie Dressen. Dressen, who had managed the team to two straight National League pennants, was demanding a two-year contract. According to the Dodger president, Walter F. O'Malley, "the Brooklyn club will not deviate under any circumstances from its policy of one-year contracts."[14]

Dressen's firing marked the first time since 1926 that a pennant-winning manager was not rehired. That year, after beating the Yankees four games to three in the World Series, the St. Louis Cardinals general manager, Branch Rickey, did not renew the contract of field general Rogers Hornsby.

In October 1953, a distribution list of sixteen people adorned the upper right-hand corner of internal FBI memos. The persons were listed by last name. To the right of each name was a small line on which a check mark could be placed to indicate the memo had been read.

J. Edgar Hoover ran the bureau in a dictatorial fashion, but four men were responsible for implementing the policies of the director: Clyde Tolson, D. M. Ladd, Louis Nichols, and Alan Belmont. They were the brain trust for one of the largest intelligence-gathering agencies in the world. Not coincidentally, their names were the top four on the distribution list.

Ladd and Belmont eschewed the public eye. Although their power was legend within the bureau, rarely, if ever, were their names in print.

Tolson was closer than anyone, in or out of the bureau, to Director J. Edgar Hoover. He joined the bureau in 1928 and within three years had been named assistant director, a position he held for the remainder of his career.

Louis Nichols was slavishly devoted to the director and even named his son J. Edgar Nichols. He became so adept at passing information to the press that he was known as "the cleanest leak in Washington."[1] Nichols was responsible for protecting the image of the bureau. That meant, among other things, he had to ensure the FBI was

193

not attached to any unsavory effort that involved spying on innocent citizens.

On the day after the Air Force announced its verdict on Milo, Belmont penned a memo to Ladd regarding Major [*sic*] Radulovich in which he admitted, "Most of the information contained in the Air Force charges is based upon Bureau investigation. Copies of all pertinent Bureau reports were furnished to the Office of Special Investigations (OSI)."[2] The memo points out that the case had attracted the attention of Sen. Ferguson. Also mentioned was that newspaper coverage had resulted in unfavorable publicity for the Air Force.

The memo was to alert Mr. Ladd that the "Secretary of the Air Force had wanted to prepare a news release for disribution on October 15, 1953, to counteract the unfavorable publicity in the Detroit area."[3] Specifically, the Air Force wanted to release additional information about Milo that was not listed in the original charges.

<hr>

Joe McCarthy's pace went unhindered by Murrow and Friendly. "Those who knew him [Murrow] well and knew how abhorrent McCarthyism was to him," writes David Halberstam, "thought he had become a kind of prisoner to broadcasting's growing political cautiousness."[4] One visitor accused Murrow of not wanting to jeopardize his own comfort. "You may be right," Murrow responded.[5] Another suggested that though McCarthy's style may be abrasive, there was merit to his message and all should listen. "You may be right," Murrow said again.[6]

Only the "See It Now" team knew that since the spring of 1953, film was discreetly being compiled on Wisconsin's junior senator. But that wasn't general knowledge. "People Murrow respected," said Joe Wershba, "were reproaching him for hanging back."[7] The frustration, however noble its root, mattered little to those who wanted Murrow and Friendly to unsheathe their sword now. Still they watched, biding their time, patiently awaiting the right moment. "I think we were look-ing for Milo Radulovich long before we knew who Milo Radulovich was," Friendly said.[8]

Unlike many newspeople based on the East Coast, Ed Murrow prowled the out-of-town newspapers. He had been following a story in the Detroit papers about an Air Force lieutenant who was being run out of the military, not for anything he did but for allegations against his family.

Then it all happened quickly.

Friendly was returning from the cutting room, Murrow hurrying to a lunch date, when they met each other at the elevator. Murrow pulled a crumpled newspaper article from the pocket of his blue overcoat and thrust it at Friendly. With classic understatement he said, "Fritzl," a name Friendly did not appreciate, "this may be your McCarthy pro-gram. The *Detroit News* has been doing a hell of a job with the story."[9]

Friendly went to his office, read, and then reread, the article by Edwin G. Pipp on the Milo Radulovich verdict. Moments later he was on the phone with Joe Wershba. Moments after that Wershba was on the phone with Milo. "Sure, c'mon out, I'll talk to you," Milo told him.[10] What was one more interview? By three o'clock that afternoon, Wershba was on a plane to Detroit, his ultimate destination, Dexter, Michigan.

Both Friendly and Wershba were guarded in their excitement. At first blush, all looked good. The lieutenant, whose loyalty was acknowledged by the Air Force, readily appeared the victim of Communist witch-hunting excess. But there was much to determine before they could say with certainty that Milo Radulovich was the lit-tle picture of their long-awaited McCarthy show—the weapon power-ful enough to strike at a king. They didn't know if he could talk on camera.

Before any resources were expended, they had to discern whether or not Milo could convey the passion of his plight. "That was always a consideration when you went to do a story," Wershba points out.

"Would the person you get be somebody who would grip the interest of the viewer? Are you reaching the audience with a feeling of more than a master's degree survey on an issue?"[11]

They met later that evening. The more Wershba talked with Milo, the more his eagerness grew. "I was enthused," the reporter recalls, "in that he was somebody who could tell his story and tell it with a sense of strength, of rightness of what he was saying, and who could do it with a feeling of humility rather than arrogance. Milo didn't have to feel like he was the biggest potato in the patch."[12] That inner strength, Wershba happily discovered, extended to Milo's wife, Nancy, as well.

At ten o'clock that evening, back in his hotel room, Joe Wershba phoned Fred Friendly at home. "We got our man, Fred."[13]

———⟫●⟪———

It was learned that the University of Kentucky's head football coach, Paul Bryant, had reluctantly convened a late-hour team meeting after the previous Saturday's game against Louisiana State University. Kentucky had battled LSU to a 6-6 tie. Bryant, however, had been under the assumption that Kentucky had lost by a score of 7-6.

Bryant discovered his error shortly after midnight during a radio interview. "How do you feel about the tie, coach?" the announcer asked. "My God, you don't mean it," Bryant responded. The coach immediately called his team together and apologized for "less than gracious" half-time remarks when he thought LSU was ahead by one point. Later Bryant said he had been too engrossed in the game to pay attention to the scoreboard.

THURSDAY, OCTOBER 15, 1953

The "See It Now" team had less than a week to put the program together, the program that would be their first frontal assault on Joe McCarthy. Charlie Mack grabbed the next flight to Detroit.

Joe Wershba was on the phone early with Fred Friendly; both knew they would talk frequently over the next few days. The reporter had been busy. He secured a copy of the hearing transcript from Milo and had already read most of it. It would be very useful in telling the story. He called Selfridge. The Air Force would allow them to film select areas on the perimeter of the base, but would not comment on the case. Fred would check with the Pentagon and try to get a statement from his end. Wershba had set up a date to film the father—not sure yet about the sister, still working on it. Yes, Dexter was Hometown, U.S.A., right off the back lot of Andy Hardy. There was even a statue in the town square honoring Dexter's war heroes.

The first order of business was to "nail down the centerpiece," the interview with Milo. Over the past few weeks, Milo had gained a degree of comfort talking with print reporters while they scribbled in their notepads. But this was television with its endless stream of clanking equipment, its bright lights, and the added apprehension that millions, not thousands, would be weighing words and expressions. Wershba knew from experience that television was another dimension and it could easily intimidate. He was concerned that Milo might back out and wanted him on film as soon as possible.

While Charlie Mack busied himself for almost an hour setting up for the interview, Joe Wershba talked to Milo and Nancy. He eased their nerves and told them to "say it just like that."

At first Milo was ill at ease. There were a few "aahhhs" as he fumbled for the right word, but then he warmed to the task. His strong sense of family, the outrage over injustice, took hold of his words: "I have maintained throughout this entire hearing that what my sister does, what political opinions or activities she engages in, are her own affair because they certainly do not influence me...if I had said 'I will cut the blood ties' everything would have been beautiful with the Air Force...if I am being judged on my relatives, are my children going to be asked to denounce me?...are they going to have to explain to their friends why their father is a security risk?"[1]

Joe Wershba's concerns proved groundless. A determined Milo Radulovich had no intention of backing out. If anything, his intensity had increased from their previous night's conversation. After the filming Wershba was more convinced than ever that they did indeed "have their man."

For nearly a month newspaper references to Nancy Radulovich inevitably made mention that she was strikingly attractive. She was "the pretty wife of" or "his pretty blond mate." In response to Joe Wershba's questions, she proved to be a convincing force in her own right. "No, I wouldn't want him to take it lying down," she responded at one point, her eyes boring into the camera. "I don't regret anything at all—him coming forward and fighting it."[2]

Needing an opposing point of view, Wershba and Charlie Mack took to the streets of Dexter. They stopped people in the downtown area, talked to business owners, even went in and out of a few bars. They were searching for someone, anyone, who believed Milo should step down. "Nearly everybody knew about the case," Wershba recalls, "but nobody would defend the Air Force."[3]

They talked to John Palmer, chief marshal of Dexter. "[I]t's still a mystery to me why they are condemning him for something that his father did," Palmer said. "Certainly, he can't condemn his father and cast him aside just because he read a newspaper that he wasn't supposed to read. I couldn't do that. Neither could any other boy who had a father."[4]

They stopped at Madeline Lewis's dry-cleaning shop. Earlier she had circulated a petition on behalf of Milo. "I felt like so many others in Dexter," she told Wershba, "that Milo really was getting a pretty bad deal on this and we had quite a lot of faith in the boy."[5]

They sought out Dr. A. G. Wall, a dentist and for twenty-nine years the mayor of Dexter. Wall said, "I can't see how they can hold a man responsible for the views and actions of his relatives, because of the fact that you can't control them."[6]

Their journey continued to a service station. Ernst Alsasser echoed the sentiments of his neighbors: "I know I wouldn't want to be held responsible for what my father did."[7]

Finally, Wershba thought, he had found his counterpoint in Steve Sorter, beer-truck driver and post commander of the American Legion. "We went into a local tavern and started talking to this burly guy at the bar. He growled back at me," Wershba said, "and I thought here's our guy. So I asked him if he would step outside where the light is better."[8] Showing the effects of an afternoon at the tavern, Sorter continued to growl at Charlie Mack's camera. Sorter, it turned out, was a Milo supporter: "I wouldn't know him if he came down the middle of the street. And that's beside the point...if the Air Corps or United States Army or whoever they are that are purging him gets away with it, they are entitled to do it to anybody. You or me or anybody else."[9]

"Tension is the greatest part of a story, clashing points of view," Wershba says. "I think in this case the tension was already in the air and the Air Force's action was the opposing point of view."[10]

A nervous Charlie Lockwood recited a carefully memorized statement to Joe Wershba and Charlie Mack. Wershba indicated it was too long and said they would have to shoot it again. He asked the attorney to shorten it. Lockwood delivered the same remarks again verbatim.

The continuity and eloquence of the attorney's two-minute, four-second statement was so well done, though, that Wershba anticipated it would be difficult to trim.

"I have never witnessed such a farce and travesty upon justice as this thing has developed," Lockwood said. "Now this whole theory of guilt by relationship is something that was adopted back in the thirteenth and fourteenth century and then abandoned as being inhuman and cruel. It was later revived in Germany under Hitler and Himmler."[11]

The letters to Milo continued.

Grace Hudson of Pasadena, California, sent Milo a carbon copy of a letter she had sent to "Chief of the Air Force, The Pentagon." In it she said, "Have you in the Air Force gone completely crazy? Your colonels admit that Lt. Radulovich's *personal loyalty is unquestioned....*He is right in saying that one would expect such a decision from the Nazi army."

Letters to the editor also continued.

Air Force Capt. Robert E. Foote wrote to the *Detroit Times*: "If Radulovich's commission can be taken away in 1953 because his father read an allegedly subversive paper in 1940, is it not possible that my commission in the U. S. Air Force can be terminated in 1954 because, in 1854, my grandmother read a book called *Uncle Tom's Cabin?*"[12]

Editorials in Detroit's major papers continued as well.

The *Detroit Times* minced few words: "A part of our heritage is the right to be confronted openly by our accusers on the issues; the right to face-to-face encounters instead of a knife between our shoulder blades."[13] Ironically, the Radulovich comment was on the editorial page only a few inches below a picture of the conservative publisher and anti-Communist crusader, William Randolph Hearst.

The *Detroit News* welcomed a statement from Charlie Lockwood that the fight for Milo's good name would be carried to the White House. "That is as it should be," said the *News*. "The issue is bigger than the man and more important than any board's narrow judgments on one individual." It went on to say, "The facts appear to be that he is cast out as a 'security risk' because he has relatives of which the Air Force does not approve. If there is any soundness in that concept, then favor within our services should go only to children of the 'best families.'"[14]

Noting the Air Force's decision to release the Radulovich verdict on the same day that twenty-six top-secret documents were discovered in the Russian zone of East Germany, the *Detroit Free Press* caustically observed, "In a great many minds the pairing of the two items may breed a feeling that, after all, Radulovich perhaps was guilty of something more than has been permitted to meet the public eye."[15]

Apart from Ed Murrow, others at CBS had begun reading the Detroit papers.

———>●<———

Based on what had loosely been termed a technicality, the children of executed spies Julius and Ethel Rosenberg were removed from their school. According to reports from Toms River, New Jersey, where the children were living with friends, both were well-behaved and popular; one of the boys was even elected president of his class. "Apparently," opined the *Detroit Times*, "the children of Toms River show better sense than some of their elders."[16]

———>●<———

The word "Recommendations" had been typed across the top of a response on nonletterhead stationery that accompanied Belmont's memo of the previous day on its return journey. The top four names on the distribution list—Tolson, Ladd, Nichols, and Belmont—had all been checked. The OSI, said the memo, should be advised as follows:

> 1. The Air Force would be opening itself to severe criticism by disclosing information publicly which was not contained in the original charges to the subject.

There were two handwritten notes scrawled under the first recommendation: "This is not our business. We should stop giving advice." Which was followed by, "I certainly agree."[17]

> 2. The Bureau cannot be placed in a position of approving news releases for the Air Force under any circumstances, and particularly if we do not see the news release.

The word "Right" was handwritten under the second recommendation.

> 3. All information in FBI reports is confidential and is to be used only for official purposes, and should not be used in a controversy between the Air Force and newspapers.

Again, the word "Right" had been handwritten under the recommendation.

Ever vigilant of the bureau's image, the director, according to another memo, had approved recommendations two and three. Scrawled across the bottom of the original memo was a note indicating that at six o'clock that evening, Frank Welch of the OSI had been advised of the bureau's decision regarding points two and three. The memo, however, was accompanied by yet another document, a brief overview of the files that had previously been shared with the OSI. It was labeled "Details."

According to the "Details" memo, Margaret, in an April 1948 entry, was described as "one of the two most dangerous employees of the [Yugoslavian] Embassy and as one who would stop at nothing to further the aims of the Communist Party."[18] It chronicled her activities in Detroit after employment as an embassy secretary in Washington. The file said she had become leader of the Henry Winston Club of the

Communist party and had also picketed federal establishments in connection with Smith Act prosecutions.

Mention was also made of John Radulovich and a statement that the information contained therein was extracted from his "main file." In language that bore a marked resemblance to that of the Statement of Reasons, the memo said that "a reliable informant advised in 1947 that John Radulovich had endeavored to spread Russian Communist propaganda and extolled the virtues of Russia."*

———————⟶ ⟶●◄ ———————

The film they had amassed was shipped off to New York at day's end. Wershba did little to hide his enthusiasm and asked Friendly to let him know first thing what Murrow thought about the interview with Milo.

Friendly writes:

> Wershba's "dope sheets" were sometimes more comprehensive than the film they accompanied, but in the Radulovich case they were unnecessary, for after each interview he called to brief us. From the beginning the material seemed promising. When our reporters were doing well they would promote their stories with phrases like "first rate" or "pretty good stuff." But when the material was truly exciting there was often a note of restraint. "Fred," Wershba said now, "please try to see this film tonight. I don't want to try to evaluate it from this end, but if there is any sound on the track and the picture is as good as Mack thinks it is, we may have something here." His last words were: "And tell the lab not to scratch the film." When a reporter says that, you know he has something.[19]

*The Statement of Reasons read: "[I]t is reported that he endeavored, on occasions, to spread Russian and Communist propaganda in the factory."

FRIDAY, OCTOBER 16, 1953

"He called me at work," Margaret Fishman says of her first contact with Joe Wershba. "I said I would talk to him, but just don't ask me the sixty-four-dollar-question—are you now, or have you ever been, a member of the Communist party?—and he agreed."[1]

Wershba tried to calm Margaret while Charlie Mack set up. Unlike the others, she was composed, relaxed, and enjoyed talking about the case. "When the lights went on I froze," she laughs. "All of the sudden I'm talking to twenty million people. I didn't know what they would think of me. After all, I was the villain."[2]

Although Margaret acknowledged the difficulty of her part in the case, she did not retreat from her well-entrenched, often stated view that whatever her activities, they should not reflect on Milo. "My political beliefs are my own private affair," she told Wershba.[3] Wershba did not ask the sixty-four-dollar question; Margaret did not volunteer the answer.

During filming, one of the lights went out, a problem that normally would have been a signal to stop. Charlie Mack quickly motioned for Wershba to continue. "In addition to being one of the best cameramen we had," Wershba says of Mack, "he was also a superior reporter. He recognized the importance of the moment."[4]

Wershba and Mack then traveled to the offices of United Auto Workers Local 154, where they interviewed Claude Bland. Unfazed by the camera, Bland voiced strong opposition to Communists in his union and scoffed at the notion that John Radulovich was a subversive. "I have known him since 1937," Bland said. "I worked with the man in the same department for two years—in '45 and '46—ate lunch with him on many occasions. I never heard him say one word regarding the Communist philosophy."[5]

Their second day of filming was drawing to a close. One interview remained, John Radulovich. Both Wershba and Mack wanted to do it that day so they could return to New York and participate in editing the hours of film they shot. Wershba called John Radulovich and he agreed to meet them that night.

———————

Five minutes into viewing the film on Milo, Friendly called Murrow. After apologizing for interrupting him just before the evening's broadcast, Friendly strongly urged that Murrow make time to see the Radulovich film—that night. Murrow said he was going home for dinner but would meet him in the cutting room later that evening.

"When Murrow saw the film he was jarred," Friendly writes. "Whenever someone appearing on one of our programs spoke with great conviction and force Ed would say, 'The guy has fire in his belly.' He said that now about Radulovich, but he was also impressed with the young officer's control."[6]

Fred Friendly and Ed Murrow agreed with Wershba. Milo Radulovich was their man.

Impressed by what he had just seen, Murrow machine-gunned Friendly with questions. What does the Air Force say? How about the sister? The father? How do the townspeople feel?

The material was great and both were certain they definitely had a program. But Murrow doubted they could do it justice in ten minutes. He suggested they devote the entire program to Milo. Friendly agreed, but thought they should make the final decision after viewing footage on the father.

Friendly would inform the Air Force of their decision to do the Radulovich program and make another effort to get a comment. He would also talk to the network about promoting the program. Murrow began work on the ending.

———————

Late in the evening Wershba and Mack were finally able to film Milo's parents, John and Ikonija. "We asked in advance what they were going to do," Wershba says, "and they said send a letter to the president. I said fine, read it."[7]

Bravely fighting a language that strangled thoughts so clear in his mind, John Radulovich, American citizen, his wife at his side, read the letter he was sending to the president.

> Mr. President. I writing to you because they are doing a bad thing to Milo. They are wrong. The things they say about him are wrong. He has given all his growing years to his country. Mr. President, I am an old man. I have spend [sic] my life in the coal mines and auto furnaces. I ask nothing for myself. I ask justice for my boy. Mr. President I ask your help.

At one point John struggled with proper pronunciation. With her hand on his arm, Ikonija Radulovich gently supplied the word to her husband of thirty years.

It was midnight. Filming completed, John Radulovich would not let the weary newsmen leave until they had joined him in eating some "good Yugoslavian salami."

Liberated from the bright lights and dreaded camera, the elder Radulovich became an animated conversationalist. Now able to trust these strangers from New York and confident they were not there to harm his family, he told Wershba, "You know why they do this to my boy Milo, they jealous! They jealous because he is lieutenant in American Air Force."[8]

Others may have been confused, but not John Radulovich. It was all so clear to him.

"'They jealous!' That stuck in my mind more than anything else, the jealousy," Wershba says. "That was more powerful coming from the father who didn't care about the politics involved, but really cared about why they were trying to destroy his son—because they were jealous. He had made it and their sons had not."

Wershba looked at Charlie Mack. It would take the cameraman nearly an hour to position his lights and equipment for that one quote, that one passionate, critical quote. "I didn't have the heart to ask Charlie to set up," he says.[9]

———————

Wershba called Friendly. It was late. He and Charlie Mack were dead tired. He prefaced his remarks with, "I don't want to prejudice you before you see it, but we just interviewed Radulovich's father...."

"Fred is the master of a statement for the moment," the reporter observes. "He says to me, 'WERSHBA, YOU'RE FIRED! I'M FIRED! MURROW'S FIRED! But we may have one of the greatest shows in the history of broadcasting.'"[10]

SATURDAY, OCTOBER 17, 1953

Fred Friendly had placed a call to the Pentagon and informed the public information officer that "See It Now" was going ahead with its broadcast of the Radulovich program. Would a high-ranking spokesman be available for a comment? The officer was somewhat surprised and pointedly asked if Mr. Murrow himself was aware of the decision. Friendly informed him that it was Mr. Murrow's idea.

Edward R. Murrow was proud of the kinship he felt with America's fighting men and women. His respect for their deeds, his ability to verbalize their fear, had earned him special regard in their eyes. "All men would be brave," he perceptively observed while on a bombing mission over Europe, "if they could leave their stomachs at home." That bond, the Pentagon had learned, extended to reserve officers whose constitutional rights Murrow felt were being abrogated.[1]

"See It Now" in general, Murrow and Friendly in particular, had enjoyed autonomy like that of longtime newspaper columnists.* Friendly indicates they were responsible only to network chief William

*There was one notable exception. The previous year a Murrow piece from Korea, highly critical of Gen. Douglas MacArthur and other command officers, was "killed" by the network. Murrow had questioned the purpose of a particular battle, quoting a highly placed military source as saying it had been waged only because someone decided a victory was needed. His transcript to CBS called the military

208

S. Paley and the ALCOA president, Irving W. Wilson. Two years earlier, in 1951, ALCOA had sought Murrow and embraced the "See It Now" concept, even participated in its development. According to their original understanding, Murrow and Friendly had tended the issues while ALCOA had manufactured the aluminum. To date, there had been no interference. Now a long-awaited broadcast was being molded that would test the boundaries of "See It Now"'s independence.

The task of informing management about the Radulovich program fell to Friendly. "The only reaction," Friendly says, "was a quick, silent gasp."[2] As a courtesy, even though the program hadn't been put together, he invited network executives to see parts of it. They declined, indicating only that they would wait like everyone else until Tuesday night. "We were notifying the CBS management about the Radulovich broadcast only because the issue was highly volatile," Friendly said. "We felt the company had a right to know that by next Wednesday morning it would probably be engulfed in criticism."[3]

Management's uneasiness with the Radulovich program was brought to a head when Friendly asked the director of advertising, Bill Golden, to place an ad for the program in the New York papers. Golden was informed by the twentieth floor—the floor that housed the network's upper echelon of management—that CBS would not

---

action meaningless and pointed out that it had cost innumerable lives. Murrow also challenged statements by "air-conditioned military officers" who said the war could be over in a few months. According to the GIs and field commanders that Murrow had talked to, "that ain't the way it looks from here."

The official reasons given for killing the piece was that it gave comfort to the enemy, could be used as Communist propaganda, and—the real blow to Murrow— the sources might be unreliable. Nobody wanted to be the one to tell Murrow. William Paley ordered the CBS news director, Ed Chester, to do it. Chester thought it should be Paley. Both were relieved when Murrow's staff volunteered to break the news. Murrow was furious and seriously considered resigning. He didn't, but the incident severely strained his relationship with Paley. Details of the episode eventually leaked and, much to Paley's chagrin, more than seven hundred correspondents of the Overseas Press Club cabled messages of outrage to MacArthur.

promote the program. Network executives were definitely distancing themselves from the program.

Murrow and Friendly turned to their sponsor, ALCOA. They told the aluminum maker that the Radulovich program was something special and asked the company to buy an ad for it. Murrow knew ALCOA had major defense contracts with the Air Force and the Radulovich program inadvertenly placed the company in a difficult position. He believed pressing ALCOA to step up its visibility regarding the program, especially this week, might cost "See It Now" its coveted sponsor. Without a sponsor the future of "See It Now" was at risk. ALCOA said it would not purchase any newspaper advertisements for the broadcast, but to Murrow and Friendly's delight offered to forgo the program's middle commercial so as not to disrupt the continuity of the show. Even that decision, Murrow and Friendly felt, would not bode well with the Pentagon.

Wershba and Mack returned from Michigan late in the day. The massive task of editing the thirty thousand feet of film they shot—about five hours' worth—had begun. Murrow had asked that a few minutes be left for him, a *tailpiece,* because, as he confided to Friendly, "We are going to live or die by our ending."[4] Murrow took the hearing transcript home with him and would write the critical ending over the weekend. On Monday, he and Friendly would dissect the weekend effort.

The United States government agreed to accept half of crooner Dick Haymes's earnings until his tax debt of $50,000 had been satisfied. The native of Argentina remained responsibile for other debts, including alimony from three previous marriages. Haymes, who recently wed actress Rita Hayworth, was singing at the Shamrock Hotel in Houston, where his salary had been attached by the Internal Revenue Service.

SUNDAY, OCTOBER 18, 1953

S hortly after the first newspaper article on the case, Milo had been contacted about an appearance on "Meet the UAW," a popular Sunday morning television show that discussed issues of importance to Detroit's auto-worker population. Arrangements were made for the October 18 show, and Milo was joined by Ken Sanborn, Charlie Lockwood, and UAW Secretary-Treasurer Emil Mazey. Guests on "Meet the UAW" sat on the famous "park bench" while being interviewed by the program's knowledgeable but folksy host, Guy Nunn. The bench was comfortable and of genuine park vintage; unfortunately it was not accustomed to accommodating four guests at once. Ken Sanborn drew the unlucky end position and was forced to wax eloquently while fighting the discomfort of "one cheek on, one cheek off" the bench. "It was a long, long interview," Sanborn chuckles.[1]

—————————— >●< ——————————

"See It Now" was a weekly pressure cooker. The fact that CBS News was spread over half of Manhattan only added to the stress of creating, reporting, editing, and writing a show in less than a week. The journalistic headquarters were on Madison Avenue. The film was developed on Ninth Avenue. The screening and editing was done on Fifth Avenue. Murrow's narration was recorded at CBS radio, near his office. Friendly says that "often the 'final mix' was not completed until an hour before a broadcast."[2]

On Sunday evening, pace in the cutting room, always feverish, had turned hectic. Only forty-eight hours separated the "See It Now" team from the Radulovich broadcast. Five hours of film had been reduced to forty-five minutes. Murrow and Friendly met to review the editing and both were impressed with the pared-down version. Murrow continued to fret over the ending, believing the success or failure of the entire show hinged on the strength of his concluding comments.

———◦———

President Eisenhower announced that government employees who invoked their constitutional safeguard against self-incrimination would be subject to dismissal from government jobs. The executive order was aimed at employees charged with disloyalty.

Atty. Gen. Herbert Brownell, Jr., referred to the directive in a speech to the National Press Club. "There is no law," Brownell said, "that requires the government to sit supinely by until the suspected employee has been convicted of disloyalty or other similar misconduct inconsistent with the interests of national security before it can separate him from the government service."[3]

The attorney general also indicated the Department of Justice intended to seek legislation during the next Congress that would compel witnesses who sought refuge under the Fifth Amendment to testify if they were assured immunity from criminal prosecution.

Murrow was at the studio early that Monday morning. By the time Friendly arrived he had dictated his third rewrite of the tailpiece. Within minutes Murrow burst into Friendly's office and thurst the copy into his partner's hands. He paced nervously while Friendly read it.

Friendly recalled that after reading the conclusion he reached up and shook Murrow's hand. "You know, Ed," he said, "this language is so precise and eloquent that I hate to see you ad-lib it."[1] They agreed Murrow would read the statement, and that he would not use a teleprompter—a device they both despised.

Later that morning Murrow called Friendly on the private line that connected their two offices. A general and a colonel were coming in to see them about the Radulovich show. Would Friendly be available for an afternoon meeting?

The meeting, according to Friendly, began with the military men admitting they did not sit with the security panel and as such were not well versed with particulars in the Radulovich case. They were concerned, nevertheless, with the story's potential negative impact on American confidence in the military. A positive public image, they argued, was critical—especially during the cold war. Murrow didn't disagree and suggested it was all the more reason they should take advantage of the offer to respond on the record. As the meeting wore on, Friendly felt the general was unconvinced that the Radulovich program would ever be broadcast.

The general continued to press his case. Murrow's brother, Air Force Brig. Gen. Lacey Murrow, was subtly mentioned. Further, Murrow was reminded that he had always enjoyed the best of relationships with the Air Force, and had even won their prestigious Distinguished Service to Airpower Award. The conversation, Friendly felt, was inching perilously close to intimidation. At meeting's end the general rose and mentioned to Murrow that the Air Force had always extended to him complete cooperation and that he was confident the newsman would do nothing to jeopardize that status. "Murrow simply let that last sentence hang there against his quiet stare," Friendly recalls. "I expect the general remembers that moment thirteen years later."*

After their visitors left, Murrow voiced doubts that the Air Force would comment on the program, verbally or in writing. He added that given the tenor of the meeting, "See It Now" couldn't postpone the program now, even if they wanted to. "I had never seen him display quite such an appetite for a broadcast," Friendly says.[2]

Murrow and Friendly did not dismiss lightly an opposing point of view. On the contrary, both were mindful of CBS's wartime covenant that provided direction when dealing with controversy: the audience should not be able to discern the news analyst's position on the issue. The guideline had served the network well.

But Murrow and Friendly were frustrated: the case for the Air Force couldn't be made without the military's cooperation, and, for whatever reason, the Air Force was not cooperating. Wershba, Friendly, and now Murrow had made repeated efforts to secure a point of view, a comment, a written statement, anything on the Milo Radulovich case. The only response had been a private meeting to

---

*The "thirteen years" refers to the intervening period after the incident and when Friendly was writing about it in his book.

deliver a subtle threat to kill the show. The wartime guideline didn't address what should be done when one side of the controversy refused to comment.

"See It Now" had not shied from topical issues during its two-year existence. A year earlier, in one of the show's sterling moments, they had earned acclaim with "Christmas in Korea." But a story on fighting men and women away from home during the holidays, however interesting and heart wrenching, did not challenge the viewer to seek a point of view. Likewise with other topics, such as juvenile delinquency and alcoholism—they were universally abhorred.

Now, with the Milo Radulovich case before them, Murrow and Friendly were keenly aware they were escorting television on its maiden voyage into the uncharted mine fields of advocacy. Television, heretofore a medium to entertain, was being contemplated as a medium to influence.

An opposing point of view for the Radulovich show was discussed at length by Murrow and Friendly. Notwithstanding the Air Force's unwillingness to participate in the program, Murrow concluded that some issues just aren't balanced. "We can't sit there every Tuesday night and give the impression that for every argument on one side there is an equal one on the other side," he said to Friendly.[3]

As the clock continued to count down to the 10:30 p.m. Tuesday broadcast, the "See It Now" team sensed that the effort was becoming something historical. Murrow, at long last, was set to strike at Sen. Joseph McCarthy. Editing continued, but it was now apparent that the program would come down squarely on one side of a controversial issue; television hadn't done that before, and management was nervous. The twentieth floor was adamant—CBS would not pay to advertise the Radulovich show. Neither would ALCOA, for that matter.[4]

Murrow and Friendly decided the show was too important not to be publicized. Consulting no one, they reached into their own pockets and came up with $1,500 to advertise the show in the *New York Times*.

The ad, like the show it advertised, was straightforward, no embroidery. Over a picture of Milo sat the caption, "The case against Lt. Milo Radulovich, AO589839." Below the picture it read, "Tonight on "SEE IT NOW," 10:30, WCBS-TV, Channel 2." It was unceremoniously signed "Ed Murrow, Fred Friendly."

Noticeably lacking, and further irking the twentieth floor, was that the ad had not included the networks's famous logo, the CBS eye. In fact, there was no mention of the network.

Partisan politics reared its head in New York this day. Robert F. Wagner, Jr., Democratic candidate for mayor of New York, accused Republican Gov. Thomas E. Dewey of attempting to engineer a parole for imprisoned labor leader Joey Fay. Wagner charged that the request for Fay's parole came from the highest sources in Washington.

Dewey quickly denied the charge and produced documents indicating that the president pro tem of the state senate, Arthur Wicks, had visited Fay no fewer than eleven times. Wicks, acting lieutenant governor, said the visits had been an attempt to prevent labor disputes involving construction projects in his district. Dewey said he was not satisfied with Wicks's answer and demanded an immediate meeting.

Wicks was said to be considering a statewide broadcast reminiscent of Vice President Richard Nixon's "tell-all" speech during 1952's presidential campaign.

The twentieth floor continued to stay away from the Radulovich show. Advertising Director Bill Golden had called Friendly early on the morning of the show and said somewhat sheepishly that he needed cash for the ad. The network had refused to advance the money to the newspaper through its regular account. Murrow and Friendly quickly complied.

Editing the film from five hours to forty-five minutes had proved to be a much easier task than paring forty-five minutes to twenty-two. The cutting room had worked all Monday night and continued their precision efforts until one hour before the broadcast. Murrow had viewed all the film but he would not see the final version until less than an hour before the show.

A few hours before airtime, the director, Don Hewitt, had heard Murrow's concluding comments and was deeply impressed. The film and audio ran on separate machines and weeks earlier they had lost sync during a broadcast. Only half joking, Hewitt threatened bodily harm to anyone responsible for losing sync during the Radulovich show.

It was a weekly horse race to get everything done by the 9:40 p.m. dress rehearsal. This week had been tighter than usual. Friendly was never even able to see the final version; the film he was watching had to be interrupted and reracked for the program.

217

Minutes before the broadcast, Murrow and Friendly had a few quiet moments together, just the two of them. They shared thoughts on the program and what it might mean to history. "I don't know whether we'll get away with this one or not," Murrow said, "and things will never be the same around here after tonight, but this show may turn out to be a small footnote to history in the fight against the senator [McCarthy]."[1]

Murrow was not a heavy user of alcohol but each week just before going on the air he had a drink. Seconds before airtime he took a gulp of Scotch and, as was their custom, passed the glass to Friendly who did likewise.

At precisely 10:30 p.m., CBS viewers were shown a television monitor on their screen that read, "stand by Dexter Michigan." The voice-over announced, "From Studio 41 in New York, Edward R. Murrow and See It Now." Murrow turned in his chair and with trademark lighted cigarette in hand bid his audience, "Good evening."

"The Case Against Lt. Radulovich," Friendly wrote, "was the shortest half hour in television history."[2]

Murrow set the scene, talking about Air Force Regulation 35-62, and how it had been used to discharge Milo from the military even though "there was no question whatsoever as to the Lieutenant's loyalty."[3]

Most of the show, however, was the handiwork of Joe Wershba and Charlie Mack. The centerpiece was Milo. The memorized statement of attorney Charles Lockwood. Margaret. The townspeople. The union official. Nancy. John Radulovich, stealing the show in his halting English, reading a letter to the president.

Underscoring the lack of due process, Murrow turned to the hearing transcript. He read the section dealing with the introduction of evidence that represented the government's case against Milo—a classified file that was received and remained in a sealed envelope. "THE LAWYER: [in reference to the file] of which the respondent is not informed, does not see and has no way of knowing what it is except as found in the statement of reasons? PRESIDENT: that is correct."

Murrow biographer Ann Sperber wrote of the Radulovich show, "It was the first time the victim was provided with a forum over the mass media—heretofore the prerogative of the accusers—spelling out what it all meant, financially, socially, in terms anyone could understand."4

Murrow introduced the ending himself: "Perhaps you will permit me to read a few sentences just at the end because I should like to say rather precisely what I mean." From a hand-held clipboard he read the brief remarks that had demanded so much of his energy over the past few days.

> We have told the Air Force that we will provide facilities for any comments, criticism or correction it may wish to make in regard to the case of Milo Radulovich. The case must go through two more Air Force Boards routine and channels before it reaches Secretary Talbott, who will make the final decision. We are unable to judge the charges against the father or the lieutenant's sister because neither we, nor you, nor the lieutenant, nor the lawyers, know precisely what was contained in that manila envelope. Was it hearsay, rumor, gossip, or hard, ascertainable fact backed by creditable witnesses? We do not know.
>
> There is a distinct difference between a loyalty and a security risk. A man may be entirely loyal, but at the same time be subjected to coercion, influence or pressure, which may cause him to act contrary to the best interest of national security. In the case of Lieutenant Radulovich, the board found that there was no question of his loyalty, but that he was regarded as a security risk. The security officers will tell you that a man who has a sister in Warsaw might be entirely loyal, but would be subjected to pressure as a result of threats that might be made against his sister's security or well-being. They contend that a man might be subjected to

the same kind of pressure, but here again, no evidence was adduced to prove that Radulovich's sister was a member of the Party, and the case against his father certainly was not made.

We believe that "the son shall not bear the iniquity of the father," even though that iniquity be proved beyond all doubt, which in this case it was not. But we believe too that his case illustrates the urgent need for the Armed Forces to communicate more fully than they have so far done the procedures and regulations to be followed in attempting to protect the national security and the rights of the individual at the same time.

Whatever happens in this whole area of the relationship between the individual and the state, we will do ourselves; it cannot be blamed upon Malenkov, Mao Tse-tung or even our allies. It seems to us—that is, to Fred Friendly and myself—that it is a subject that should be argued about endlessly.

With only seconds remaining, Murrow looked up from his clipboard and, with the slightest trace of an impish grin, said, "You may have noticed we left out the middle commercial and saved it for the end. We hope you might find it interesting now."

Moments later the "all clear" sign was given and the tremendous tension and pressure of the previous week had been broken. Friendly vividly recalls the moment: "If twenty men in a control room can figuratively lift a man on their shoulders, it happened in Studio 41 that night. Technicians and stagehands came over to Murrow, who was bathed in sweat and smoke, and shook his hand. Some had tears in their eyes."[5]

The calls started. Switchboards in New York, Philadelphia, and Washington lit up. CBS telephone operators in New York stopped counting at a thousand. Reporters from CBS, and other networks as well, phoned to congratulate Murrow. Most calls were supportive, but not all. Some believed Murrow and CBS were handmaidens of the Communist party, and said so.

Laura Z. Hobson, author of *Gentleman's Agreement*, the powerful anti-Semitic novel of the previous decade, was so moved that she penned a note to Murrow that very night. "During the last minutes when you were speaking from the screen," she wrote, "I actually said out loud, 'Bless you, damn it, bless you.'"[6]

Similarly, columnist Harriet Van Horne wrote in a private letter to Murrow, "In a sense you are his Zola. And thus we are all in your debt....Considering the climate of opinion we live in these days, you are an extraordinarily brave man."[7]

No calls came from the twentieth floor.

Murrow, Friendly, and their "See It Now" colleagues finally slipped away for the postshow ritual at the Pentagon bar. Still in makeup, Murrow entered the popular media watering hole amid the hosannas of his peers. Some cheered, others rushed over to shake his hand.

———⋙●⋘———

Milo Radulovich and his family were not among the callers to Murrow and Friendly that evening. The network affiliate in Detroit, WJBK, replaced "See It Now" with a show called "My Favorite Story," a half-hour dramatic series hosted by actor Adolphe Menjou. That evening's episode was titled "The Postmistress."

———⋙●⋘———

In a paper delivered to the Association of Life Insurance Medical Directors gathered at the Statler Hotel in New York, medical researcher Dr. E. Cuyler Hammond said establishing a definitive cause between smoking and lung cancer was still two years away. Dr. Hammond sug-

gested that the steady increase in cancer-related deaths could be a result of an aging population.[8]

Hammond cited studies that had linked cancer with smoking, but said none were conclusive because they had only shown a correlation. So far, Hammond said, no statistician had been able to state whether the correlation was merely of academic interest or was so large that it posed a frightening public health problem.

Hammond also said he felt sure that if smoking proved to be seriously harmful, the tobacco companies would undertake research to discover the injurious ingredients and remove them from the product.

The *New York Times* responded quickly. Without mentioning the previous night's "See It Now" program, its editorial on the morning after began, "GUILT BY RELATIONSHIP—through a kind of blood taint—is one of the less attractive features of totalitarian 'justice.' It is therefore distressing to find something uncomfortably akin to this principle playing a part in the security program conducted by our own government." It went on to say that the government's case against Milo "is to carry things uncomfortably close to the totalitarian technique."[1]

———————◦———————

There was still no official comment from the twentieth floor, and with some justification. Friendly indicated concerns had begun to drift in from a few of the affiliates who felt that a decision to broadcast such a controversial program should have been made by management, not Murrow and Friendly. The network, some stations felt, had abdicated its responsibility.

From their standpoint, management had been placed in a no-win situation. Praise for the program had been heaped on Murrow and Friendly. Yet those who disagreed with the Radulovich program—and there were some—had directed their venom at the network. Friendly wrote, "Obviously the company's anguish was complicated by the press; the liberals castigated them for not supporting us, the McCarthyites for not stopping us."[2]

ALCOA had received a few negative phone calls, but their responses were mostly supportive. One woman, Friendly said, had even inquired about purchasing an ingot of aluminum as a gesture of gratitude.

According to Congressman Kit Clardy, Michigan's Communist picture was far worse than he and his colleagues on the House Un-American Activities Committee had originally thought. Clardy announced that he was completing final plans for subcommittee hearings on Communism in Michigan, scheduled to begin on November 30.

Clardy anticipated calling a number of witnesses, and Bereniece Baldwin, he assured, would be among them. The Detroit housewife/Communist infiltrator had testified before the full committee in Washington on many occasions. "It is no stretch of the imagination," Clardy said of Baldwin, "to assume she will name a few more people in organized labor."[3]

THURSDAY, OCTOBER 22, 1953

Maj. Gen. Joseph F. Carroll, deputy inspector general of the Air Force, traveled to Michigan to meet with the *Detroit Free Press*. The general and a civilian aide sat with the paper's executive editor, Lee Hills, and acting editorial page director, Royce Howes.

Since the Radulovich story began a month earlier, *Detroit Free Press* editorials had been strident in their criticism of the Air Force's decision to discharge Milo from the service and, conversely, strongly supportive of his efforts to fight that discharge.

According to Howes, during the two-hour closed-door session, General Carroll intimated that the government had undisclosed information adverse to Lieutenant Radulovich, and it would be in the paper's best interest to stop championing the lieutenant's cause. In a terse statement after the meeting, Howes indicated the Air Force had produced no additional information.

The general's version of the meeting was different. He claimed the Radulovich case had not been specifically mentioned. Carroll said he had gone to the paper to explain that the security-risk criteria applied in cases like Radulovich's was not unilateral action by the Air Force, but of broader national policy. He did admit, however, that the paper's outspoken comments on the case had prompted his trip to Detroit.[1]

The Air Force Association announced it intended to conduct a study of the Lt. Milo Radulovich hearing. According to the Detroit squadron commander, Lt. Col. Irving Kempner, "If this case is as it appears—if Radulovich was prejudged and had to prove himself not guilty—then we will ask the national headquarters to take action."

Kempner called the association's national headquarters in Washington and voiced the concerns of his members. He wanted to know if the Air Force had additional information on Milo. If they didn't, he had told them, he would demand the association take a position that called for Milo's immediate exoneration.

Kempner's threat would not be viewed as hollow. The thirty-five thousand-member association had long been valued by the Air Force for its lobbying clout on Capitol Hill. Michigan's award-winning Vandenburg chapter had worn the distinction of being one of the more valued affiliates across the country.

———————⟫●⟪———————

The *Detroit News* again took to their editorial page in defense of Milo, this time with an attack on Air Force Regulation 35-62. "The regulation is self-contradictory," said the News. "It employs words to mean whatever it pleases, neither more nor less. It applies the word 'honorable' to a type of discharge which at the same time dishonors the man by calling him a poor risk."[2]

———————⟫●⟪———————

In a memo to Tolson—duly routed to and checked by Belmont and Ladd—Nichols wrote that Paul Leach of the *Chicago Daily News* had called and asked for information, and any advice the bureau could provide, about a story on Milo Radulovich. Nichols reminded Tolson that "most of the information contained in the Air Force charges against Milo Radulovich is based upon Bureau investigation."[3] He also pointed out that two nights before, Edward R. Murrow had devoted a full half hour to the Radulovich case. "In view of this background," Nichols wrote, "Leach was advised there was no comment the Bureau could make on this matter whatsoever."[4]

⟶➤●◄⟵

The French Indochina war continued to spark controversy in Paris. As the French National Assembly prepared to debate the country's ongoing involvement in the unpopular conflict, the government maintained that the shortest route to a settlement was through a strengthening of the French and Indochinese forces.

French involvement in the Indochina war had been underwritten financially by the United States. Harold Callender observed: "Rarely if ever has a war been fought in the paradoxical conditions of that in Indo-China. There a European power fights to defend a former Oriental colony in the interest of a Western coalition led by an anti-colonial power. The states of Indo-China depend upon France for their defense while France depends upon the United States to finance that defense."[5]

Secretary of Defense Charles E. Wilson traveled to the University of Michigan to deliver the School of Engineering's centennial convocation. In a press conference before the speech, Wilson was questioned on the status of University of Michigan student Milo Radulovich. Wilson said a final decision on the case might come at any time and that he expected it would sustain the board's finding that Radulovich be discharged.

The secretary's comments about Milo included the following statement.

> It is one of these difficult kinds of problems where you don't want to do an individual an injustice, but you don't want the nation to be harmed. It looks as though we were giving the individual too much of a break. In cases of doubtful loyalty, the interests of the nation should come first. Working for the government is a privilege, not a right. There are other things you can do for a living. We've been a little soft in resolving cases in favor of the individual rather than the nation. We're going to be strict. We're going to be fair, but we're going to resolve cases in favor of the government.[1]

In a direct reference to Milo, Wilson also said, "There apparently was a conflict of interest here in which the family and the country were involved. Perhaps someone who couldn't resolve this conflict between his family and his country would be better off making a living somewhere else."[2]

Wilson's remarks at the press conference differed markedly from those delivered later in the day. In the conclusion of his convocation address, he said:

> There is a third great pioneering movement....It is our great pioneering experiment in government and in human freedom. It recognizes the essential dignity and inherent importance of the individual and his inalienable personal rights. Ours was perhaps the first government ever established to promote the welfare of all the citizens rather than the aggrandizement of the state or the rulers thereof or to benefit a privileged few. In the declaration of principles that made possible the United States of America this great discovery or principle was recognized in the words 'to secure these rights governments are instituted.' The rights referred to are life, liberty and the pursuit of happiness—individual rights that are above and beyond the rights than may be conferred upon. . .any other group. The Constitution of our country was designed in part to protect the citizens against any attempt by even government itself to invade these inalienable rights. Our political invention, based on the religious concept of the sacredness of the individual, has given our people personal freedom and has gone far toward fulfilling the age-old hopes and aspirations of man. In our political system the state is the servant of the people; the people are not the serfs of the state.[3]

Reached at his home in Dexter, Milo said that if Air Force Secretary Harold Talbott had made his ruling, he had not been made aware of it. Milo also said that if he were not exonerated of the charges, he intended to carry his battle into the federal courts.

—⟫●⟪—

If Secretary of State Wilson had perused the Detroit newspapers on the morning of his visit, or if Maj. Gen. Joseph Carroll had decided to begin monitoring those same newspapers to gauge the impact of his visit earlier in the week, both would have discovered an entire section of letters to the editor in the *Detroit Free Press*, all supportive of Milo.[4]

SATURDAY, OCTOBER 24, 1953

Tight-lipped military officials, previously unwilling to discuss the Milo Radulovich case—even in private—broke their silence in an "off the record" interview with *Detroit News* reporter Gordon A. Harrison. "Unnamed sources" told Harrison that the appeal of Lieutenant Radulovich would be denied. All agencies had completed their reviews and Secretary Talbott's decision was expected within a few days.[1] The evidence against Milo, said the sources, warranted dismissal as a security risk.

The case against Lieutenant Radulovich, Harrison's sources revealed, was far more severe than had been publicly expressed. They said that all the facts in the case had not and could not be publicized.

The government's position was described as wholly untenable. According to Harrison's Pentagon sources, the Air Force had not been able to dismiss Radulovich on the basis of disclosed evidence without igniting a public outcry. Conversely, they had been prevented by law and reasons of national security from justifying their case in public. After the ruling was announced, they said, the Air Force had planned to brace itself for yet another onslaught of public contempt.

The unusually talkative officials discussed what they believed was a far more exhaustive review of evidence by the Air Force than would have been undertaken had the Radulovich case occurred in another branch of the military. After the first complaints, Air Force intelligence officers had conducted their own investigation to determine if

231

there was sufficient evidence to proceed. After they had conferred with the FBI, all evidence was reviewed again by Air Force legal officers. The Air Force, according to Harrison's sources, was on solid legal ground.

The officials said the lengthy review of the Radulovich case was by no means a formality, that in other cases decisions often had been reversed and at various junctures in the appeal process. In light of an extensive internal examination by Air Force lawyers and intelligence officers, the unanimity of opinion regarding Radulovich, they said, warranted considerable weight.

Charlie Lockwood knew a coordinated campaign when he saw it. The comments by Defense Secretary Wilson at the previous day's press conference, the unexplained willingness of previously mum sources to go "off the record"—to Lockwood, a veteran of many court-of-public-opinion battles, it was all too coincidental.

"Wilson and the Pentagon say the case has already been decided and they haven't even got our information," Lockwood commented.[2] Under provisions of Air Force Regulation 35-62, Milo and his attorneys had twenty days from the date of the ruling—or until November 3—to present additional evidence. Lockwood said Wilson's statements, coupled with the Pentagon leak, was clear evidence that a decision on the case had been reached before the hearing even began.

———————

White House Press Secretary James C. Hagerty disclosed that between May 27 and September 30 of the current year, 1,456 government workers had been fired or forced to resign for security reasons. Of that number, 863 workers had been dismissed and the remaining 593 had resigned because of security checks. "In all of the resignation cases the agencies and departments had unfavorable reports on these employees," Hagerty said.[3] He also pointed out that the government did not intend to release any of the names.

U nnamed sources" had once again become available for off-the-record comments on the Milo Radulovich case. A *Detroit Free Press* article said persons close to Air Force Headquarters in Washington believed that scheduled reviews by the Air Force Personnel Board, the judge advocate general, and Air Force Secretary Harold Talbott would uphold the verdict that had directed Milo's dismissal. They also indicated that a statement on the case could be expected in a day or two.[1]

Attorney Charles Lockwood announced that he intended to take the Radulovich case into federal court. He cited Defense Secretary Wilson's statement two days earlier as evidence that top military officials had arrived at a verdict long before Milo's guaranteed appeals had been exhausted. Lockwood said the move was needed to safeguard the lieutenant's constitutional rights. "I am going to make every effort to have the proceedings transferred to the Federal Court because it is all too apparent that the entire proceeding has been prejudged and that the defendant has not had his day in court," Lockwood explained.[2]

Lockwood also cited portions of a telegram he had sent to Talbott about the provision in AFR 35-62 that guaranteed Milo an opportunity to supply additional material. In it he said, "On Oct. 13, 1953, Lt. Milo Radulovich was notified by the Air Force that he had been given 20 days in which to file any brief, argument or further information before the Air Force Personnel Board. We demand that this agreement be kept."[3]

Lockwood and cocounsel Ken Sanborn also attacked recent claims by the Air Force about additional evidence that purportedly justified Milo's discharge. "Under the regulations we are entitled to be confronted by all the evidence they have," Lockwood said. "Now in order to alibi themselves they intimate they have to keep some back for security reasons."[4] Sanborn harkened back to the hearing where the board president, William Doolan, had expressly denied there were additional charges beyond what had been included in the Statement of Reasons.

———————

Milo had been the beneficiary of media attention for more than a month, ever since Russell Harris's article on September 23. Whenever the Radulovich story had seemed in danger of leaving the public eye, appropriate nourishment in the form of additional information, a new twist, arrived. The original article had been followed by the hearing. Then came the hearing verdict. Although each event had added to the body of the story, it also gave the press an opportunity to revisit the case, to recite yet another time the injustice of what the government had done to this nice young man with a pretty wife and two children.

Because of the "See It Now" show, the Milo Radulovich story was alive and well once again. Newspapers across the country had taken note of the broadcast and not only stepped up their support for Milo but also renewed their attacks on the Air Force.

The *Chicago Daily Sun-Times* said in an editorial, "Murrow deserves much credit for bringing the case forcefully to the attention of the American public....No American who is loyal—as the Air Force Board concedes Radulovich is—can be made disloyal by the acts of others. Like virtue, loyalty is a personal thing."[5]

In his *New York Times* column on the Sunday after the "See It Now" broadcast on Milo, Jack Gould wrote of more than the Radulovich case. He also awarded the program, along with Murrow and Friendly, a page in history. The Radulovich show, he wrote, "was not just a superb and fighting documentary. It was a long step forward in television journalism." He noted it was the first time a television program had taken "a vigorous editorial stand in a matter of national importance and controversy." He concluded that "everyone connected with the program can be proud."[6]

Edward R. Murrow aside, the Air Force had also fanned the flame of public interest. Its claim of additional evidence against Milo that could not be released for fear of jeopardizing national security did not go unnoticed by the press. In yet another editorial on Milo, the *Detroit News* said, "The Air Force says there are better reasons [for separating Milo from the military], but are of such a hush-hush nature they cannot be revealed....When supposedly competent evidence is thus suppressed, and the people are asked to take on faith the good will and virtue of their institutions, there is no court of last resort for the preservation of human rights under the Constitution. What has happened to Radulovich can happen to any other man."[7]

———————

In 1946, life had been exciting for handsome, young, unmarried lieutenants in the nation's capital. Women substantially outnumbered the men. Clerks and stenographers, recruited from high schools and secretarial institutes across the country to staff the many bureaus of government, accounted for the imbalance.

New gold bars on Lt. Milo Radulovich's crisply starched uniform, coupled with his unmarried status, had secured his place on a number of invitation lists to the many parties in carefree postwar Washington. "I dated very little while growing up," Milo says. "My dad was always after me to hit the books. When I got away from home, dating was one of the things I tried to catch up on."

Additionally, Margaret Radulovich had made sure her brother was invited to the diplomatic receptions at the Yugoslavian Embassy where she worked as a secretary, although he attended only one. "The young staff had more fun after all the dignitaries left," she recalls. "We'd talk and dance Viennese waltzes and the tango all night long."

Given his active social life, Milo did not think it out of the ordinary when he got a call one October afternoon in 1946 from a Mrs. Betty Razun inviting him to a party that evening. Although Mrs. Razun was a stranger, Milo was not uncomfortable with the invitation, especially when she said the gathering was for people of Yugoslavian descent. Always at the ready to expand his social calendar, he quickly accepted.

Milo called a friend, Walter Boskovich, a clerk and chauffeur in the Military Attaché's Office at the Yugoslavian Embassy, to see if he would also like to attend. Boskovich was committed to a social function at the embassy that evening and begged off.

The party was fun; a few drinks, some idle chatter, certainly nothing out of the ordinary. There was some political talk but that was to be expected given the turmoil in Yugoslavia at the time. Most of the attendees were pro-Mihailovic, the Royalist general whose army had been defeated by Tito's Partisans.

A few days later Milo spoke to Margaret and told her about the party, casually volunteering that politics had been discussed. The crowd appeared to be pro-Mihailovic, he told her, but he didn't participate in any of the political discussions.

About a month later, shortly after eight o'clock one morning, Milo received a phone call from Mrs. Razun. She was upset and denounced him for calling the embassy to say that the party he had attended was a "Chetnik" meeting.* The implication was clear: Mrs. Razun had

*Chetnik being a name used to describe pro-Mihailovic fighters in Yugoslavia.

accused Milo of spying for the embassy—the Tito-controlled, Communist embassy. Moreover, she said he had used his uniform as a front, and then refused to elaborate on her comment. Milo bristled at the charge and their conversation turned testy. Unbeknown to Milo, a colonel had been listening on the line. Although he refused to identify himself, the colonel interrupted the conversation and berated Milo for being impolite to Mrs. Razun. Milo shrugged off the colonel's comments. "He was just trying to impress the lady," he said.

After the call from Mrs. Razun, Milo quickly phoned his friend Walter Boskovich and told him of the conversation. Boskovich assured him that he had told no one of Milo's attendance at the party.

United States military personnel are instructed to immediately report any questionable contacts to their immediate supervisor. Lieutenant Radulovich followed procedure and reported the incident to his commanding officer, Capt. Anthony Pauson. On Pauson's advice Milo prepared a written statement for counterintelligence that recounted the party and subsequent phone call.

The next day, while Milo was being interviewed by FBI Special Agent Langdon C. Tennis, another piece of information was dislodged. He recalled experiencing some discomfort at the party when a woman had pointed at him and whispered loud enough to hear that his sister worked at the embassy.

Lieutenant Radulovich had carefully adhered to standing military orders and thought the matter closed. In January 1947, he returned to Texas for flight school, but left a few months later without graduating and returned to Washington in late spring where he was assigned to the Pentagon.

Among the young ladies who had gone to the nation's capital after the war was Nancy Tuttle of Lewiston, Maine. Strikingly attractive, she was a telephone operator and at the urging of a girlfriend, had transferred to Washington. Nancy moved into the same building as Milo but if it weren't for a friend, they would never have met. But meet they did.

Concerns over conspiracies and colonels trying to impress clerks quickly faded. With the cherry blossoms of Washington as a backdrop, the handsome lieutenant courted the pretty New Englander and they fell in love.

Movies, dinners, trips to Virginia Beach, sight-seeing in one of the world's great cities, and all through the eyes of young love: those were fun times remembered warmly by Milo.

Notions of being a pilot behind him, Lt. Milo Radulovich had developed a fascination with weather. He applied for and was accepted to study meteorology at New York University. Milo moved to New York in early September 1947, but his heart remained in a Washington rooming house. A few weeks later he took the train to Washington and on September 27 married Nancy in the rectory of the Church of the Nativity.

The marriage did not sit well back in Detroit. Nancy was not Serbian, much less Montenegrin. Worse than that, she was Roman Catholic. John Radulovich was so upset that he refused to talk to Milo. The nuptials did not set well with the Tuttles back in Maine, either. "Marrying a man with a long foreign name was not 'old New England style,'" Milo laughs.

The following May, Milo graduated from meteorology school. Ironically, he drew an assignment to Selfridge Field in Mount Clemens, Michigan, not far from his home in Detroit. The new assignment had afforded his growing family the chance to get to know his parents, and his brothers and sister. Things were tense for a while but on August 9, the coolness vanished forever when Diane Radulovich was born.

In 1947, Ikonija Radulovich had taken ill and Margaret returned home to care for her mother. This was fine with her father, who had begun to fear for Margaret's safety. A growing repressive political atmosphere in the old country, he felt, did not bode well for those who worked at the Yugoslavian Embassy.

Although Milo saw Margaret occasionally when they lived in Washington, that dwindled. The new marriage understandably had occupied most of his free time. After Margaret had moved back to Detroit, Milo and Nancy would sometimes come to Sunday dinner at the home of their parents. But men in the Radulovich house didn't talk politics with the women, and the dinners were mostly social.

When viewed through the looking glass of the FBI—the party at Mrs. Razun's, her phone call, Milo's conversations with Margaret and Walter Boskovich, Milo's courtship and marriage to Nancy—all looked much different.

On November 6, 1946—the day Mrs. Razun called—Milo penned his account of the party and the Razun phone call. He pointed out that some political discussions had taken place at the party but he had not participated in them. A few days after the party, Milo wrote, he visited his sister and told her of the evening's events. He also said in the report that he had mentioned the invitation to Walter Boskovich and invited him along that evening, and that Margaret and Walter were the only two people he told about the party. Finally, Milo recounted the call from Mrs. Razun and how she had accused him of spying for the embassy and using his uniform as a front.

The following day, Milo was interviewed by Special Agent Tennis, whose report was mostly a recitation of Milo's statement. During the interview, however, Milo recalled the incident at the party when he was singled out as the brother of someone who worked at the embassy. In an "Agent's Note" at the conclusion of the report, Tennis commented: "The fact that this woman, reportedly knowing Lt. RADULOVICH's sister, who attended the gathering was not known to Lt. RADULOVICH by name is unsatisfactorily explained."[8]

Three weeks before Milo had written out his account of the party and phone call from Mrs. Razun, the Milorad Radulovich file had already received its first entry. In an internal FBI memo from E. G. Fitch to Mr. Ladd, dated October 15, 1946, Col. L. R. Forney had informed the Military Intelligence Division (MID) that an informant had accused Milo of giving information to the Yugoslav Military Attaché. The informant's name is blacked out on the memo, but Forney indicates that he [Forney] "can establish contact with the informant and set up the same arrangement with the informant and the Bureau as now exists with [name blacked out]." Scrawled across the bottom of the memo is a message that says, "Don't start invest[igation] now—wait for more data from informant."[9] Mrs. Razun did not invite Milo to any additional parties.

On November 15, a week after Milo had written his account of the Razun incident, he was mentioned again, this time in a confidential internal memo from Fitch to Ladd. Mention was made that Milo had given information to the Yugoslavian legation. There was no notation, however, that for his part Milo had carefully followed military procedure and volunteered this information in his own sworn statement. Reading the FBI file, an assumption could easily be drawn that this vital piece of *intelligence* was "dug up" during an investigation. The report also noted that his sister had worked for the Yugoslavian legation and that "his father is a prominent Serbian Communist in Detroit."[10]

The reference to John Radulovich as a "prominent Serbian Communist" is ridiculed by both Milo and Margaret. "That's just stupid," Milo says. "He could barely speak English. Some Communist leader." Margaret echoes her brother: "It's laughable, but it doesn't surprise me."

John Radulovich first caught the attention of the FBI in an incident involving his sons Walter and Sam. A confidential informant advised the bureau that he first came in contact with the Radulovich family in 1943 at a time when the Serbian Orthodox Church had been conducting a church school for Serbian children. John Radulovich, said the informant, withdrew his children from the school because Chetnik songs were being sung. The report said, "Subject [John Radulovich] termed such songs as fascist and reactionary and states he would not have his children participate in them. Subject is of Montenegran [*sic*] nationality and is described as being stubborn and uneducated, follows the line of Communism in his activities. He belongs to the Serbian Progressive Club 'Vaso Pelagich' described by the informant as a pro-communist club for Serbians in Detroit."[11]

At the time two separate factions sought the support of Serbs around the world—the Monarchists, who were controlled by Draza Mihailovic, and the Communists, who were led by Marshal Tito. Wary of Mihailovic's ties to the Nazis, the United States supported Tito. Margaret says the school incident involved her brother's refusal to stand for a Chetnik battle song of the Mihailovic loyalists.

An angry John Radulovich wrote an article in *Slobodna Rec* about the incident. "After that," Margaret says, "the word was out. People wouldn't go near John Radulovich." Although acknowledging her history of involvement in Communist-related causes, she firmly believes the action taken against Milo stemmed from vengeful members of Detroit's close-knit Serbian community who had not forgotten the church school episode.

In his review of Ray Bradbury's Fahrenheit 451, *Orville Prescott wrote, "We fear the future. We fear the absolute power of states more tyrannical than the tyrannies of the past because they strive to rule men's minds as well as their bodies. And writers [such as Bradbury] who can imagine the dreadful details of such a future more vividly than the rest of us, write books capable of troubling our sleep indefinitely."[12]*

Fahrenheit 451 told of a fireman whose job it was to burn books. Books, in Bradbury's not too distant future, were banned as useless and threatening to the establishment. The title refers to the temperature at which paper burns.

MONDAY, OCTOBER 26, 1953

The Milo Radulovich discharge story made *Newsweek*.[1] Titled "One Man's Family," the article focused on efforts by the Air Force to convince Milo that denouncing his family would have been in his best interest.

Actor Larry Parks, who hadn't worked since his startling admission two years earlier that he had been a Communist, announced that he had been signed to do a television movie. The star of The Jolson Story *said that we all must pay for our mistakes and he felt no bitterness toward anyone. After his testimony, Parks was commended for his honesty and cooperation by the House Un-American Activities Committee.*

Charlie Lockwood announced formation of the Radulovich Defense Committee. The intent had been to form a cadre of legal expertise from a group of prominent Detroit lawyers who had offered their help. A number of lawyers responded. Lockwood welcomed the assistance and said it would be particularly helpful before taking the case to federal court, where he had hoped to receive a fair hearing.

When asked about the military appeal that had been pending, Lockwood said he believed the Air Force had already reached a verdict and that had prompted him to petition the federal courts to consider the Radulovich case. The attorney also said that he intended to appeal the case right up to the president, but given Eisenhower's military background he felt it would be only a formality.

Lockwood also challenged the Air Force's contention that all the information on Milo had yet to be released. Referring to the telegram he had sent Talbott, Lockwood said, "I told the secretary that statements the Air Force has more evidence other than that published 'was a lie' in exactly those words."[1]

<hr />

Apart from the case, things had not been going well for the Radulovich family. Milo's godfather had stopped speaking to him. Word was out in the Serbian community to stay away from John Radulovich's house: it was being watched. And, when a drunken

243

neighbor became abusive to Margaret, Milo had to throw him out of the house.

Margaret and husband, Al, had gone to visit her parents. When they arrived, a neighbor, known for his frequent drunkenness, was already there. "He kept calling me 'the commissar'," Margaret says, "'the commissar, the commissar.'" It got so bad that John Radulovich thought it best that Margaret leave. Margaret and Al were preparing to depart when Milo entered. Seeing that his sister was upset, and quickly discerning why, an angry Milo ordered the neighbor from the house.

"Yeah, I got mad," Milo says. "The guy was drunk and he had no business saying the things he did."

⸺⸻⸺

"[J. Edgar] Hoover was very close to Hearst columnist George Sokolsky and checked matters with him, through [Louis] Nichols almost daily for twenty years," writes Reeves."[2] The FBI considered Sokolsky reliable. He could be trusted to use leaked information in his column and, of critical importance to Hoover, he protected the bureau as his source. "Sok" and "Edgar" were philosophical soul mates in the battle against communism.

It was a two-way street. Sokolsky's privileged status at the FBI was a veritable gold mine for a national columnist—an endless stream of tidbits from the bureau's bottomless pit of information from their files on the famous and powerful. Sokolsky's path to those files went through the office of Louis B. Nichols, Hoover's liaison with the press and protector of the bureau's image. Nichols, in an internal memo, once referred to Sokolsky as "a great American. A Great Jew, too."

In a phone call to Nichols about the Radulovich case, Sokolsky had indicated he felt it reprehensible and un-Christian to visit the sins of the father on the son.[3] Further, he thought the Air Force's action of saying that Milo was not a security risk and then firing him was unexplainable. Sokolsky had already written a story in which he charged the Air Force had woefully mishandled the Radulovich case. After the article appeared, Sokolsky told Nichols the Air Force had called him and tried to refute the contents of his story, but during the conversation had volunteered that the FBI was the source of its case.

Sokolsky asked Nichols if the bureau had additional information on Milo, and also for any advice on how he should proceed. In full knowledge that the Air Force had acted on material provided by the FBI, Nichols advised Sokolsky "that the investigation had been handled essentially by the military authorities…and that it would not be possible to give him any guidance except to be cautious."

However untruthful, Nichols's response had come as no surprise. In June 1949, the bureau had been publicly embarrassed over a court-ordered release of its files. The case involved Judith Coplon, a Justice Department employee who had been accused of giving information to the Russians. She claimed the papers in question were not a threat to national security and, despite strenuous objections from the bureau, a judge ordered the documents released.* It was the first time FBI files had ever been viewed by the public. According to Anthony Summers, Hoover's concern wasn't national security; he was worried about the files "because they were a mishmash of unchecked tittle-tattle."[4] During the trial it was learned the FBI had bugged privileged communications between Coplon and her attorney. The records and disks of the conversations were destroyed but in such a manner that Hoover would had to have known about it. Summers says the incident brought Truman as close as he ever came to firing Hoover.

Nichols recommended to Tolson: "I think if we have not already done so, Liaison should secure full details from the Air Force and ascertain the basis for their actions in dismissing him [Milo], and if it is on their own material rather than that set forth in our report, then I think we should make an issue out of this with the Air Force, which should not of course, divulge our source of information [Sokolsky]."[5]

---

*Hoover appealed unsuccessfully to the president.

———⫸⊙⫷———

Was the Air Force scrambling to salvage whatever dignity it could from what had become a public-relations disaster? Was it attempting to sow a seed of doubt in the American people and suggest that perhaps the Air Force had been on far more stable ground in the Radulovich case than the country had been led to believe? Was it carefully orchestrating a campaign of leaks to the press that conveniently involved "classified" information the cloak of national security would prevent from ever being released? Or did it have solid evidence, as it had strongly intimated over the past week, that Milo and his family deserved a security-risk label?

The Milo Radulovich FBI file was riddled with inaccurate and inane entries. Documentation was loose at best and depended heavily on hearsay and unnamed sources. One of the few threads of consistency was the significance that had been attached to any comment Milo may have uttered in favor of Tito, despite the fact that Tito enjoyed the support of the United States government.

If there were a hidden time bomb in the Radulovich file with the ability to transmute public opinion—as the Air Force had suggested—it was well hidden.

Informants were divided into categories; some were referred to as "reliable," others as "believed reliable." One "reliable" informant said in a report,[6] "Margaret's two older brothers, Milorad and William had been active in the Communist cause prior to leaving their home in Detroit."*

---

*The "reliable" informant sorely missed the mark. Margaret had no older brothers— she was the oldest child in the family. Milo left home shortly after graduation from high school. Other than wrestling, he participated in few extracurricular activities. To suggest he was an active Communist in high school is bordering on ludicrous. Margaret had no brother named William. Further, it was obvious to Milo that the informant was more than likely a Serb. Only a Serb would refer to Milo as Milorad.

There was an order to put a mail cover on Milo's residence for thirty days, but no evidence that it was ever done. One report from a neighbor indicated that a well-dressed man with a heavy briefcase visited the Radulovich house each week and remained for about five minutes. When he left, the family usually read pamphlets that had been left and then discussed them in a foreign language. "That was the insurance man," Margaret laughs. "We all had those nickel policies and he came around and collected the premium every week. And the language sure wasn't foreign to us." The same neighbor was asked if she had ever heard the family make any remarks that could be considered derogatory toward the United States government. She said Mrs. John Radulovich was once overheard to say that "the bigshots are running everything." Several references indicated Milo supported Tito, but then so did the United States government. The fact that Milo's parents were not enamored with his choice of Nancy as a bride is also mentioned frequently.*

Throughout Milo's file were references to his father and sister. The litany of charges that later surfaced as the Statement of Reasons was easily identified and mentioned frequently. The mail delivered to the home of John Radulovich had been monitored and cataloged. Reports listed delivery of the *Worker* and the *Daily Worker*; both, however, had been addressed to Margaret. John Radulovich, said one report, had signed a petition that would have provided a place on the 1946 ballot for the Communist party. The petition with his name was in the file.

In a report dated November 1, 1949, a "reliable informant" stated that John Radulovich was very active in all Communist activities among Serbian groups. He was, the informant added, strongly pro-Tito. The same report indicated that during Margaret's tenure of employment at the Yugoslavian Embassy, all American employees were either pro-Communist or pro-Tito.† Margaret had been singled

---

*There is no mention, however, that after Diane was born differences were forgotten.
†Given the fact that Tito was in power, being pro-Tito should not have been considered out of the ordinary.

out as one of the two most dangerous women employees in the Yugoslavian Embassy, and that she would stop at nothing to further the aims of the Communist party.[7]

A report dated May 24, 1950, illustrates how information was gathered and recorded. An unnamed classmate of Milo's from officer's candidate school in Texas sat with agents who prepared and filed the following report.[8]

> —the informant had know Milo since 1946.

> —the informant considered Milo to be radical in his beliefs and a type of person who could be easily led into Communism, although he did not consider Milo to be a Communist.

> —the informant said Milo had on numerous occasions criticized both the government and the armed forces, although he could provide no specific instances.

After their commissions, Milo and the informant had been stationed in the Washington, D.C., area. They ended up living at the same boardinghouse. The report continued:

> —the informant heard rumors around the boarding house that Milo had twice visited the Russian embassy and that he had attended a number of Communist front meetings, although he could not state the source of any of these rumors.

> —the informant said Milo often went out in the evening alone. When asked where he was going, Milo often replied to see his sister.

"That's ludicrous," Milo says of the charges in the file. "I visited the Russian Embassy twice! How do things like that get started?"

Whether the Milo Radulovich file qualified as a "mishmash of unchecked tittle-tattle," if released it would have been embarrassing to a number of governmental agencies.

―――――⟩●⟨―――――

At the annual meeting of Southern Indiana, Inc., a business promotion-
al organization in the Hoosier State, Sen. William E. Jenner dismissed
notions that the Senate Internal Security Subcommittee was involved
in witch-hunting. "We are hunting rats," said the Indiana senator.
"Communist rats. And the ridding of these rats is not just a committee
job—we need the support of all Americans."[9]

In his speech Jenner disclosed that most of the Communists in
education who had been called before the subcommittee were originally reported by university presidents. Those presidents, said Jenner,
were unable to cope with Communist teachers.

THURSDAY, OCTOBER 29, 1953

From the day in 1946 when Joe McCarthy had declared his candidacy for the United States Senate against incumbent Robert La Follette, William T. Evjue, owner, editor, and publisher of the *Capital Times*, had been an avowed enemy. The Madison, Wisconsin, paper had dogged McCarthy throughout the campaign with charges that some of his relatives had contributed well beyond their means. Evjue also had cast a jaundiced eye at McCarthy's claims of wartime heroism in the Pacific theater. Evjue's scrutiny and criticism had continued throughout McCarthy's Senate career.

The *Capital Times* had finally weighed in on the Radulovich case. Evjue wrote: "Here is a man [Milo] whose name and life are being destroyed because of alleged acts of others over whose conduct he had no control. Here is a man who must suffer because in this country we have adopted the principle of guilt by blood relationship, one of the most primitive and barbaric of any rule in any system of justice."[1]

Charlie Lockwood used his weekly *Eastside Shopper* column to discuss the Milo Radulovich case. After he had quoted Colonel Doolan in the hearing transcript as saying the Air Force had no additional information on Milo, Lockwood vented his own feelings: "Let me make a prediction—you are going to hear a great deal about the Radulovich case in the days ahead, and sooner or later Lt. Radulovich will be completely vindicated."[2]

———⫸●⫷———

Charles Lockwood and Ken Sanborn submitted their supplemental brief to the Air Force five days early. It had been drafted by Sanborn and was an eloquent overview of the case. Sanborn systematically listed each of the government's points, and then meticulously refuted them. He also cited the comments of Defense Secretary Charles Wilson from the previous week as evidence the military had decided the fate of Lieutenant Radulovich long before his appeals had been exhausted.

Sanborn minced few words. "From what has transpired," he wrote, "we can only assume that as soon as this brief is filed an adverse decision will be announced. This will be in keeping with the shameful and undemocratic practices and procedures so far indulged in by the Air Force, and will complete the whole disgraceful and sordid record of the Radulovich case."[3]

———⫸●⫷———

A suit was filed in the Superior Court of Los Angeles by three persons against Bing Crosby, charging the crooner with driving his foreign-made car "at a wanton and reckless rate of speed in violation of traffic controls and while under the influence of intoxicating liquors."

The suit stemmed from an early morning accident three weeks earlier in which Crosby's car collided with a car driven by city fireman Frank Verdugo. Verdugo and the two other passengers in his car suffered serious injuries and were still hospitalized. Crosby was not injured in the crash.

On September 27, shortly after the first flurry of publicity had sur-faced about Milo, Harriet Chidester read of the case in a *New York Times* article and was moved to write a letter to "The Commanding General, U.S. Air Force, Washington, D.C." She had called the charges "preposterous and dangerous," adding, "This is not even guilt by association. It is guilt by association once removed." She concluded by saying, "Those who want him dismissed should at the very least be severely reprimanded."[1]

Instead of answering the letter, the Air Force chose to investigate Harriet Chidester. In a communication to "the Honorable J. Edgar Hoover," Air Force Lt. Col. Ralph Ravenburg, of the OSI, wrote, "A search of the files of this office has not revealed any record pertaining to Harriet Chidester. It would be appreciated if any information avail-able to your agency concerning that individual would be furnished this office."[2]

The controversial movie The Moon Is Blue *was banned in New Jersey. New Jersey police confiscated the film, claiming it was "obscene, inde-cent, immoral and tending to corrupt the morals of citizens."[3] After a private showing, Superior Court Judge Thomas J. Stanton character-ized the film as "somewhat boring" even though he upheld the police action.*

The trial of six Michigan Communists had begun in Detroit's federal court. The six, who had been charged under the federal Smith Act, were accused of conspiring to teach and advocate violent overthrow of the government.

In opening remarks the prosecution said it would show specific instances where the defendants attended Communist meetings, recruited new members, and distributed party propaganda—activities they would have to prove were a clear and present danger to the country. The government had already successfully prosecuted nearly fifty Communists in seven other Smith Act trials across the country.

Only three of the defendants were represented by counsel; the other three had chosen to defend themselves. The decision to reject formal counsel by the three had been reached two weeks earlier after a clash of opinions about legal strategy with their attorney, Ernest Goodman.

"I agreed to handle the case," Goodman explained, "on the basis that I would be fighting in that courtroom for the First Amendment—for the right to teach the overthrow of government by force and violence. That should be protected by the Constitution. And they agreed."[1] However, the six had decided among themselves that the legal proceedings were the embodiment of fascism in America and wanted their defense based on that premise. Goodman told his clients they should seek other counsel.

254

Two days later a compromise was reached. It was decided three of the defendants would be represented by Goodman and fight the charges on the basis that their First Amendment rights had been violated. The other three would mount a defense based on a contention that the proceedings and the court had been rooted in fascism.

Judge Frank A. Picard had granted the prosecution and both factions of the defense an hour each for opening remarks. Because of the unusually long statement of Nat Ganley, one of the defendants who had chosen to represent himself, Picard did not adjourn the first day's proceedings until after 6:00 p.m.

On Monday, October 19, television's host supreme, Arthur Godfrey, fired singer Julius La Rosa—on the air. At program's end, just as La Rosa had completed his number, Godfrey announced, "That was Julie's swan song." Longtime bandleader Archie Bleyer was also fired from two of Godfrey's three shows. Godfrey claimed La Rosa and Bleyer had violated agreements by pursuing outside employment without permission.

Bleyer admitted to making a record with "breakfast clubber" Don McNeill in Chicago. "McNeill is on ABC and in competition with us," Godfrey said. "Archie is an outstanding gentleman, but he used my show just to get money and make records."[2]

Most of the publicity, however, centered on the twenty-three-year-old La Rosa. In the weeks that followed the firings, Godfrey continued his public criticism of La Rosa, claiming the singer had lost his humility. "When he used to hit the wrong note, he used to turn his head, and you could see tears coming down his cheeks," Godfrey explained. "He hasn't done that for a year."[3]

Rumors had also surfaced that Godfrey was upset over La Rosa's romantic interest in Dorothy McGuire of the singing McGuire Sisters, also members of the "Godfrey family." McGuire, who was married, denied the involvement. La Rosa, however, said he intended to marry her.[4]

J. Edgar Hoover was not about to be blindsided. The director had become concerned over the growing notion that Air Force action against Milo had stemmed from reports generated by the FBI. In an internal memo to his top brain trust—Tolson, Ladd, Belmont, and Nichols—Hoover said, "In view of the recent dismissal from the Air Force Reserve of Lieutenant Radulovitch [sic], and the alleged statement having been made by the Armed Services that this action was taken upon a report submitted by the FBI, I desire that a detailed brief, containing all the facts in this matter, be prepared, properly indexed, so it may be readily available for reference. Very truly yours, John Edgar Hoover, Director."

With Hoover directly involved, and with claims swirling around that the information used to discharge Milo had originated from FBI files, the Radulovich case had quickly been elevated in importance within the bureau. In a memo to Ladd, Belmont wrote that columnist George Sokolsky had been advised that the bureau had conducted very little of the Radulovich investigation and that the Air Force should be contacted to determine where it got its information. "If it was found that the Air Force had actually based their action upon military reports and then had claimed that their action was based upon FBI reports," Belmont wrote, "we should make an issue of this with the Air Force." Then he added, "The Director agreed."[1]

Belmont also pointed out that after the "See It Now" broadcast on Milo, which had been critical of the Air Force, General Carroll had traveled to Detroit to "clarify the situation in order to prevent further unfavorable publicity."[2] He concluded the memo with an admission that there had been very little derogatory information on Milo, and that Air Force action was based mainly on the files of Margaret and John, "all of which was obtained from FBI reports."[3] At some point during the memo's circulation through the bureau, someone had underlined the last statement.

In Detroit's Smith Act trial, contempt action was threatened by the federal judge, Frank A. Picard. The head of the Michigan Communist party, Saul Wellman, had bolted from his chair and called government witness and former Communist John Lautner a "stoolpigeon." Picard told Wellman that any further use of the name would result in contempt charges.

The outburst came as Lautner had been reading a list of persons who made up the hierarchy of Michigan's Communist party after it had been reorganized in 1945. Wellman had been angered by Lautner's failure to note the asterisks next to certain names, which designated World War II veteran status.

THURSDAY, NOVEMBER 5, 1953

In a rare instance of public opposition to Milo, Air Force Tech. Sgt. John A. Pedersen defended the government's action. In a letter to the *Detroit Free Press,* Pedersen wrote, "There is no more room in our armed forces today for people who cannot be trusted implicitly and who for this reason must fall under the heading 'security risk.'"[1]

------⇒⊃●⊂⇐------

Air Force Secretary Harold Talbott had invited Ed Murrow to lunch. They discussed the Radulovich case, but Talbott mostly reiterated the Air Force policy about security risks. When Murrow got back to the office he told Friendly it had been a gracious lunch but that he had detected a note of sadness when Talbott had spoken of the intransigence of the Air Force position about Milo. When asked by Friendly if he thought there was any possibility of a reversal, Murrow replied, "Not a chance."[2]

------⇒⊃●⊂⇐------

One of the first things Milo had learned about Charlie Lockwood was that there were no shades of meaning with him—he said exactly what he meant. His weekly *Eastside Shopper* column did little to dispel that notion.

"Powerful business and financial interests in this country are using witch hunts, legislative investigations, loyalty probes, etc. etc. not

257

only to uncover subversives, but also to produce fear hysteria and confusion," he wrote. "Let any reader of this newspaper start to agitate for better housing, for the enforcement of the pure food and drug acts, for equitable tax laws, for better wages and working conditions, for world-wide reduction of armaments, freedom of speech and assembly, for better medical care, and for wider public employment of our natural resources—let anyone show a marked interest in these subjects and see how soon he is labeled and regarded with suspicion."[3]

The rich and powerful were not spared the sharpness of Lockwood's pen—in particular, Defense Secretary Charles Wilson: "Wilson also said that in cases where there are conflicting loyalties or interests between one's family and one's state, the state must come first. It seems most peculiar to me that Secretary of Defense Wilson should bring up the subject of conflicting interests when he was the one who moved heaven and earth to retain his huge holdings in GM stock at the very time he was taking a most important government position which involved vast dealings with General Motors. Of course what are divided interests for humble Milo J. Radulovich are something different when applied to the Honorable Charles E. Wilson."

———————<><>———————

Ever since Abraham Lincoln was president, the Citadel had enjoyed a sterling reputation for turning out American military leaders. Through the years not much had changed at the South Carolina military college, especially for a freshman. Still known as a "Doowillie, Dumbrod, Dumbsmack, or Duwack," the lowest of the low still had to crawl for upper classmen.

A new president prepared to assume command of the tradition-steeped school. Gen. Mark Clark had arrived at the Citadel by way of World War II, Korea, and a ticker tape hero's welcome in Manhattan. Clark succeeded eighty-six-year-old Gen. Charles P. Summerall, one-time U.S. Army chief of staff.

MONDAY, NOVEMBER 9, 1953

Inevitably the Radulovich story had begun to fade from the nation's press. For the first time in nearly two months, there was nothing new in the case. Milo had returned to the University of Michigan, where he was desperately trying to get caught up with his studies.

The *Detroit Free Press* had called Milo for an update, but there wasn't much to say. He told the reporter that after the Murrow program, he had received a lot of mail, more than 150 letters from across the country. "One guy wrote and said it was God's will," he laughed. Another guy offered me asylum in Canada."[1]

Since the case had begun nearly two months earlier, Milo's deepest concern had been reserved for his father. "It's hardest on my Dad," he said. "His so-called friends who have known him for 30 years have stopped seeing him. They're all immigrants and are scared. They haven't the faintest idea of their rights. My Dad can hardly speak English. How could he have spread Communist propaganda in the factory where he works?"[2]

Milo also said the first shock of the military's attempt to discharge him had gradually given way to reality. "Unless I find an exceptional employer in the future," he lamented, "I'll have a rough time getting a job."[3]

Although scheduled to graduate the following June, Milo admitted the case had taken a severe toll on his classes, and graduation was now in serious doubt.

———⟩●⟨———

"What's good for the country is good for General Motors." Uttered by Defense Secretary Charles E. Wilson only a few months earlier, his statement had already begun to haunt him. Wilson maintained the comment had been distorted.

In an appearance before the Senate Armed Services Committee, the former General Motors chief claimed to have said "for years I have thought that what was good for our country was good for General Motors, and vice versa." He pointed out that some reporters had focused only on the "vice versa" and amplified it out of context.[4]

In a memo to the FBI director, Mr. Ladd let it be known that he was not the obstacle in securing information that had been requested on Milo Radulovich nearly two weeks earlier. "The Detroit Office was requested to submit a current report on the subject's [Milo] sister and her husband in order to prepare the detailed brief," Ladd wrote. "Detroit was advised to submit these reports by November 20, 1953, at which time this brief will be prepared."* Hoover's original request had been sent to Tolson, Ladd, Belmont, and Nichols, but Ladd's memo was directed only to Hoover.

G. David Schine, hotel heir and controversial member of Senator Joseph McCarthy's investigative staff, was inducted into the Army as a private. Schine was ordered to report for basic training at Fort Dix, New Jersey. According to an army spokesman, Schine would be treated like any other inductee.

*Memo from Ladd to Hoover, November 16, 1953.

261

TUESDAY, NOVEMBER 17, 1953

It had all the markings of high political drama—a sitting attorney general of the United States versus a former president. Washington had been consumed for the past ten days with Atty. Gen. Herbert Brownell's charge that President Harry Truman had, in 1946, appointed Harry Dexter White to the sensitive post of U.S. Director of the International Monetary Fund, and had done so in full knowledge that White was a Communist spy. In a nationwide radio address, Truman had called Brownell a liar and accused him of embracing McCarthyism for nothing more than political advantage. Brownell had been scheduled to answer Truman in testimony before the Senate Internal Security Subcommittee. In a surprise move, J. Edgar Hoover had accompanied Brownell to the standing-room-only Senate Caucus Room. Hoover's presence and his testimony had turned the hearing into a bombshell news day.*

Joe Wershba had covered the hearing. As he was leaving the committee room, Don Surine of Senator McCarthy's staff blocked his path. In a hurry to get the film back to New York for that evening's "See It Now" broadcast, Wershba politely but unsuccessfully tried to maneuver around Surine.

---

*At one point Hoover was asked if he thought Truman knew that White was a spy. Incredibly, he said that to answer such a question would be to break a long-standing FBI tradition of offering no evaluation, only situations and facts.

"I covered McCarthy in the Senate and I knew Surine," Wershba says. "We had been at a couple of gatherings but you could never get close to him. He was the gray, dark eminence with a big act of the brooding genius who was digging up all this stuff."[1]

Surine startled Wershba by asking if he knew that Murrow had once been on the Soviet payroll. That got Wershba's attention.

A former FBI agent, Surine directed the activities of McCarthy's vast informer network out of a basement office in the Capitol. His duties—unlike those of his highly visible staff counterpart, Roy Cohn—kept him out of the limelight.

They went to Surine's office where a photostat of a 1935 front-page story from the *Pittsburgh Sun Telegraph* was produced. The headline read "American Professors, Trained by Soviet, Teach in U.S. Schools." Ed Murrow was in a picture with several others: Surine had been all too willing to identify them—"Communist, Communist fronter, pro-Communist."[2]

The story referred to some American educators involved in a summer exchange program with Moscow University. The International Institute of Education, where Murrow had been employed at the time, administered the program. Arrangements on the Russian end had been through VOKS, the Soviet agency for cultural relations with foreign countries. "Mind you, Joe, I'm not saying Murrow is a Commie himself," Surine offered, "but he's one of those goddamn anti-anti-Communist, and they're just as dangerous."[3]

Surine had also referred to Murrow's brother Lacey, who was a brigadier general in the Air Force. He then implied to Wershba that if Murrow would forget about "this Radwich [Radulovich] junk," no one would have to know about his Communist background.

Wershba uncharacteristically bypassed Friendly and went directly to Murrow with the information. "I was more scared than I let on," he says. "This was my rent money, here."

Murrow had been fighting a severe cold and managed only a subdued response: "So that's what they got on me."

—————————<><>—————————

According to Bernice Fitz-Gibbon, advertising director of Gimbels Department store, graduates of girls' colleges had been hunting jobs the wrong way. The first step, she advised, was to get in touch with someone who mattered, a giant of industry, someone who could take three hours for lunch.

"What is that type of employer looking for in a secretary?" Fitz-Gibbon asked. "Short-hand speed? Dependability? Industry? Don't be silly. First and foremost, he's looking for a LOOKER." Did this mean all top executives are lecherous old wolves? Of course not, she responded, the graduates will be perfectly safe. "It does mean your intelligent, attractive girl will have a well-paid job until she marries. The big problem today is that too many college placement bureaus never dream of putting their brightest liberal-arts graduates into 'lush' secretarial jobs or the retail store business, but send them into 'fusty,' dusty publishing houses."[4]

Fitz-Gibbon's remarks were gleaned from an address to the deans and placement directors of a hundred women's colleges.

WEDNESDAY, NOVEMBER 18, 1953

After conferring with Murrow, Friendly had pumped Wershba for every last detail of the Surine encounter.

Jesse Zousmer, one of the network's top reporters, had already been dispatched to Pittsburgh in search of the infamous front-page article. Inside the *Sun Telegraph*'s archives, Zousmer discovered that the page in question had been torn out of the large book that housed past editions.

Wershba and Murrow—whose cold had dramatically improved overnight—met at the water fountain later that morning. Wershba vividly recalls the moment: "I remember him gritting his teeth and pounding one fist into the other—'The question is, when do I go against these guys.' I think that's when he made up his mind that he and Fred were going to do the story on McCarthy."

"Apparently something has slowed up the Air Force," Charlie Lockwood wrote to his cocounsel, Ken Sanborn. "I am leaving for Florida on Saturday and will be gone for four weeks."[1]

News on Milo had dwindled considerably. It had been nearly a month since Defense Secretary Wilson had assured reporters that a decision was only a couple of days away—nearly a month since an orchestrated program of leaks from the Pentagon had let it be known

265

that Air Force Secretary Talbott had decided to discharge Milo and announce that decision within a few days.

"If we get an adverse decision it might be well to appeal to the President," Lockwood had suggested. "I will keep my fingers crossed while I am strolling along the white sands of the Gulf of Mexico."

———————◦———————

On November 6, J. Edgar Hoover had requested information on Harriet Chidester, the erstwhile champion of Milo Radulovich who had written the "Commanding General" of the Air Force on his behalf. In a blunt telegram labeled "urgent" to the New Haven office, Hoover wrote, "Your reply not received to date. Handle at once and advise by immediate return when necessary information will be furnished." It was tersely signed, "Hoover."[2]

———————◦———————

Mrs. Thomas J. White, a Republican member of the Indiana State Textbook Commission, called Robin Hood *subversive and urged it be removed from bookshelves across the state. Robbing from the rich and giving to the poor was the Communist line, she claimed. "It's just a smearing of law and order and anything that disrupts law and order is their meat."*[3]

Sen. Richard Russell, a Democrat from Georgia, announced that the Senate Armed Services Committee had ordered a complete review of the Lt. Milo Radulovich case. "I understand a complete report has been requested from the Defense Department on the case," Russell wrote in a letter to Charles Lockwood. "I am sure our common objective—a fair treatment of this individual [Milo] and a maintenance of security standards necessary to the national welfare—will be achieved."[1]

⸺⸺⸺

The meeting had been set up as a private briefing on the Radulovich case. Attendance, by design, had been limited—just the major who had traveled to Detroit from the Pentagon and Irv Kempner and Phil Rosenberg from Michigan's Vandenburg chapter of the Air Force Association.

The major had begun the meeting by stating that he was under orders to thoroughly answer all questions put to him on the Radulovich case. He also said that all the information the Air Force had on Milo Radulovich was in his briefcase, and that they were welcome to examine the entire file.

Kempner and Rosenberg asked what damning information there was on Milo beyond the relationship he had with his father and sister.

The major thought for a moment and then said Milo had been seen coming in and out the Yugoslavian Embassy and that he had also socialized with people employed there.

Kempner grilled the major. Did the Air Force know if any of Milo's embassy friends had been important? The major didn't know. Did the Air Force know what information Milo was privy to that could have compromised national security? Again the major didn't know.

The meeting lasted an hour and ended affably. Kempner had two final questions, though. Was there anything in the Milo Radulovich file that hadn't been mentioned? Was there anything in the briefcase that pertained to the case that hadn't been mentioned? The answer to both questions was no. "Then you are making a hell of an error," Kempner said trying to control his anger. "If this is all you have, you are going to embarrass the hell out of the Air Force."

For whatever reason, President Dwight D. Eisenhower had discarded his prepared speech to the B'nai B'rith Anti-Defamation League in Washington. Instead he invoked a folksy, straight-from-the-shoulder style to the distinguished gathering and bluntly spoke his mind about the right of all Americans to face their accusers.

Eisenhower talked of growing up in Abilene, Kansas, where Wild Bill Hickock had once been the marshal. "If you don't know about him, read your westerns more," the president suggested.[2] "That town had a code," he continued, "and I was raised as a boy to prize that code. It was: Meet anyone face to face with whom you disagree. You could not sneak up on him from behind, do any damage to him without suffering the penalty of an outraged citizenry. If you met him face to face and took the same risk he did, you could get away with almost anything as long as the bullet was in front."

During the speech Ike returned time and again to the notion of facing one's accuser. "If we are going to continue to be proud that we are

Americans there must no weakening of the codes by which we have lived, the right to face your accuser face to face."

——————>•<——————

Now it can be told. According to the Soviet zone magazine Berliner Illustrierte, *actress Marilyn Monroe had been assigned by Sen. Joseph McCarthy to distract Americans from high prices and other evils of western life. In a full-page exposé, the magazine claimed Monroe's wiles had been foisted on the American people at the height of the previous year's presidential election and prevented voters from exercising freedom of choice at the polls. The magazine also charged that while McCarthy was violating the individual rights of the American people, no one noticed because unruly fans had been tearing Monroe's clothes from her body during the premiere of one of her films in New York.[3]*

The "See It Now" team had worked through the night in preparation for its program of November 24, 1953, "An Argument in Indianapolis." Most had gone home to change clothes and would return to the studio shortly. There was a degree of tension in the air; like the Milo Radulovich program of a month earlier, the program about Indianapolis had become tinged with controversy.

It was eight o'clock in the morning. Fred Friendly had just stepped into the shower. His wife interrupted him and said that Ed Murrow was on the phone and needed to talk to him right away. Friendly said to tell Murrow he was in the shower and would return the call in ten minutes. A few moments later she interrupted again; the shower excuse was no good—Murrow's face was covered with shaving lather. He needed to talk to Friendly now.

Two of the country's most recognized and influential journalists— one dripping on the floor in front of the phone while holding a towel around his waist, the other with shaving lather on his face—discussed a phone call Murrow had just received from Air Force Secretary Harold Talbott. The secretary had requested a camera crew for an announcement he was about to make regarding Milo Radulovich. Murrow and Friendly both quickly concluded that Talbott would not have asked to go on camera if he intended to discharge Milo. Charlie Mack was sent immediately.

That night the start of "See It Now" was delayed for a special announcement from Secretary of the Air Force Harold E. Talbott. Talbott agonizingly waded through obligatory references to "individual rights" and "individual liberties" before mercifully reaching the point: "I have decided that it is consistent with the interests of the national security to retain Lieutenant Radulovich in the United States Air Force. He is not, in my opinion, a security risk....I am also convinced that the record does not support the conclusion that Lieutenant Radulovich's father has engaged in activities of such a type as to bear upon the decision in this case."[1]

Word spread rapidly. Milo learned he had been exonerated when Gayle Greene of the *Detroit Free Press* called him for a response. "Like having a 20-ton dump truck lifted off my back," he said. "It's like having your future handed back to you. I thought I was all washed up. It's just miraculous."[2]

An impromptu party developed. The same neighbors that had stood beside him for the past three months, that had signed a petition on his behalf, that had told the many reporters who came to their doors that Milo could be trusted—those same neighbors now joined him and his family to celebrate the good news.

Milo's mother called and said that "lies never make much headway." John Radulovich offered "thank-you, thank-you. I just do not have the words to say what I feel." Milo tried to call his sister but didn't know the number—"so much for a close association" one of his neighbors quipped.

About noon, United Auto Workers Secretary-Treasurer Emil Mazey checked the Teletype machine in his office and learned of Milo's exoneration. He took great pleasure in being the one who told Ken Sanborn.

Charlie Lockwood had learned of Milo's exoneration over the radio while riding in his car near Miami.

Joe Wershba found out in the cutting room, while piecing together "An Argument in Indianapolis." There were a few whoops and hollers but that night's program demanded their attention for the moment. "I remember feeling that we had done something useful," he said.[3]

Col. William Doolan had no comment on the announcement. Nor did Selfridge Air Force Base.

Once the news had settled in, questions quickly surfaced about who had made the decision. Despite speculation that Eisenhower had intervened on Milo's behalf, Talbott steadfastly maintained that the decision had been his and his alone.

Talbott's denials did little to stem the growing belief that the president's fingerprints were firmly imbedded in the decision. It was widely assumed that Eisenhower's speech the previous night to B'nai B'rith in which he had underscored the right of all Americans to face their accusers was intended as a strong message to those who would be deciding the matter. Talbott's ruling had come only a few hours after Eisenhower delivered what pundits had already taken to calling the "fair play" speech.

"A reliable Pentagon source," wrote Don O'Connor, "said the decision to retain reserve Lt. Milo J. Radulovich came from 'higher-up'—apparently President Eisenhower himself."[4] When the source was asked if "higher-up" meant Eisenhower, he responded, "The President's speech should have been a tipoff."

The source called the Radulovich decision far-reaching and indicated that it would require a review of every pending security case, a figure that was said to be in the thousands. Included in that count was the case of M. Sgt. Victor Harvis who, like Milo, had been tabbed a security risk because of organizations his father had joined twenty years earlier.

Another unnamed Pentagon official predicted the Radulovich decision would lead to major changes in personnel practices. "They [the

Air Force] regard it as the inauguration of a policy of confronting security suspects with the substance of charges against them," the official said.[5]

Frank Welch of the OSI advised the FBI that the Radulovich exoneration had been cleared with President Eisenhower before Talbott's decision and that the decision reflected the views of the president. He went on to say that sixteen of the last nineteen Air Force security cases resulting in discharges had been based on associations. The Radulovich decision, he believed, could change the military's entire security policy.[6]

Despite a rolling tide to the contrary, Joe Wershba wasn't one of those who thought the president had intervened on behalf of Milo. "I would like to believe that Eisenhower told Talbott to clean this thing up. There's no case against this kid. Drop it. And that would have been to Ike's credit," Wershba says. "But I don't believe he did."[7]

Wershba had covered McCarthy, Hoover, and Eisenhower before the Radulovich case. He cited a 1952 Wisconsin campaign speech in which presidential candidate Eisenhower had been persuaded to delete a paragraph that included a strong statement of support for Gen. George Marshall, secretary of state in the Truman administration. "Ike had made Marshall," Wershba says, "and was one of his strong supporters." Marshall over the past few years had been on the receiving end of a number of McCarthy attacks. Eisenhower's advisers felt they should play it safe and not challenge or embarrass McCarthy on his own turf, even if the reticence came at Marshall's expense.

Wershba recounted an incident at CBS shortly after the Radulovich exoneration announcement. "Someone in the newsroom asked if the President was going to comment on Milo. Murrow gritted his teeth and said, 'the President is not going to say one damn word about McCarthy.'"

At day's end Milo drew on Shakespeare to express his feelings on the only real charge the Radulovich family had fought during the past three months. "Who steals my purse steals trash/But he that filches from me my good name/Robs me of that which not enriches him/And makes me poor indeed."[8]

⸺⟫●⟪⸺

Would the polio vaccine work? It was hoped that at least a million second graders across the country would provide an answer by summer's end, 1954.

The vaccine developed by Dr. Jonas Salk of the University of Pittsburgh, was set to be tested on second graders in the deep South. Second graders had been chosen because of the high incidence of infantile paralysis in their age-group—the deep South because the dreaded child paralyzer seemed to strike early and often in the southern states.

EPILOGUE

Forty-three years have passed since that night in 1953 when Air Force Secretary Harold Talbott publicly exonerated Milo. It would be nice to report that the American penchant for happy endings was fulfilled in the Milo Radulovich story. But that verdict has yet to be received.

Not long after the exoneration Milo moved his family to California. Jobs were plentiful there, but not for him. Interviews would go well. Job offers would be tendered. A brutally honest man, Milo would always volunteer information about the case. When he did, personnel officers would disappear into rooms with his file. When they came out he was told there had been a mistake, the position had already been filled. On one occasion, when he had come back the next day to start work, there was even a red dot on his file—and no job.

Milo sold insurance. He worked in a shipyard. But he was unhappy. Weather remained his true career ambition. Just as he and Nancy were preparing for a move to the East Coast—packing had nearly been completed—he spied an ad in the paper for an opening at a private weather service. Not wanting to set himself up for another rejection, he contemplated ignoring it. At the last minute, however, he applied.

The owner, a gruff man, was impressed with Milo's credentials and offered him a job. True to form, Milo embarked on his often-told tale of the case. This time he was stopped halfway through the story.

"I don't care about all that crap," his new boss said. "All I care about is if you can do the job." Milo worked for the private weather service for ten years. When the operation was moved to Utah, he joined the National Weather Service. He retired in 1994.

———————

In 1957, Margaret Fishman had been identified as a Communist by an FBI undercover agent. She was called to testify before the House Un-American Activities Committee in Chicago. When asked by the committee counsel to look at a man who had earlier testified that she was a Communist, Margaret responded, "I don't feel so inclined, thank you." Later when asked if she had ever received from her brother Milo Radulovich any property, manuals, or documents of the United States Air Force, she responded, "You know better."

The Fishman home in Detroit continues as a thoroughfare for battles involving human rights. On any given day their house could be the site of a campaign meeting for a city council candidate or a temporary shelter for a Bosnian refugee who needs a job or an interpreter.

Now a retired City of Detroit employee, Al Fishman recently joined other labor notables and was arrested outside the *Detroit Free Press* building. They were marching on behalf of unions who were striking Detroit's two main newspapers.

The fire burns bright in the Fishman household.

———————

Charlie Lockwood died in 1983 at the age of eighty-eight. After his successful representation of Milo Radulovich, Lockwood went on to become involved in fifteen similar cases, and won them all. In 1977, at the age of eighty-two, he wrote to Ernest Goodman, "I will always be grateful for your sending Milo to me. It was truly the most rewarding case I ever had."

———>●<———

Ken Sanborn went on to a distinguished career on the Michigan bench. Appointed in 1972 to probate court, he rose to sit on both district and circuit courts. Not long after the Radulovich case, he ran successfully for a seat in the state legislature. Unlike most Republicans, Ken Sanborn enjoyed consistent support from labor throughout his political career.

———>●<———

Joe Wershba left CBS in June 1954. He spent five years as a free-lance filmmaker and then five more writing a column for the *New York Post*. In 1964, he won the prestigious Sydney Hillman Award, an annual honor for the best television program involving human rights. The story involved Clarence Gideon and his right to have a lawyer at his trial. Wershba had won the award once before, in 1954, for "The Case Against Lt. Milo Radulovich." Shortly after Edward R. Murrow's death in 1965, Wershba worked on the memorial program. That tribute, he insisted, include Murrow's carefully crafted ending to the Milo Radulovich program.

———>●<———

A year after his son was exonerated by the Air Force, John Radulovich died. Newspeople are noted for looking at life through suspicious and acerbic eyes. A picture of John Radulovich hung on the wall of the cutting room at CBS for a number of years after his appearance on "See It Now."

———>●<———

Fred Friendly went on in 1964 to become president of CBS News. Later he took a distinguished professorship at the prestigious Columbia Graduate School of Journalism. He would go on to raise the "Socratic Dialogues" to new heights with his landmark PBS series. Each year Friendly's graduate students at Columbia are treated to a screening of "The Case Against Lt. Milo Radulovich," with special commentary from "the dean of American journalism."

On April 11, 1991, Friendly taped "Ethics in the Media: Hard News, Hard Choices" at the Hyatt Regency in Sacramento. Before the show, Milo, then a resident of Sacramento, wrote on the back of his business card, "Milo Radulovich, See It Now, October 1953," and sent it backstage to Friendly.

Aware that Milo was in the audience, Friendly related the story of Lieutenant Radulovich during the show and asked Milo to stand and be recognized. Later, at a reception, Milo Radulovich and Fred Friendly shook hands for the first time.

Friendly inscribed his program that evening: "To Milo: who taught me something about the Bill of Rights."

"Murrow and I agreed," Friendly says, "the Milo Radulovich program was one of the best things we ever did."

———>●<———

Emboldened by the Milo Radulovich program, "See It Now" devoted its entire half-hour program on March 9, 1954, to Sen. Joseph McCarthy. The broadcast consisted of McCarthy film clippings with Murrow providing only the briefest narration—primarily to correct or clarify points made by the senator. Consequently, if McCarthy accepted the offer for an on-air rebuttal, he would, in essence, be debating himself.

Murrow's tailpiece was riveting, just as it had been five months earlier at the end of the Radulovich program. "This is no time for men who oppose Senator McCarthy's methods to keep silent," he said. "There is no way for a citizen of a republic to abdicate his responsibilities." He concluded by invoking Shakespeare: "Cassius was right. The fault, dear Brutus, is not in our stars but in ourselves. Good night and good luck."

Within twenty-four hours CBS reported the largest response ever to any program in network history, 12,348 comments—15 to 1 in favor of Murrow. According to Alexander Kendrick, "Many felt that McCarthy's eventual censure by the Senate was merely ratification of the censure delivered that night on television."[1]

Friendly said, "We never could have done the McCarthy program without the Milo Radulovich program."

In April 1965, Edward R. Murrow died at the age of fifty-seven. Of the countless expressions of sympathy received by his wife, Janet, one stood out: "Wherever men cherish human freedom and dignity, Ed Murrow's spirit will forever stand. To him, we owe what life and freedom is ours. Milo and Nancy Radulovich."

In 1954, Homer Ferguson was defeated in his bid for reelection to the United State Senate by Patrick V. McNamara. Ken Sanborn believes Ferguson would have been returned to the Senate if he had offered public support to Milo Radulovich.

As we walk along the nearly deserted streets of Sacramento on a pleasant May evening, the moods of Milo Radulovich change frequently. He is obviously pained at the recall of events in his life that he would prefer be consigned forever to 1953.

But his eyes dance when the conversation turns to his family. He lives near two of his three daughters and speaks fondly of them. He is especially close to his grandson, Scotty. Family is important to him.

I was told to expect an intelligent man, and was not disappointed. Milo is well read and knowledgeable about current events, especially of the carnage in Bosnia, a subject he returns to time and again.

We meet a homeless man rummaging through a cigarette receptacle outside a large building. "What are you doing there?" Milo asks.

"Nothing, sir," the man replies, frightened.

Milo pulls a few dollar bills from his pocket and gives them to the man. "Here," he says, "get something to eat."

There is a brief, uneasy silence, which he breaks. "We have to do something to help these people."

The next day we walk through Old Sacramento, killing time before meeting his daughter, Janet, and her husband, Brian.

"Look at these people," Milo says. "Every one of them is a story. They laugh. They love." He pauses. "And they hurt, too."

Notes

AUGUST 21, 1953
   1. Interview with Vera Layton, October 7, 1994.

AUGUST 22, 1953
   1. "The Un-Americans," a BBC production, 1992. Broadcast on "The Time Machine" on Arts & Entertainment Network (cable TV).
   2. *Detroit Free Press*, August 23, 1953.
   3. Thomas C. Reeves, *The Life and Times of Joe McCarthy: A Biography* (Briarcliff Manor, N.Y.: Stein and Day, 1982), 247.
   4. *Detroit News*, August 23, 1953, and *Detroit Free Press*, August 23, 1953.

AUGUST 23, 1953
   1. *Detroit News*, August 17, 1953.
   2. *New York Times*, August 12, 1953.
   3. *Detroit News*, August 20, 1953.
   4. *New York Times*, August 12, 1953.

AUGUST 24, 1953
   1. Interview with Ron Rothstein, October 26, 1994.
   2. Ibid.
   3. *Time*, August 31, 1953.

AUGUST 25, 1953
   1. Statement of Reasons.
   2. Interview with Milo Radulovich, May 22, 1993.
   3. *Detroit News*, August 25, 1953.

AUGUST 26, 1953
   1. *Detroit News*, August 26, 1953.

AUGUST 27, 1953

1. Interview with Ron Rothstein, October 26, 1994.
2. *Detroit News*, August 27, 1953.
3. Ibid.

AUGUST 31, 1953

1. *Michigan State Bar Journal*, September 1950, pp. 73–74.
2. New material in capitals.
3. As quoted in the *Michigan State Bar Journal*, vol. 30, no. 9, September 1951, pp. 70–74.
4. Dean of the University of Michigan Law School and commissioner-at-large for the State Bar of Michigan.
5. *Michigan State Bar Journal*, vol. 30, no. 9, December 1951, p. 19.
6. *CIO News*, March 13, 1952.
7. HUAC hearings, 2878–92.
8. Interview with Coleman A. Young, September 1, 1994.
9. Michigan Public Act 117 of 1952.
10. *Detroit Free Press*, April 10, 1952.
11. *Detroit Free Press*, August 31, 1953.
12. *Detroit News*, August 31, 1953.

SEPTEMBER 1, 1953

1. *Detroit Free Press*, September 1, 1953.

SEPTEMBER 7, 1953

1. *Detroit Free Press*, September 7, 1953.

SEPTEMBER 8, 1953

1. Interview with Ernest Goodman, July 27, 1994.
2. Interview with Charles P. Lockwood, November 14, 1994.
3. Interview with Ernest Goodman, July 27, 1994.

SEPTEMBER 10, 1953

1. Interview with Ernest Goodman, July 27, 1994.
2. Coleman Young and Lonnie Wheeler, *Hard Stuff: The Autobiography of Mayor Coleman Young* (New York: Penguin Group, 1994), 90.
3. Ibid.
4. During our conversation Goodman was quick to correct himself whenever he used the term "media." He pointed out that television news was still a novelty and radio dealt mostly with headlines. Newspapers were still the primary source of news for Americans, hence the ongoing emphasis on newspapers.

5. Interview with Ernest Goodman, July 27, 1994.

6. *Newsweek*, September 7, 1953.

SEPTEMBER 11, 1953

1. Interview with Charles P. Lockwood, November 14, 1994.

2. Ibid.

SEPTEMBER 12, 1953

1 The top ten TV shows of 1953 were: (1.) I Love Lucy, (2.) Dragnet, (3.) Arthur Godfrey's Talent Scouts, (4.) You Bet Your Life, (5.) Bob Hope Chevy Show, (6.) Milton Berle, (7.) Arthur Godfrey and His Friends, (8.) The Ford Show, (9.) Jackie Gleason, (10.) Fireside Theater.

2. Neal Gabler, *Winchell: Gossip, Power and the Culture of Celebrity*, (New York: Alfred A. Knopf, 1994), 202.

3. Ibid., 201.

4. Ibid.

5. Anthony Summers, *Official and Confidential: The Secret Life of J. Edgar Hoover* (New York: G. P. Putnam's Sons,1993), 84.

6. Ibid., 468–9.

SEPTEMBER 13, 1953

1. *Detroit Free Press*, September 12, 1953.

2. Ibid.

3. Ibid.

SEPTEMBER 15, 1953

1. *Detroit Free Press*, September 15, 1953.

2. Ibid.

3. Ibid.

4. Interview with Harry Lunn, January 21, 1995.

5. Memo, September 15, 1953.

SEPTEMBER 18, 1953

1. During the 1952 presidential campaign, Republicans labeled Stevenson's intellectual supporters "eggheads."

2. *Detroit News*, September 18, 1953.

3. Ibid.

4. Ibid.

SEPTEMBER 21, 1953

1. *Newsweek*, September 14, 1953.

SEPTEMBER 23, 1953

1. *Detroit News*, September 23, 1953.
2. Ibid.
3. Robin Roberts, a friend of both Milo and Sanborn—and a roommate of Milo's for a while—enjoyed campus luminary status based largely on his ability with a basketball. Sanborn laughs and says, "We found out later he also played a little baseball."
4. Reeves, *Life and Times*, 345.
5. William Manchester, *The Glory and the Dream: A Narrative History of America*, 1932–1972, (New York: Bantam Books, 1975), 527.
6. Reeves, *Life and Times*, 351.
7. *Detroit News*, August 16, 1953.
8. Ibid.
9. *Detroit News*, September 23, 1953.
10. Ibid.
11. *Time*, September 21, 1953.

SEPTEMBER 24, 1953

1. *Detroit News*, September 24, 1953.
2. *Detroit Free Press*, September 24, 1953.
3. Ibid.
4. *New York Times*, September 24, 1953.
5. *Detroit Times*, September 24, 1953.
6. Ibid. The eighth commandment is "Thou shalt not bear false witness against thy neighbor."
7. *Detroit News*, September 24, 1953.
8. *Detroit Times*, September 24, 1953.
9. *Detroit News*, September 24, 1953.
10. Ibid.

SEPTEMBER 25, 1953

1. *Detroit Free Press*, September 25, 1953.
2. Ibid.
3. Interview with Al Fishman, July 10, 1995.
4. Ibid.
5. Correspondence from Jewel E. West to Kenneth N. Sanborn, September 25, 1953.

SEPTEMBER 26, 1953

1. *Detroit News*, September 26, 1953; also *Detroit Times*, September 26, 1953.
2. *Detroit News*, September 26, 1953.

SEPTEMBER 27, 1953
1. *Detroit Times*, September 28, 1953.
2. *Detroit Free Press*, September 28, 1953.

SEPTEMBER 28, 1953
1. Air Force Regulation No. 35-62 (Washington: Dept. of the Air Force, December 21, 1951), Section IV, par. 14, (a) Milo being an officer, the document was titled, "Notice of Proposed Termination of Appointment."
2. Ibid., Section III, par. 11.
3. Ibid., Section IV, par. 14, (d) (2).
4. Ibid., par. 17.
5. Ibid., Section IV, par. 14, (d) (3) (4).
6. Ibid., Section I, par. 4, (b).
7. Ibid, par. 14, (b).
8. Ibid, Section II—Loyalty Cases, par. 6.
9. *Detroit News*, September 29, 1953.
10. Interview with Lt. Col. Irving H. Kempner, USAF (Ret.), August28, 1995

SEPTEMBER 29, 1953
1. Reeves, *Life and Times*, 512.
2. *Detroit Free Press*, September 18, 1953; *Detroit News*, September 17, 1953.
3. Reeves, *Life and Times*, 512.
4. Most quotes are from the hearing transcript; where that is not the case, it will be so noted.
5. Of note, while making a point involving similarities between administrative hearings and courts-martial, Doolan referred to Ken Sanborn as "Lieutenant Sanborn."
6. *Detroit Times*, September 29, 1953.
7. Interview with Ken Sanborn, December 3, 1992.
8. Interview with Ken Sanborn, April 9, 1993.
9. The account here is garnered from recollections of Milo Radulovich and from the *Detroit Times,* September 30, 1953.
10. *Detroit Free Press*, September 30, 1953.
11. Accounts of speculation surrounding Earl Warren's appointment to the Supreme Court were garnered from the September 29, 1953, editions of the *Detroit Free Press* and *Detroit News*.
12. *Detroit Free Press*, September 29, 1953.
13. *Michigan Daily*, September 30, 1953.
14. *Newsweek*, September 28, 1953.

SEPTEMBER 30, 1953
   1. *Eastside Shopper*, September 30, 1953.
   2. *Detroit News*, September 30, 1953.
   3. *Michigan Daily*, September 30, 1953.

OCTOBER 1, 1953
   1. *Detroit News*, October 2, 1953.
   2. Jurkovic's charges against the Air Force are taken from the October 1, 1953, editions of the *Detroit Times* and *Detroit News*.
   3. *Detroit Times*, October 1, 1953.
   4. Ibid.
   5. Ibid.

OCTOBER 2, 1953
   1. Hearing transcript, 59.
   2. *Detroit Free Press*, October 1, 1953.
   3. *Detroit Times*, October 2, 1953.
   4. *Detroit News*, October 2, 1953.
   5. *Detroit Times*, October 2, 1953.
   6. All quotes are from the brief dated October1, 1953, submitted by Charles C Lockwood and Kenneth N. Sanborn.
   7. *Washington Post*, October 2, 1953.

OCTOBER 3, 1953
   1. *Detroit Free Press*, October 3, 1953.
   2. *Washington Post*, October 3, 1953.

OCTOBER 4, 1953
   1. Letter from Emil Mazey to Harold E. Talbott, October 2, 1953.
   2. *Detroit Free Press*, October 4, 1953.

OCTOBER 5, 1953
   1. *Time*, October 5, 1953.
   2. *Detroit Free Press*, October 5, 1953.
   3. Ibid. (ellipses part of original text).
   4. *Washington Post*, October 5, 1953.

OCTOBER 6, 1953
   1. *Detroit Free Press*, October 6, 1993.
   2. *Washington Post*, October 7, 1953.

OCTOBER 8, 1953

1. *Detroit News*, October 8, 1953.
2. Ibid.
3. *Detroit Times*, October 8, 1953; also see edition of October 7, 1953.
4. *Detroit News*, October 8, 1953.
5. Ibid.

OCTOBER 9, 1953

1. *Detroit Free Press*, October 9, 1953.
2. Ibid.

OCTOBER 10, 1953

1. *Detroit Times*, October 10, 1953.

OCTOBER 12, 1953

1. See David Halberstam, *The Powers That Be* (New York: Alfred A. Knopf, 1979), 137.
2. Reeves, *Life and Times*, 223.
3. Ibid., 224.
4. *Denver Post*, February 11, 1950.
5. For an account of McCarthy's performance on the Senate floor that evening, see Reeves, *Life and Times*, 235–242.
6. Ibid., 242.
7. *Washington Post*, March 29, 1950.
8. Reeves, *Life and Times*, 267.
9. Manchester, *The Glory and the Dream*, 526.
10. Alexander Kendrick, *Prime Time* (New York: Avon Books, 1969), 75.
11. Manchester, *The Glory and the Dream*, 529.
12. Ibid., 527.
13. *McCarthy: Death of a Witch Hunter*, a film by Emile de Antonio, 1986.
14. Ibid.
15. Halberstam, *The Powers That Be*, 141.
16. David Halberstam, *The Fifties* (New York: Villard Books, 1993), 55.
17. Reeves. *Life and Times*, 245.
18. Manchester, *The Glory and the Dream*, 525.
19. Halberstam, *The Fifties*, 51.
20. Reeves, *Life and Times*, 207.
21. "The Un-Americans," BBC.
22. Victor S. Navasky, *Naming Names* (New York: The Viking Press, 1980), 152.
23. Ibid., 153–154. All quotes of the Bogart letter and Sokolsky column are from Navasky's account.

24. "Edward R. Murrow: This Reporter," documentary produced by Susan Steinberg as part of the PBS series "American Masters," 1990.

25. Ibid.

26. Ibid.

27. Ibid.

28. Joseph E. Persico, *Edward R. Murrow: An American Original* (New York: McGraw-Hill, 1988), 287

29. Ibid., 288.

30. Ibid., 293.

31. A. M. Sperber, *Murrow: His Life and Times* (New York: Freundlich Books, 1986), 351.

32. Interview with Wershba, April 8, 1993.

33. Persico, *Edward R. Murrow,* 302.

34. "Edward R. Murrow: This Reporter."

35. Ibid.

36. *New York Times Magazine,* April 1967.

37. Ibid.

38. Ibid.

39. "Edward R. Murrow: This Reporter."

40. Ibid.

41. Ibid.

42. Interview with Fred W. Friendly, Jr., March 15, 1993.

43. Halberstam, *The Powers That Be,* 142.

44. Sperber, *Murrow,* 318.

45. Summers, *Official and Confidential,* 91–92.

46. Interview with Wershba, April, 8, 1993.

47. Sperber, *Murrow,* 318.

48. "Edward R. Murrow with the News," December 21, 1948, as quoted in Sperber, *Murrow,* 319.

49. Ibid. and memo to the file, December 22, 1948, as quoted in Persico, *Edward R. Murrow,* 330. Also see Kendrick, *Prime Time,* 57.

50. Interview with Wershba, April, 8, 1993.

51. Persico, *Edward R. Murrow,* 1.

OCTOBER 13, 1953

1. Interview with Ken Sanborn, April 8, 1993.

2. *Detroit Free Press,* October 14, 1953.

3. *Detroit Times,* October 14, 1953.

4. *Detroit Free Press,* October 14, 1953.

5. *Detroit Times,* October 14, 1953.

6. *Detroit Free Press,* October 14, 1953.

7. *Michigan Daily*, October 14, 1953.

8. *Detroit News*, October 14, 1953.

9. Ibid.

10. Copy of Findings and Recommendations.

11. Ibid.

12. *Detroit News*, October 14, 1953.

14. Interview with Ken Sanborn, April 9, 1993.

15. *Detroit News*, October 14, 1953.

OCTOBER 14, 1953

1. Summers, *Official and Confidential*, 166.

2. FBI internal memorandum from A. H. Belmont to Mr. Ladd. Subject: Milo Radulovich Internal Security—YU, October 14, 1953.

3. Ibid.

4. Halberstam, *The Powers That Be*, 142.

5. Fred W. Friendly, Jr., *Due to Circumstances Beyond Our Control* (New York: Random House,1967), 3.

6. Ibid.

7. Interview with Wershba, April 8, 1993.

8. Interview with Friendly, March 15, 1993.

9. Ibid.

10. Interview with Wershba, April 8, 1993.

11. Ibid.

12. Ibid.

13. Ibid.

OCTOBER 15, 1953

1. "See It Now," October 20, 1953.

2. Ibid.

3. Interview with Wershba, April 8, 1993.

4. "See It Now," October 20, 1953.

5. Ibid.

6. Ibid.

7. Ibid.

8. Interview with Wershba, April 8, 1993.

9. "See It Now," October 20, 1953.

10. Interview with Wershba, April 8, 1993.

11. "See It Now," October 20, 1953.

12. *Detroit Times*, October 15, 1953.

13. Ibid.

14. *Detroit News*, October 15, 1953.

15. *Detroit Free Press*, October 15, 1953.
16. *Detroit Times,* October 15, 1953.
17. Follow-up of original Belmont-to-Ladd memo.
18. FBI internal memorandum.
19. Friendly, *Due to Circumstances*, 6.

OCTOBER 16, 1953
1. Interview with Margaret Fishman, April 12, 1993.
2. Ibid.
3. "See It Now," October 20, 1953.
4. Interview with Wershba, April 8, 1993.
5. "See It Now", October 20, 1953.
6. Friendly, *Due to Circumstances*, 7.
7. Interview with Wershba, April 8, 1993.
8. Ibid.
9. Ibid.
10. Ibid.

OCTOBER 17, 1953
1. Friendly, *Due to Circumstances*, 8.
2. Ibid., 9.
3. Ibid., 10.

OCTOBER 18, 1953
1. Interview with Ken Sanborn, December 3, 1992.
2. Friendly, *Due to Circumstances*, 12.
3. *New York Times*, October 16, 1953.

OCTOBER 19, 1953
1. Friendly, *Due to Circumstances*, 13.
2. Ibid., 10.
3. Ibid.
4. Ibid.

OCTOBER 20, 1953
1. Friendly, *Due to Circumstances*, 1.
2. Ibid., 14.
3. All quotes from the show are from "See It Now," October 20, 1953.
4. Sperber, *Murrow*, 418.
5. Friendly, *Due to Circumstances*, 15.

6. Letter from Laura Z. Hobson to Edward R. Murrow, October 20, 1953, as quoted in Sperber, *Murrow,* 419.

7. Harriet Van Horne in a letter to Edward R. Murrow, as quoted in Sperber, *Murrow,* 419.

8. *New York Times*, October 16, 1953.

OCTOBER 21, 1953

1. *New York Times*, October 21, 1953.
2. Friendly, *Due to Circumstances*, 17.
3. *Michigan Daily*, October 21, 1953.

OCTOBER 22, 1953

1. *New York Times*, November 25, 1953.
2. *Detroit News*, October 22, 1953.
3. Nichols-to-Tolson memo, October 22, 1953.
4. Ibid.
5. *New York Times*, October 21, 1953

OCTOBER 23, 1953

1. *Michigan Daily*, October 24, 1953.
2. *Detroit Free Press*, October 24, 1953.
3. *Michigan Daily*, October 24, 1953.
4. *Detroit Free Press*, "As Others See It," October 23, 1953.

OCTOBER 24, 1953

1. The story was researched and written by Gordon Harrison of the *Detroit News*, Washington Bureau. It appeared in the October 24, 1953, edition.
2. *Detroit News*, October 25, 1953.
3. *Detroit Free Press*, October 24, 1953. Article by James M. Haswell.

OCTOBER 25, 1953

1. *Detroit Free Press*, October 25, 1953.
2. Ibid.
3. Ibid.
4. Ibid.
5. *Chicago Daily Sun-Times*, October 23, 1953.
6. *New York Times*, October 25, 1953.
7. *Detroit News*, October 25, 1953.
8. Confidential report of Special Agent Langdon C. Tennis on Milo J. Radulovich, 2d lt., November 7, 1946.

9. FBI internal memorandum from E. G. Fitch to Mr. Ladd, regarding Milorad Radulovich, Internal Security—X, October 17, 1946.

10. Fitch to Ladd, confidential memo regarding Milo John Radulovich, November 15, 1946.

11. Confidential FBI report on John Radulovich, June 27, 1950.

12. *New York Times*, October 21, 1953.

OCTOBER 26, 1953

1. *Newsweek*, October 26, 1953.

OCTOBER 27, 1953

1. *Michigan Daily*, October 27, 1953.

2. Reeves, *Life and Times,* 245–246.

3. The references here to the Sokolsky-Nichols conversation of October 27 are found in Nichols's memo to Clyde Tolson, October 29, 1953, regarding "Milo J. Radulovich, Internal Security."

4. Summers, *Official and Confidential*, 172.

5. Nichols's memo to Tolson, October 29, 1953.

6. FBI file, "Milo John Radulovich," November 1, 1949.

7. FBI report, November 1, 1949, "RE: Milo John Radulovich."

8. FBI file on Milo Radulovich, dated May 24, 1950.

9. *New York Times*, October 22, 1953

OCTOBER 29, 1953

1. *Capital Times,* October 29, 1953.

2. *Eastside Shopper*, October 29, 1953.

3. "Supplemental Brief of Respondent on Review of the Board Findings," submitted by Charles C. Lockwood and Kenneth N. Sanborn, October 29, 1953.

NOVEMBER 2, 1953

1. Letter from Harriet Chidester to Commanding General, U.S.   Air Force, September 27, 1953.

2. Letter from Lt. Col. Ravenburg to J. Edgar Hoover. Although undated, Ravenburg's letter was date-stamped November 2, 1953.

3. *Newsweek*, October 26, 1953.

NOVEMBER 3, 1953

1. Interview with Ernest Goodman, July 27, 1994.

2. *New York Times*, October 22, 1953.

3. *Newsweek*, November 2, 1953.

4. Godfrey's firing of La Rosa continued as a news item for nearly three weeks. Also see *New York Times*, television critic Jack Gould's column, October 26, 1953, and *Time*, November 2, 1953.

NOVEMBER 4, 1953

1. Internal FBI memo from A. H. Belmont to Mr. D. M. Ladd, regarding Milo J. Radulovitch [*sic*], Internal Security, November 4, 1953.

2. Belmont-to-Ladd memo.

3. Ibid.

NOVEMBER 5, 1953

1. *Detroit Free Press*, November 5, 1953.

2. Friendly, *Due to Circumstances*, 17.

3. *Eastside Shopper*, November 5, 1953.

NOVEMBER 9, 1953

1. *Detroit Free Press*, November 9, 1953.

2. Ibid.

3. Ibid.

4. Ibid.

NOVEMBER 17, 1953

1. Interview with Wershba, April 8, 1993.

2. Sperber, *Murrow*, 416.

3. Ibid.

4. All quotes are from *Time*, November 16.

NOVEMBER 18, 1953

1. Letter from Charles C. Lockwood to Ken Sanborn, November 18, 1953.

2. Telegram from J. Edgar Hoover to New Haven office, November 18, 1953.

3. *Newsweek*, November 23, 1953.

NOVEMBER 23, 1953

1. *Michigan Daily*, November 21, 1953.

2. All quotes from Eisenhower's speech are from a transcript published in the *New York Times*, November 24, 1953.

3. *Time*, November 30, 1953, and *Newsweek*, November 30, 1953, p. 53.

NOVEMBER 24, 1953

1. Official statement released by the Department of Defense, November 24, 1953, and read by Air Force Secretary Harold Talbott on "See It Now," November 24, 1953.

2. *Detroit Free Press*, November 25, 1953.

3. Interview with Wershba, April 8, 1993.

4. *Detroit Times*, November 25, 1953.

5. *Detroit Free Press*, November 25, 1953.

6. FBI memo from Mr. Keay to Mr. Belmont, November 25, 1953.

7. Interview with Wershba, April 8, 1993.

8. Othello, act III, scene 3.

EPILOGUE

1. Kendrick, *Prime Time,* 67.

Index